The Critical Eye

Appreciating Prose and Poetry

DON SHIACH

Nelson

Thomas Nelson and Sons Ltd
Nelson House Mayfield Road
Walton-on-Thames Surrey
KT12 5PL UK

© Don Shiach 1984
First published by Thomas Nelson and Sons Ltd 1984

I(T)P Thomas Nelson is an International
Thomson Publishing Company

I(T)P is used under licence

ISBN 0-17-433096-0
NPN 15

Printed in Croatia

Contents

Contents

Contents

Acknowledgements

The author and publisher would like to thank the following for their helpful contributions as advisers:

Paul Clarke, Collyer's Sixth Form College, Horsham, West Sussex
Joyce Fisher, Washington School, Tyne and Weir
Dave Freestone, Malory School, Downham, Bromley, Kent
Jenny Hockley, Langley College of Further Education, Slough, Berkshire
Donald Mackenzie, Adviser in English, Tayside Regional Council

Thanks are due for permission to reprint the following copyright material:

The Would-be Gentleman by Molière from MOLIÉRE: THE MISER & OTHER PLAYS, trans. John Wood (Penguin Classics 1962) pp. 18–19, © John Wood, 1953, reprinted by permission of Penguin Books Ltd; *Cash Help* (DHSS leaflet S.B.1), an extract reprinted by permission of the Department of Health and Social Security; *Mastermatch* advertisement reproduced by permission of Masterview; *The Dark Hours* from ESSAYS OF FIVE DECADES by J.B. Priestley, an extract reprinted by permission of William Heinemann Ltd; *The Turtle who Conquered Time* from VINTAGE THURBER edited by Helen Thurber © Hamish Hamilton 1963 reprinted by permission of Hamish Hamilton Ltd; *Once there was a King* by Rabindranath Tagore, an extract reprinted by permission of Macmillan, London and Basingstoke; *A Farewell to Arms*, an extract reprinted by permission of the Executors of the Ernest Hemingway Estate and Jonathan Cape Ltd; *Nausea* by Jean-Paul Sartre, an extract reprinted by permission of Hamish Hamilton Ltd; *The Habit of Loving* © Doris Lessing 1957, an extract reprinted by permission of Curtis Brown Ltd on behalf of Doris Lessing; *Sunset Song* by Lewis Grassic Gibson, an extract reprinted by permission of Curtis Brown Ltd, London on behalf of the Estate of Lewis Grassic Gibbon; *The Ginger Man* by J.P. Donleavy, an extract reprinted by permission of Neville Spearman Ltd; *Rain* by W. Somerset Maugham, an extract reprinted by permission of the Executors of the Estate of W. Somerset Maugham and William Heinemann Ltd; *A Passage to India* by E.M. Forster, an extract reprinted by permission of Edward Arnold (Publishers) Ltd; *The Beautiful and the Damned* by F. Scott Fitzgerald, an extract reprinted by permission of the Bodley Head Ltd from THE BODLEY HEAD SCOTT FITZGERALD, Vol. IV; *Vile Bodies* by Evelyn Waugh, published by Chapman & Hall Ltd, an extract reprinted by permission of A.D. Peters & Co. Ltd; *The Quiet American* by Graham Greene, an extract reprinted by permission of William Heinemann Ltd, The Bodley Head Ltd, and Laurence Pollinger Ltd; *Trespasses* by Paul Bailey, © 1969 Paul Bailey, an extract reprinted by permission of Jonathan Cape Ltd and Deborah Rogers Ltd; *The Bell* by Iris Murdoch, an extract reprinted by permission of Irish Murdoch and Chatto and Windus Ltd; *Them* by Joyce Carol Oates, published by Victor Gollancz Ltd, an extract reprinted by kind permission of Murray Pollinger Literary Agency; *Sanctuary* by William Faulkner, an extract reprinted by permission of Curtis Brown Ltd, London on behalf of Random House; *Catch 22* by Joseph Heller, an extract reprinted by permission of Joseph Heller and Jonathan Cape Ltd; *The Goebbels Diaries* edited by Hugh Trevor Roper, an extract reprinted by permission of Martin Secker & Warburg Ltd; *A Very Easy Death* by Simone de Beauvoir (André Deutsch 1956), an extract reprinted by permission of André Deutsch; *Goodbye to All That* by Robert Graves, an extract reprinted by permission of Robert Graves; *Leningrad Diary* by Vera Inber, an extract reprinted by permission of Hutchinson Publishing Group Ltd; *Dispatches* by Michael Herr, an extract reprinted by permission of Pan Books; *Diaries of Evelyn Waugh* edited by Michael Davie, an extract reprinted by permission of Weidenfeld & Nicolson Ltd; *Mental Nursing* advertisement reproduced by permission of the Department of Health and Social Security; *England at First Glance* from THE ENGLISH PEOPLE by George Orwell, an extract reprinted by permission of the estate of the late Sonia Brownell Orwell and Martin Secker & Warburg Ltd; *How to Commit Murder in the Mass Media*

Acknowledgements

from ADVERTISEMENTS FOR MYSELF by Norman Mailer, reprinted by permission of André Deutsch; *High Noon at the Nuclear Corral* from VOLE magazine reprinted by permission of Laurence McGinty; *The tragedy of El Salvador* from THE SUNDAY TIMES (editorial 21 February 1982) © Times Newspapers Limited, reprinted by permission of Times Newspapers Limited; *US Extends aid to army in Salvador* by Jane McIntosh from LABOUR WEEKLY (issue for 5 February 1982) reprinted by permission of Labour Weekly; *Mondays, Thursdays* by Keith Waterhouse, an extract reprinted by permission of Michael Joseph; *Praxis* by Fay Weldon © 1978 by Fay Weldon, an extract reprinted by permission of Hodder and Stoughton Limited; *To the Lighthouse* by Virginia Woolf, an extract reprinted by permission of The Literary Estate of Virginia Woolf and The Hogarth Press; *The Big Sleep* by Raymond Chandler, an extract reprinted by permission of Helga Greene and Hamish Hamilton Ltd; *Riddley Walker* by Russell Hoban, an extract reprinted by permission of Russell Hoban and Jonathan Cape Ltd; *The Centaur* by John Updike (André Deutsch 1972), an extract reprinted by permission of André Deutsch; *Riotous Assembly* by Tom Sharpe, an extract reprinted by permission of Martin Secker & Warburg Ltd; *A Cool Million* by Nathanael West, an extract reprinted by permission of Martin Secker & Warburg Ltd and Farrar, Straus & Giroux Inc.; *Cakes and Ale* by W. Somerset Maugham, an extract reprinted by permission of The Executors of the Estate of W. Somerset Maugham and William Heinemann Ltd; *You Can't Go Home Again* by Thomas Wolfe, an extract reprinted by permission of William Heinemann Ltd; *You're the Top* by Cole Porter, © 1934 Harms Inc., U.K. Publisher Chappell Music Ltd. Published by permission; *White Christmas* © W.R. Rodgers 1941, reprinted by permission of Mrs Lucy R. Cohen; *O What is that Sound* reprinted by permission of Faber and Faber Ltd from COLLECTED POEMS by W.H. Auden; *Beyond the End* from COLLECTED EARLIER POEMS 1940–1960. Copyright © 1957 by Denise Levertov. Reprinted by permission of New Directions Publishing Corporation; *The Taxi* by Amy Lowell, published by Houghton Mifflin Company; *The Fight of the Year* by Roger McGough, reprinted by permission of A.D. Peters & Co Ltd; *Prelude I* reprinted by permission of Faber and Faber Ltd from COLLECTED POEMS 1909–1962 by T.S. Eliot; *Morning at the Window* reprinted by permission of Faber and Faber Ltd from COLLECTED POEMS 1909–1962 by T.S. Eliot; *The Abortion* by Anne Sexton, reprinted by permission of A.D. Peters & Co Ltd; *The Wife's Tale* reprinted by permission of Faber and Faber Ltd from DOOR INTO THE DARK by Seamus Heaney; *Do the Dying Cry?* by Taner Baybars from OUTPOSTS, reprinted by permission of Taner Baybars; *Death in Leamington* from COLLECTED POEMS by John Betjeman, reprinted by permission of John Murray (Publishers) Ltd; *Thistles* reprinted by permission of Faber and Faber Ltd from WODWO by Ted Hughes; *The Death-bed* by Siegfried Sassoon, reprinted by permission of George Sassoon; *A Refusal to Mourn* from COLLECTED POEMS by Dylan Thomas, reprinted by permission of J.M. Dent & Sons Ltd; *Officers' Mess* from THE COLLECTED EWART 1933–1980 (Hutchinson) reprinted by permission of Gavin Ewart; *The Wind Sprang up at Four O'Clock* reprinted by permission of Faber and Faber Ltd from COLLECTED POEMS 1909–1962 by T.S. Eliot; *Prayer Before Birth* reprinted by permission of Faber and Faber Ltd from the COLLECTED POEMS OF LOUIS MACNEICE; *Tell me not here, it needs not saying* reprinted by permission of The Society of Authors as the literary representative of the Estate of A.E. Housman and Jonathan Cape Ltd, publishers of A.E. Housman's COLLECTED POEMS; *The Quaker Graveyard in Nantucket I* reprinted by permission of Faber and Faber Ltd from POEMS 1938–1949 by Robert Lowell; *Winter* by Ruth Stone reprinted by permission of Ruth Stone; *Carnal Knowledge* reprinted by permission of Faber and Faber Ltd from FIGHTING TERMS by Thom Gunn; *Apocalypse* reprinted by permission of D.J. Enright, Chatto and Windus Ltd and Watson, Little Ltd; *Poem* by Robin Blaser from THE NEW AMERICAN POETRY 1945–60, reprinted by permission of Robin Blaser; *Night Mail* reprinted by permission of Faber and Faber Ltd from COLLECTED POEMS by W.H. Auden; *Poetry of Departures* by Philip Larkin reprinted from THE LESS DECEIVED by permission of The Marvell Press, England; *Mary's Song* from WINTER TREES by Sylvia Plath © Ted Hughes 1971 published by Faber and Faber Ltd; *I, being born a woman and distressed* by Edna St Vincent Millay from COLLECTED POEMS, Harper & Row © 1923, 1951 by Edna St Vincent Millay and Norma Millay Ellis; *The Rolling English Road* by G.K. Chesterton published by Methuen & Co. Ltd, reprinted by permission of Miss D.E. Collins; *Trench Idyll* by Richard Aldington © Madame Catherine Guillaume published by Allen and Unwin Ltd; *Preparations for Victory* from UNDERTONES OF WAR by Edmund Blunden, reprinted by permission of A.D. Peters & Co. Ltd; *The Marriage of Black and White Part IV* from FRANTZ FANON'S UNEVEN RIBS by Taban Lo Liyong, reprinted by permission of Heinemann Educational Books; *A Welsh Testament* by R.S. Thomas from SELECTED POEMS 1946–1968 (Hart-Davis, MacGibbon) reprinted by permission of Granada Publishing Ltd; *The Lake Isle of Innisfree* by W.B. Yeats, reprinted by permission of Michael Yeats and Macmillan London Ltd; *To the Ancestral North* from THE DESCENT INTO THE CAVE, Oxford University Press 1957 © James Kirkup and from TO THE ANCESTRAL NORTH: POEMS FOR AN

Acknowledgements

AUTOBIOGRAPHY, Asahi Press, Tokyo 1983; *The Howling of Wolves* reprinted by permission of Faber and Faber Ltd from WODWO by Ted Hughes; *On the Lake* reprinted by permission of Curtis Brown Ltd, on behalf of the Estate of Victoria Sackville-West; *If He Let Us Go Now* Copyright © 1975 by Shirley Williams Reprinted from THE PEACOCK POEMS by permission of Wesleyan University Press.

Every effort has been made to trace owners of copyright and if any omissions can be rectified the publishers will be pleased to make the necessary arrangements.

Illustrations
Cover illustration: Alan Adler
Tamara Capellaro pp 35, 123, 131; Mike Gornall p 171; Dominic Mansell p 210; Stephen Mildrew p 185; Ian Penny p 177; Deborah Pollard pp 57, 179; Christine Roche p 106; Laini Stoddart p 44; Gary Wing pp 6, 121; Stephen Wright pp 146; Andrew Yaniw p 31.

Photographs
Keystone Press Agency Ltd pp 11, 73; National Film Archive/Stills Library pp 76, 129, 228.

Introduction
What are Prose and Poetry?

The difference between prose and poetry is certainly no longer easy to define. The boundaries between the two have been eroded in twentieth-century literature, as writers of all types have sought to break away from traditional forms and types of expression. In the past, this was not the case: for some people the difference between prose and poetry appeared to be clearly defined.

To see this, let us look at an extract from a play by Molière, the seventeenth-century French playwright. It is from *The Would-be Gentleman* and the characters involved are Mr Jourdain, a parvenu aiming to be accepted by high society, and a philosopher who has skills with language which Mr Jourdain wishes to make use of.

Mr Jourdain	And now I must tell you a secret. I'm in love with a lady of quality and I want you to help me to write her a little note I can let fall at her feet.
Philosopher	Very well.
Mr Jourdain	That's the correct thing to do, isn't it?
Philosopher	Certainly. You want it in verse, no doubt?
Mr Jourdain	No. No. None of your verse for me.
Philosopher	You want it in prose then?
Mr Jourdain	No. I don't want it in either.
Philosopher	But it must be one or the other.
Mr Jourdain	Why?
Philosopher	Because, my dear sir, if you want to express yourself at all there's only verse or prose for it.
Mr Jourdain	Only verse or prose for it?
Philosopher	That's all, sir. Whatever isn't prose is verse and anything that isn't verse is prose.
Mr Jourdain	And talking, as I am now, which is that?
Philosopher	That is prose.
Mr Jourdain	You mean to say that when I say 'Nicole, fetch me my slippers' or 'Give me my night-cap' that's prose?
Philosopher	Certainly, sir.
Mr Jourdain	Well, my goodness! Here I've been talking prose for forty years and never known it, and mighty grateful I am to you for telling me! Now, what I want to say in the letter is, 'Fair Countess, I am dying for love of your beautiful eyes!' but I want to put it elegantly, so that it sounds genteel.

10

20

1

Philosopher	Then say that the ardour of her glances has reduced your heart to ashes and that you endure night and day –
Mr Jourdain	No. No. No! I don't want that at all. All I want to say is what I told you. 'Fair Countess, I am dying for love of your beautiful eyes'.
Philosopher	But surely it must be elaborated a little.
Mr Jourdain	No, I tell you I don't want anything in the letter but these very words, but I want them to be stylish and properly arranged. Just tell me some of the different ways of putting them so that I can see what I want.
Philosopher	Well, you can put them as you have done, 'Fair Countess, I am dying for love of your beautiful eyes', or perhaps 'For love, fair Countess, of your beautiful eyes I am dying', or again 'For love of your beautiful eyes, fair Countess, dying I am', or yet again 'Your beautiful eyes, fair Countess, for love of, dying am I', or even 'Dying, fair Countess, for love of your beautiful eyes, I am'.
Mr Jourdain	But which of these is the best?
Philosopher	The one you used yourself, 'Fair Countess, I am dying for love of your beautiful eyes'.
Mr Jourdain	Although I've never done any study I get it right first time.

What Mr Jourdain wants to communicate to the Countess – the content of his message – is straightforward and might, translated into a twentieth-century idiom, be expressed in these terms:

I'm mad about your eyes!

Clearly, characters in a seventeenth-century play would not talk like this but we are given enough examples of Mr Jourdain's spoken style for us to be sure that the words he would have naturally used for his message would be considerably less refined than those he suggests to the philosopher. Indeed, that is the reason he has hired the services of this man: he is desperately concerned that what he does shall be 'the correct thing to do' (5) and he wants his message phrased 'elegantly, so that it sounds genteel' (26) and, consequently, acceptable to the rank of person he is addressing. He has already chosen the words for his message:

Fair Countess, I am dying for love of your beautiful eyes! (24–25)

and he is roundly dismissive of the elaboration suggested by the philosopher:

Philosopher	Then say that the ardour of her glances has reduced your heart to ashes and that you endure night and day –
Mr Jourdain	No. No. No! I don't want that at all. (27–29)

All that Mr Jourdain wants is for the words he has selected to be 'stylish and properly arranged' (34). In compliance with this request, the philosopher suggests a variety of ways in which these words can be ordered in one sentence, before admitting, to Mr Jourdain's comic self-satisfaction, that the original version was the best.

Mr Jourdain has clear preconceptions – however misguided they may be – of the appropriate way to express oneself. In the same way, many people have clear ideas about what poetry is.

If the term 'poetic' had to be applied to any of the three versions of Mr Jourdain's love-note (including the twentieth-century 'translation') it would most likely be applied to the last two. Why? Since the three sentences are all saying essentially the same thing, what is it about these two that makes them sound 'poetic'?

The most obvious difference is, of course, in the language: the last two versions use an exaggerated, heightened language that is not the language of everyday life. People seldom say that they are 'dying for love' of someone's eyes, any more than they announce that their heart has been 'reduced to ashes'. This intense, stylised language is commonly associated with poetry. Another factor may be the rhythm of these two versions. In each sentence the emphasis falls naturally on the key words ('dying', 'love', 'beautiful eyes'; 'ardour', 'reduced', 'heart', 'ashes', 'endure') and this rhythmic quality is another feature people commonly associate with poetry. Finally, people might point to the 'emotional content' of the last two versions and suggest that this intensified emotion is the hallmark of much poetic writing.

Choice of language, rhythm, emotional content: these are some of the ways in which poetry is commonly held to differ from prose. However, the differences are by no means as clear-cut as this might suggest. For example, does a statement automatically become poetry because it is expressed in heightened, stylised language? Or, alternatively, is it not possible for a poem to be written in everyday, 'spoken' language? There are prose extracts later in this book that use a language more stylised than that met in much poetry, and there are poems written in the distinct style of everyday speech. Similarly, a statement does not necessarily become poetry merely because it is laid out like a poem. What is the difference between the following two versions?

The ardour of your glances has reduced my heart to ashes

The ardour of your glances
Has reduced my heart to ashes

Both stress the same key words, both have a similar rhythm: is the second really poetry merely because it has the accepted form of a poem? Rhythm can play as important a part in prose as in poetry: there are prose extracts later in this book which have a startling rhythmic quality and modern poems which appear to have no recognisable rhythm at all. Even emotional content is no certain guide since prose, as well as poetry, can aim for a heightened and intense effect.

In short, it is increasingly difficult to maintain that prose and poetry can always be divided easily into two distinct categories, as the philosopher in the extract does. This book, while suggesting that prose may be more suited to express certain things than poetry (and vice versa) does not attempt such a division. Instead, it attempts to illustrate the startling variety of both prose and poetry and to point out, in each extract, the inter-connection between style and content. What is being said in the three versions of the love-note that we have been examining may be essentially the same, but it is clear that their different language, form and rhythm dramatically alter the way they sound and, therefore, affect their 'emotional content'. This is an important point to remember: the emotional content of any piece of writing is inextricably linked with the sort of language, rhythm and form it has, in other words, with its style.

In both prose and poetry, a good style consists of the effective use of language, whatever the content or purpose of the writing may be. The style of the writing must be appropriate to the content and purpose of the piece. Mr Jourdain wants his words to be stylish in order to impress the Countess. For him, a stylish note is one which will satisfy the expectations of members of the aristocratic society by whom he is anxious to be accepted:

I want to put it elegantly, so that it sounds genteel. (25–26)

But a piece of prose or poetry does not have to be ornate to be in a good style. Prose and poetry are put to many uses – to inform, describe, analyse, amuse, persuade, arouse. Some subjects do lend themselves to literary elaboration. Some require a straightforward direct style; the purpose of the piece of writing may well make adornment inappropriate. In all cases, however, the overall aim of the good stylist is to communicate effectively with the reader.

Chapter 1
The Variety of Prose

Narrative Prose

Prose is often associated with the telling of a story – narrative prose. The childhood desire to hear or read a good story is something that stays with most people, so it is not surprising that successful novelists are usually good story-tellers.

Emily Brontë was just such a novelist; one of the main reasons why her novel *Wuthering Heights* is still read today is because of its powerful story. The nineteenth-century reading public, for whom Brontë was writing, demanded a strong narrative, with pace and tension.

In the following passage, the narrator tells of a terrible night he spent in Wuthering Heights, the house from which the novel takes its name. As you read the passage, notice how skilfully Brontë brings out the nightmarish quality of the experience of someone who, half awake and half dreaming, finds it difficult to believe the evidence of his own senses.

■ This time, I remembered I was lying in the oak closet, and I heard distinctly the gusty wind, and the driving of the snow; I heard, also, the fir-bough repeat its teasing sound, and ascribed it to the right cause: but it annoyed me so much, that I resolved to silence it, if possible; and, I thought, I rose and endeavoured to unhasp the casement. The hook was soldered into the staple: a circumstance observed by me when awake, but forgotten. 'I must stop it, nevertheless!' I muttered, knocking my knuckles through the glass, and stretching an arm out to seize the importunate branch; instead of which, my fingers closed on the fingers of a little, ice-cold hand! The intense horror of nightmare   10
came over me: I tried to draw back my arm, but the hand clung to it, and a most melancholy voice sobbed, 'Let me in – let me in!' 'Who are you?' I asked, struggling, meanwhile, to disengage myself. 'Catherine Linton,' it replied, shiveringly (why did I think of *Linton*? I had read *Earnshaw* twenty times for Linton); 'I'm come home: I'd lost my way on the moor!' As it spoke, I discerned, obscurely, a child's face looking through the window. Terror made me cruel; and, finding it useless to attempt shaking the creature off, I pulled its wrist on to the broken pane, and rubbed it to and fro till the blood ran down and soaked the bedclothes: still it wailed, 'Let me in!' and maintained its tenacious   20
gripe, almost maddening me with fear. 'How can I?' I said at length.

'Let *me* go, if you want me to let you in!' The fingers relaxed. I snatched mine through the hole, hurriedly piled the books up in a pyramid against it, and stopped my ears to exclude the lamentable prayer. I seemed to keep them closed above a quarter of an hour; yet, the instant I listened again, there was the doleful cry moaning on! 'Begone!' I shouted, 'I'll never let you in, not if you beg for twenty years.' 'It is twenty years,' mourned the voice: 'twenty years. I've been a waif for twenty years!' Thereat began a feeble scratching outside, and the pile of books moved as if thrust forward. I tried to jump up, but could not stir 30 a limb; and so yelled aloud, in a frenzy of fright. To my confusion, I discovered the yell was not ideal: hasty footsteps approached my chamber door; somebody pushed it open, with a vigorous hand, and a light glimmered through the squares at the top of the bed. I sat shuddering yet, and wiping the perspiration from my forehead: the intruder appeared to hesitate, and muttered to himself. At last, he said in a half-whisper, plainly not expecting an answer, 'Is any one here?' I considered it best to confess my presence; for I knew Heathcliff's accents, and feared he might search further if I kept quiet. With this intention, I turned and opened the panels. I shall not soon forget the 40 effect my action produced.

WUTHERING HEIGHTS *Emily Brontë* □

This extract is a good example of how economical Brontë's narrative style is in portraying action, emotion and descriptive detail. Combining straight narrative and dialogue in telling her supernatural story, she builds tension as the narrator, finding that he cannot escape from the situation, is driven to desperation in his attempts to rid himself of the phantom. Mirroring the action, the narrator's mood swiftly passes from sleepy irritation to horror and finally grim determination. Brontë includes just enough descriptive detail to enhance the atmosphere of the story without bogging it down.

Look at the passage again and pick out examples which illustrate Brontë's skill in depicting action and emotion and in building up atmosphere.

Informative Prose

The narrative passage from *Wuthering Heights* is an example of a piece of prose which the author wrote in order to stimulate and entertain her readers and it is written in a suitable style for this. The extract which follows has a very different purpose and so it is naturally very different in style. Its purpose is to communicate information and for this, a plain, unvarnished style is appropriate so that the facts are conveyed clearly.

The extract is from a leaflet issued by the Department of Health and Social Security and the intention of the writer of the leaflet is to explain what supplementary benefit is to people who are thinking of applying for it.

What is supplementary benefit?

It is cash you can get if the money you have coming in is less than you need to live on.

You can't get it if you are in full-time work. But if you have any children you may be able to get FIS (Family Income Supplement) instead. Get leaflet FIS.1 from a post office or social security office.

You can claim supplementary benefit if you are:
- over pension age
  or
- unfit for work
  or
- bringing up children on your own
  or
- unemployed and can't get work
  or
- working only part-time
  or
- needed at home to look after a disabled relative.

Did you know:
- You don't need to have paid national insurance contributions.

- Savings up to £2000 won't affect your benefit at all.

- Owning your home won't stop you getting benefit.

- If you get supplementary benefit, you and your family can get other things free – like school meals, milk for the under-fives, visits to the dentist, glasses and prescriptions.

If you want to know more:
Ask at your social security office. Or go to a Citizens Advice Bureau or other advice centre. Detailed information is given in *Supplementary Benefits Handbook*. You can see this at your local library.

DHSS LEAFLET SB.1. ☐

Consider how effectively the information is communicated and include in this an analysis of the level of language used and the way it is set out on the page.

Poetic Prose

The next passage, which is taken from D.H. Lawrence's novel *The Rainbow*, may seem to have more in common with poetry than with prose, but prose as well as poetry can use language of beauty if that suits the writer's purpose; prose can have poetic qualities and still remain prose.

Lawrence was a prose writer who often wrote 'poetically' in his novels and short stories. In the following extract, he uses beautiful language with sensuous images to achieve a concentrated, heightened effect. This is reinforced by his use of a very definite rhythm in his sentences – another feature which is more often associated with poetry than with prose.

■ In the round dew-pond the stars were untroubled. She ventured softly into the water, grasping at the stars with her hands.

And then suddenly she started back, running swiftly. He was there, beside her, but only on sufferance. He was a screen for her fears. He served her. She took him, she clasped him, clenched him close, but her eyes were open looking at the stars, it was as if the stars were lying with her and entering the unfathomable darkness of her womb, fathoming her at last. It was not him.

The dawn came. They stood together on a high place, an earthwork of the stone-age man, watching for the light. It came over the land. But 10 the land was dark. She watched a pale rim on the sky, away against the darkened land. The darkness became bluer. A little wind was running in from the sea behind. It seemed to be running to the pale rift of the dawn. And she and he darkly, on an outpost of the darkness, stood watching for the dawn.

The light grew stronger, gushing up against the dark sapphire of the transparent night. The light grew stronger, whiter, then over it hovered a flush of rose. A flush of rose, and then yellow, pale, new-created yellow, the whole quivering and poising momentarily over the fountain on the sky's rim. 20

The rose hovered and quivered, burned, fused to flame, to a transient red, while the yellow urged out in great waves, thrown from the ever-increasing fountain, great waves of yellow flinging into the sky, scattering its spray over the darkness, which became bluer and bluer, paler, till soon it would be a radiance, which had been darkness.

The sun was coming. There was a quivering, a powerful, terrifying swim of molten light. Then the molten source itself surged forth, revealing itself. The sun was in the sky, too powerful to look at.

And the ground beneath lay so still, so peaceful. Only now and again a cock crew. Otherwise, from the distant yellow hills to the pine trees at 30 the foot of the downs, everything was newly washed into being, in a flood of new, golden creation.

It was so unutterably still and perfect with promise, the golden-lighted, distinct land, that Ursula's soul rocked and wept. Suddenly he glanced at her. The tears were running over her cheeks, her mouth was working strangely.

'What is the matter?' he asked.

After a moment's struggle with her voice,

'It's so beautiful', she said, looking at the glowing, beautiful land. It was so beautiful, so perfect, and so unsullied.   40

                                        THE RAINBOW *D.H. Lawrence* □

Lawrence uses heightened language to try to express emotion coloured with sensuousness. Both the type of language he uses and the rhythms of his prose reflect this:

> It was so unutterably still and perfect with promise, the golden-lighted distinct land, that Ursula's soul rocked and wept. (33–34)

Lawrence is trying to show us what Ursula's character is like, but not by conventional character analysis. He intends to go beyond that to deeper emotional and physical truths:

> ...it was as if the stars were lying with her and entering the unfathomable darkness of her womb, fathoming her at last. It was not him. (6–8)

Look at the passage in the light of what has been said about Lawrence's aims. Can you find examples where the language is poetic and sensuous and where it has repetitive rhythms? Does the kind of sentence construction which Lawrence uses contribute anything?

Persuasive Prose

Prose that is intended to persuade is perhaps most often seen in commercial advertising. But persuasive prose is also, of course, to be found in many other places; for example in the publications issued by political parties and pressure groups, in the literature of religious organisations and in the articles and editorials of newspapers and magazines.

The language of all writing that is meant to be persuasive is very carefully chosen, whether the reader is being asked to adopt a new soap powder or to vote for a different party at the next election. In the case of advertisements, especially, key words are included which are deliberately chosen for their appeal to the consumer.

The advertisement on the opposite page is for a dating service. Discuss how it uses language to try to persuade readers to use its services.

Looking for that special someone?

Finding the ideal partner can take time. You shouldn't **just** leave it to chance, hoping the **right one** will turn up sometime, somehow.

You should contact Mastermatch

At Mastermatch we'll do all we possibly can to find your ideal partner. This is how we go about it.

♥ we ask you to fill in a reasonably detailed – and strictly confidential – questionnaire, giving details of yourself and the kind of person you're looking for.

♥ we invite you to a friendly counselling session at our club in which we can fill out the picture given in your completed questionnaire.

♥ all your data is analysed and fed through our own computer, to discover which of our members matches or complements you most.

♥ we send you very detailed profiles of any people we suggest you meet and they are sent details of you – without names or addresses at this stage. **So that you know a great deal about each other even before you decide to meet.**

♥ No names and addresses are given until both parties agree to meet.

We do all we can to find someone who will **really** suit you. And we'll give you advice, should you ask, on how to make that first meeting free from embarrassment or awkwardness. You can depend on Mastermatch . . . because we don't leave happiness to chance.

Fill in your FREE Partner Analysis Test NOW

without any obligation, and you'll receive FREE details of the type of person whose interests, personality and even looks will be complementary to you. Please answer the questions carefully and accurately as this is very important in helping us to assess your details and send you an accurate analysis. POST TODAY and you could be well on the way to finding your ideal partner.

To MASTERMATCH Please send me under plain cover my free partner test and full details about your introduction system ☐ the club's London social events ☐ Winter ski-chalet parties ☐

1. Your interests

Pastime Interests		Arts Interests	
Playing music, T.V. & Radio	☐	Ballet, Cinema & Theatre	☐
Parties/Dancing, Pubs, Clubs etc	☐	Creative writing, Acting	☐
Card Games	☐	Social work, Psychology	☐
Travel, Motoring & Camping	☐	Literature & Poetry	☐

Descriptive Prose

The next piece is a descriptive passage from one of Charles Dickens' novels, *Bleak House*, which was published only a few years after *Wuthering Heights*. By this time in his writing career, Dickens had acquired a vast readership; all ages and classes of people read his novels.

In this passage, Dickens gives us a vivid picture of the deserted Inns of Court in London in the legal holiday when the lawyers are out of town.

■ It is the long vacation in the regions of Chancery Lane. The good ships Law and Equity, those teak-built, copper-bottomed, iron-fastened, brazen-faced, and not by any means fast-sailing Clippers, are laid up in ordinary. The Flying Dutchman, with a crew of ghostly clients imploring all whom they may encounter to peruse their papers, has drifted, for the time being, Heaven knows where. The Courts are all shut up, the public offices lie in a hot sleep, Westminster Hall itself is a shady solitude where nightingales might sing, and a tenderer class of suitors than is usually found there, walk.

The Temple, Chancery Lane, Sergeants' Inn, and Lincoln's Inn even 10 unto the Fields, are like tidal harbours at low water; where stranded proceedings, offices at anchor, idle clerks lounging on lopsided stools that will not recover their perpendicular until the current of Term sets in, lie high and dry upon the ooze of the long vacation. Outer doors of chambers are shut up by the score, messages and parcels are to be left at the Porter's Lodge by the bushel. A crop of grass would grow in the chinks of the stone pavement outside Lincoln's Inn Hall, but that the ticket-porters, who have nothing to do beyond sitting in the shade there, with their white aprons over their heads to keep the flies off, grub it up and eat it thoughtfully. 20

There is only one Judge in town. Even he only comes twice a week to sit in chambers. If the country folks of those assize towns on his circuit could see him now! No full-bottomed wig, no red petticoats, no fur, no javelin-men, no white wands. Merely a close-shaved gentleman in white trousers and a white hat, with sea-bronze on the judicial countenance, and a strip of bark peeled by the solar rays from the judicial nose, who calls in at the shell-fish shop as he comes along, and drinks iced ginger-beer!

BLEAK HOUSE *Charles Dickens* □

One of Dickens' aims is to stimulate the reader by the imaginative qualities which he brings to bear in this extract. He adds an extra tier of colourful description to his picture of an idle and hot part of London with his vision of the courts as ships laid up in harbour on the mud.

But Dickens goes further than this; by skilfully describing various aspects of the ships, he mounts an attack on the legal system:

The good ships Law and Equity, those. . . brazen-faced, and not by any means fast-sailing Clippers. . . . (1–3)

In the lines above, Dickens pretends to be describing ships, but he intends the reader to understand that being 'brazen-faced' and 'not by any means fast-sailing' are two characteristics of lawyers. He uses the ships to make two allegations about defects in the legal system; that lawyers are shameless in their conduct and slow to act.

Look at the rest of the extract again; study Dickens' use of imaginative detail and pick out other examples where he uses a comparison with ships to make a point about the law.

Reflective Prose

Prose is used also in writing that contemplates or reflects on some subject, usually in the form of an essay. The essay used to be a very common literary medium for a kind of gentle, discursive writing. Max Beerbohm, an essayist of some stature, had this to say about the craft of essay writing:

> In essay writing, style is everything. The essayist's aim is to bring himself home to his readers, to express himself in exact terms. Therefore, he must find exact words for his thoughts and cadences which express the very tone of his emotions. Himself is the thing to be obtruded and style the only means to this end.

Tone means the mood, emphasis or slant the writer chooses to give to the topic. A writer can use a detached, impersonal tone or a very emotional, personally committed tone; tone can be deferential or subversive, gentle or abrasive.

The following extract is from *The Dark Hours*, an essay by J.B. Priestley in which he contemplates sleeplessness and his own methods of combating it.

■ This last week I have had a succession of bad nights. It is not merely that I cannot easily find sleep. This I never could do, except during those times when I have spent the whole day in the open. Who, having enjoyed them, does not remember those hours of sleep, a divine unconsciousness, that fell on him, came down like a vast benevolent sandbag on the top of his head, at the Front? Sleep then was not simply a dark little ante-room through which one passed in order to arrive at the next morning's breakfast table, but a sojourn in the Blessed Isles. I remember – it must be twelve years ago – the best sleep I ever had. We had been three weeks or so in the trenches, the clayey kind, full of 10 water and with hardly a dug-out; and though there had been no real fighting, there had been any number of those daft alarms and excursions that hearty generals, talking over the wine and cigars in some distant château, praised to one another, in the belief that Englishmen always preferred magnificence to war. We had been so long without adequate sleep that our eyes were for ever hot and staring under leaden lids. Well, one dark night we were relieved at last, and went swaying down miles of cobbled road. Some of the fellows dropped out, others slept as they staggered on, and finally a remnant of us arrived at some place that was nothing to us but a dark assemblage 20 of barns and windowless houses, familiar enough yet as unreal as a place on the moon. A gulp or two of hot sweet tea, a moment's glow of rum, then down we fell so mud-caked that we were as stiff as mummies on the hard floors, and down too came the lovely velvet curtain, blotting out the whole lunatic show of babbling statesmen and lads with glazing eyes. I slept for eighteen hours.

In the ordinary way, however, I have to woo my sleep, and that is one reason why I have read so many books, chasing Morpheus down innumerable labyrinths of eighteenth-century moralising or twentieth-century introspection. Those no-sooner-have-I-touched-the-pillow 30 people are past my comprehension. There is something suspiciously bovine about them. When they begin to yawn about half-past ten, as they always do when I am with them (and I make you a present of the inevitable comment), I feel that they forfeit all right to be considered as fellow-creatures, spirits here for a season that they may exchange confidences at the hour when all the beasts that perish are fast asleep. I do not complain about having to approach sleep so stealthily, tip-toeing through a chapter or so. After all, this is only to prolong the day, and I cannot help thinking that such a reluctance to part for ever from the day, though it be only an unconscious reluctance, is proof of an 40 affectionate nature, unwilling to dismiss a servant, however poor a thing. Nor do I complain – though I like it less – about waking too early, beginning the day before it is fairly ready for me, nothing but a grey little monster with the chill on it and still opposed to all our nobler activities. I have been told that as the years wither me away, I shall have more and more of these early wakings, and I cannot say that the prospect pleases me. But for the moment I will submit to it without complaint, for there are worse things, and all this last week I have been suffering from them. I have been finding myself awake, not at the end of one day nor at the beginning of another, but sometime between 50 them, in the mysterious dark hours.

THE DARK HOURS *J.B. Priestley* □

Look at the tone of Priestley's essay and how that is reflected in the style of the writing. As you do this, bear in mind Beerbohm's opinion on essay writing, particularly his statement that 'The essayist's aim is to bring himself home to his readers, to express himself in exact terms.'

Prose and the Stream of Consciousness

In the final extract of this introductory chapter, prose is used to communicate the thoughts of a character in a novel. The writer, B.S. Johnson, is using the stream of consciousness technique, which is an attempt to reproduce the actual train of thoughts of a character. As our thought processes are not always orderly and logical, and certainly not grammatical, the stream of consciousness technique usually involves the use of prose that breaks normal rules of construction, syntax and form.

The following extract, from *House Mother Normal*, deals with the thoughts of an 85-year-old woman living in an old people's home, under the supervision of a rather despotic housemother.

■ ... me and then   get this down me and
then I'll   be all right
                         spuds and mashed and   with knees
try hard   peas, peas, peas
shovel peas in, more   then I'll be all right
                more?

                                         more
        general sold his   cockerel
                         the meat is good, more meat, that's
the thing, must eat to get right, get this down me and then   10
I'll be all right, that's it, ask for more meat. *More meat?*

He's not going to eat his, no, I'll have his, must eat, how he
can leave it I don't know, here Oh!   twitcher!
        no ...   *eee!* my hand
the backs of my hands!   Hurts   not for long, I've
got over worse, I'm the toughest.
                    They said it was just a craze,
wanting to eat, it would never   catch on, la la la!
Catchy.
                         I always did believe   20
in ruining your own work, it was one of my fondest beliefs,
if you do that then you don't have to beholden to somebody,
do you?

        Scrape the plate, the mash off, mash off corners

                                Swinging on
ropes, nothing much on, just something round his
                              unmentionables, as we
used to call them, into all that mucky water and crawlies,
out in the bare colds or   rocks was it,
only a picture after all.

15

Another one I saw had Charlie Chimpanzee
in it, when I was that high.   Then we had Gilbert
Harding being rude, we enjoyed it! Diving into the
crawlies and the water all covered by scum, those jungle
creepers!   How we used to laugh!
She ought to show us films here,
though some would abuse the privilege, they never do.
It would never do.

da-da, ma-ma
atrisket, my love bisquit, brown bread and waistcoat,   40
crumbs to his watch-piece.

My name's Gloria, Glory
for short. It's too far this time.   May I never?
My true love went once round fingering, blue hair he
had with his long black eyes, four foot   three
in his bloomers, I remember him so clearly, it was in
a pub we first met, I was with my mates at the time, he
was with his.   Yellow jumper and pale skirt
This for two or more I was with him,
standing in the dark. Milk stout was all our tipple, then.   50
He was my first, it was raining at the time.

HOUSE MOTHER NORMAL *B.S. Johnson* □

How do the layout of the passage and the way that language is used differ from
more normal story-telling techniques? Does the stream of consciousness
technique have any advantages over conventional narrative in what the author
can communicate to the reader?

Chapter 2
Narrative Prose

This chapter looks at narrative prose; this is prose that tells a story. Many writers clearly use the story as a means of discussing issues which are important to them but the ability to interest readers in a story is the most essential skill of the novelist and the short story writer.

In mass market best-selling novels, it is the plot or story-line which is much the most important element; a 'good story' is what is responsible for attracting readers. On the other hand, the novelists who rank among the most important of our writers also invest their stories with other qualities, so that they go beyond the mere telling of a tale. These writers use a story to explore human emotions and character truthfully, as they perceive them.

However, whether it is classic or best-selling writing that is in question, the author's creative presence or voice is crucial; it is the author who shapes the story, chooses the point of view from which the story is to be told, selects the incidents and chooses what is to happen to the characters. The author's shaping hand or voice is an important presence in all fictional writing.

That voice is more obtrusive in the writing of some authors than others. For example, as will be seen later in the chapter, writers of the nineteenth century were very fond of commenting directly as *the author*, a person outside the story, on the characters and action in their own narrative. With this kind of direct comment, the reader becomes very aware of the author's voice directing attention to some feature of a particular character or to a moral which is to be drawn from the story.

In this century, the tendency has been for the author to withdraw from being a direct presence in the novel or short story. However, a writer can never really disappear from his or her own work and become a kind of neutral observer. The author's voice is always there, selecting language, incidents, characterisation and point of view.

Fables are whimsical stories, often originally invented to amuse children, that teach a moral lesson through the telling of a humorous simple tale. Although fables are intended to convey a moral, in the best ones the strength and flow of the narrative holds the reader's interest.

The fable that follows is by James Thurber, an American humorist who wrote fables for adults.

■ A turtle appeared in a meadow one summer's day and attracted the attention of all the creatures in the grass and in the trees, because the date 44 B.C. was carved on his shell. 'Our meadow is honoured indeed,' exclaimed a grasshopper, 'for our visitor is the oldest of all living creatures.'

'We must build a pavilion in his honour,' said a frog, and the catbirds and the swallows and the other birds built a stately pleasure dome out of twigs and leaves and blossoms for the very important turtle. An orchestra of crickets played music in his honour, and a wood thrush sang. The sounds of jubilee were heard in nearby fields and woods, 10 and as more and more creatures turned up from farther and farther away to have a look at the ancient turtle, the grasshopper decided to charge admission to the pavilion.

'I will be the barker,' said the frog, and, with the help of the grasshopper, he composed an impressive spiel. 'Yesterday and yesterday and yesterday,' it began, 'creeps in this carapace from day to day to the first syllable of recorded time. This great turtle was born two thousand years ago, the year the mighty Julius Caesar died. Horace was twenty-one in 44 B.C., and Cicero had but a single year to live.' The bystanders did not seem very much interested in the turtle's ancient 20 contemporaries, but they gladly paid to go in and have a look at his ancient body.

Inside the pavilion, the grasshopper continued the lecture. 'This remarkable turtle is a direct descendant of one of the first families of Ooze,' he chanted. 'His great-grandfather may have been the first thing that moved in the moist and muddy margins of this cooling planet. Except for our friend's ancestors, there was nothing but coal and blobs of glob.'

One day a red squirrel who lived in a neighbouring wood dropped in to look at the turtle and to listen to the ballyhoo. '44 B.C., my foot!' 30 scoffed the squirrel, as he glared at the grasshopper. 'You are full of tobacco juice, and your friend the frog is full of lightning bugs. The carving of an ancient date on the carapace of a turtle is a common childish prank. This creep was probably born no earlier than 1902.'

As the red squirrel ranted on, the spectators who had paid to get into the pavilion began departing quietly, and there was no longer a crowd listening to the frog out front. The crickets put away their instruments and disappeared as silently as the Arabs, and the wood thrush gathered up his sheet music and flew off and did not return. The sounds of jubilee were no longer heard in the once merry meadow, and 40 the summer seemed to languish like a dying swan.

'I knew all the time he wasn't two thousand years old', admitted the grasshopper, 'but the legend pleased the people, young and old, and many smiled who had not smiled for years.'

'And many laughed who had not laughed for years,' said the frog, 'and many eyes sparkled and many hearts were gay.' The turtle shed a turtle tear at this and crawled away.

'The truth is not merry and bright,' said the red squirrel. 'The truth is cold and dark. Let's face it.' And, looking smug and superior, the iconoclast scampered impudently back to his tree in the wood. From 50 the grass of the meadow, voices once carefree and gay joined in a rueful and lonely chorus, as if someone great and wonderful had died and was being buried.

Moral: *Oh, why should the shattermyth have to be a crumplehope and a dampenglee?*

THE TURTLE WHO CONQUERED TIME *James Thurber* □

As well as providing an entertaining story in his fable, Thurber sets out, gently, to subvert the genre. Usually, the moral that is to be gleaned from a fable is meant to be morally uplifting; it is seen that hard work, thrift or some such virtue is rewarded. But in Thurber's modern fable, the tone and the moral at the end are quite different.

Thurber, the author, does not directly intrude into the telling of the story, but he is very much a presence in the fable in the tone he gives to it, the way he allows the story to develop and in the moral at the end.

1 Does the story move quickly or does the author dwell on details with descriptive touches and analysis? Illustrate your answer by referring to specific sections of the text.

2 Thurber combines a rather grand and elevated style with some American colloquialisms and a modern idiom in his telling of the fable to achieve a witty effect. Select examples of these from the text and say why you think they are effective.

3 'Oh, why should the shattermyth have to be a crumplehope and a dampenglee?' (54–55)

Comment on the effect produced by the use of the words 'shattermyth', 'crumplehope' and 'dampenglee' in the moral attached to the fable. How is the tone of the moral in line with the general tone used in the telling of the fable?

● Write a modern version of one of the following fables:

the ugly duckling   Cinderella   the golden goose

the fox and the crow   the ant and the grasshopper

Fairy-tales and folk-tales from every land and culture depend largely for their lasting popularity on their narrative appeal. People respond to a good story that is told well and with pace. Most people also respond to familiar elements in fairy-tales and in stories in general; we have certain expectations about plots, incidents, twists of fortune and endings to stories.

In the following passage, Rabindranath Tagore uses his memories of the fairy-tales that his grandmother told to him as a child to draw conclusions about what it is in them that people enjoy.

■ 'Once upon a time there was a king.'

When we were children there was no need to know who the King in the fairy story was. It didn't matter whether he was called Siladitya or Salivahan, whether he lived at Kashi or Kanauj. The thing that made a seven-year-old boy's heart go thump with delight was this one sovereign truth, this reality of all realities: 'Once there was a king.'

But the readers of this modern age are far more exact and exacting. When they hear such an opening to a story, they are at once critical and suspicious. They apply the searchlight of science to its legendary haze and ask: 'Which king?'   10

The story-tellers also have become more precise. They are no longer content with the old indefinite, 'There was a king,' but assume instead a look of profound learning and begin: 'Once there was a king named Ajatasatru.'

The modern reader's curiosity, however, is not so easily satisfied. He blinks at the author through his scientific spectacles and asks again: 'Which Ajatasatru?'

When we were young, we understood all sweet things; and we could detect the sweets of a fairy story by an unerring science of our own. We never cared for such useless things as knowledge. We only cared for   20 truth. And our unsophisticated little hearts knew well where the Crystal Palace of Truth lay and how to reach it. But today we are expected to write pages of facts, while the truth is simply this:

'There was a king . . . . . . And the king had a queen.'

That was good to begin with. He had only one!

It is usual for kings in fairy stories to be extravagant in the number of queens they have. And whenever we hear that there are two queens our hearts begin to sink. One of them is sure to be unhappy. But in Grannie's story there was no danger of that. He had only one queen.

The next detail of Grannie's story was that the king had no son. At   30 the age of seven I did not think one need bother if a man had no son. He might only have been in the way.

Nor was I greatly excited when I heard that the king had gone into the forest to practise austerities in order to obtain a son. There was only one thing that would have made me go into the forest, and that was to get away from my tutor!

But the king had left behind with his queen a little girl, who grew up into a beautiful princess.

Twelve years passed away, and the king went on practising austerities, and never thought of his beautiful daughter. The princess   40 had reached the full bloom of her youth. The age of marriage had passed, but the king had not returned. And the queen pined away with grief and cried: 'Is my golden daughter destined to die unmarried? Ah me, what a fate is mine!'

Then the queen sent men to the king entreating him to come back if only for a single night, and to eat one meal in the palace. And the king consented.

With the greatest care, the queen cooked with her own hand sixty-four dishes. She made a seat for him of sandalwood and arranged the food in plates of gold and cups of silver. The princess stood behind his 50 seat with the peacock-tail/ fan in her hand. After his twelve years' absence, the king entered the house, and the princess waving the fan, lighted up all the room with her beauty. The king looked in his daughter's face and forgot even to eat.

At last he asked his queen: 'Pray, who is this girl whose beauty shines as the golden image of the goddess? Whose daughter is she?'

The queen beat her forehead and cried: 'Ah, how evil is my fate! Do you not recognise your own daughter?'

For some time the king remained in silent amazement, but at last he exclaimed: 'My tiny daughter has grown to be a woman.'   60

'How could it be otherwise?' the queen asked with a sigh. 'Do you not know that twelve years have passed?'

'But why did you not give her in marriage?' asked the king.

'You were away,' the queen replied. 'And how could I find her a suitable husband?'

At this the king, strangely excited, vowed that the first man he saw the following day when he went out of the palace, should marry her.

But the princess merely went on waving her fan of peacock feathers and the king finished his meal.

The next morning, as the king went out of his palace he saw the son 70 of a Brahman gathering sticks in the forest outside the palace gates. He was about seven or eight years old.

The king said: 'I will marry my daughter to him.'

Who can interfere with a king's command? At once the boy was called, and the marriage garlands were exchanged between him and the princess.

At this point I came up close to my wise Grannie and asked her eagerly: 'What then?'

In the bottom of my heart there was a devout wish that I might be that fortunate seven-year-old wood-gatherer. The night resounded 80 with the patter of rain. The earthen lamp by my bedside was burning low. My grandmother's voice droned on as she told the story. And all these things served to create in a corner of my credulous heart the belief that I had been gathering sticks in the dawn of some indefinite time in the kingdom of some unknown king, and that in a moment garlands had been exchanged between me and the princess, beautiful as the

Goddess of Grace. She had a gold band on her hair and gold earrings in her ears. She wore a necklace and bracelets of gold, and a golden waist-chain round her waist, and a pair of golden anklets tinkled with the movements of her feet.   90

If my grandmother had been an author, how many explanations would she not have had to offer of this little story! First of all, every one would ask why the king remained twelve years in the forest? And then, why should the king's daughter remain unmarried all that time? Such a delay would be regarded as absurd.

Even if my Grannie could have got so far without quarrelling with her critics, still there would have been a great hue and cry about the marriage itself. In the first place, it never happened. And in the second, how could there be a marriage between a princess of the Warrior Caste and a boy of the priestly Brahman Caste? Her readers would have   100 imagined at once that the writer was preaching against our social customs in an indirect and unfair way. And they would write letters to the papers.

So I pray with all my heart that my grandmother may be born a grandmother again, and not through some cursed fate be born again in the person of her luckless grandson.

With a throb of joy and delight, I asked Grannie: 'What then?'

ONCE THERE WAS A KING *Rabindranath Tagore* □

In the introduction to the Tagore extract, the expectations that most people have about fairy-tales are mentioned. Tagore analyses those expectations of readers within the framework of the narrative. The 'I' of the story is repeatedly detaching himself from the narrative and examining both how the story works and his own expectations of the narrative element.

It could be said that there are two levels of narrative in this story; first, there is the first person narrator, the 'I', the man looking back to his boyhood; secondly there is Grannie, who is actually telling the story of the king. In this extract, then, the author's presence is emphatic, drawing attention to the very art of story-telling he is practising.

1 'At this point I came up close to my wise Grannie and asked her eagerly; 'What then?'
    In the bottom of my heart there was a devout wish that I might be that fortunate seven-year-old wood-gatherer.' (77–80)

This passage reveals two of the most important reasons why people read stories. What are they?

2 According to Tagore, how do 'the readers of this modern age' differ in their response to story-telling from the time when he was a child? Explain which response he thinks is better and why.

3 'If my grandmother had been an author . . .'(91)

  a According to Tagore what further explanations would his grandmother have had to supply if she had been an author?
  b What does this imply about our expectations and demands of fairy tales?

● Consider one of the following genres or conventional types of fiction:

  detective stories   science fiction   romantic novels

  adventure and spy stories   crime novels.

  Write a brief essay outlining and commenting on the most familiar elements in any one of these categories of fiction.

The art of short story writing is as hard to define as the art of story-telling itself. However, it may be said that there are two main types of short story. The first is the traditional short story that is basically an anecdote within a definite literary form and which usually has a twist or surprise ending. The second is the more modern type of short story which is more formless and impressionistic and aims for atmosphere and mood rather than the telling of a definite story.

Although they do not have the lengthy extent of a novel to work with, the best writers of short stories achieve a kind of resonance, a reverberation which makes the story memorable for the reader beyond the bare details of the plot. They do this by creating atmosphere, by stirring up emotions and by provoking moral or intellectual considerations.

The short story that follows is by O. Henry, a famous American short story writer who specialised in the traditional form of short story.

■ Miss Martha Meacham kept the little bakery on the corner (the one where you go up three steps, and the bell tinkles when you open the door).

Miss Martha was forty, her bank-book showed a credit of two thousand dollars, and she possessed two false teeth and a sympathetic heart. Many people have married whose chances to do so were much inferior to Miss Martha's.

Two or three times a week a customer came in in whom she began to take an interest. He was a middle-aged man, wearing spectacles and a brown beard trimmed to a careful point.   10

He spoke English with a strong German accent. His clothes were worn and darned in places, and wrinkled and baggy in others. But he looked neat, and had very good manners.

He always bought two loaves of stale bread. Fresh bread was five cents a loaf. Stale ones were two for five. Never did he call for anything but stale bread.

Once Miss Martha saw a red and brown stain on his fingers. She was sure then that he was an artist and very poor. No doubt he lived in a garret, where he painted pictures and ate stale bread and thought of the good things to eat in Miss Martha's bakery. 20

Often when Miss Martha sat down to her chops and light rolls and jam and tea she would sigh, and wish that the gentle-mannered artist might share her tasty meal instead of eating his dry crust in that draughty attic.

Miss Martha's heart, as you have been told, was a sympathetic one.

In order to test her theory as to his occupation, she brought from her room one day a painting that she had bought at a sale, and set it against the shelves behind the bread counter.

It was a Venetian scene. A splendid marble palazzio (so it said on the picture) stood in the foreground – or rather forewater. For the rest there 30 were gondolas (with the lady trailing her hand in the water), clouds, sky, and chiaroscuro in plenty. No artist could fail to notice it.

Two days afterward the customer came in.

'Two loafs of stale bread, if you blease . . . You haf here a fine bicture, madame,' he said while she was wrapping up the bread.

'Yes?' says Miss Martha, revelling in her own cunning. 'I do so admire art and' (no, it would not do to say 'artists' thus early) 'and paintings,' she substituted. 'You think it is a good picture?'

'Der balace,' said the customer, 'is not in good drawing. Der bairspective of it is not true. Goot morning, madame.' 40

He took his bread, bowed, and hurried out.

Yes, he must be an artist. Miss Martha took the picture back to her room.

How gentle and kindly his eyes shone behind his spectacles! What a broad brow he had! To be able to judge perspective at a glance – and to live on stale bread! But genius often has to struggle before it is recognized.

What a thing it would be for art and perspective if genius were backed by two thousand dollars in the bank, a bakery, and a sympathetic heart to —— But these were day-dreams, Miss Martha. 50

Often now when he came he would chat for a while across the showcase. He seemed to crave Miss Martha's cheerful words.

He kept on buying stale bread. Never a cake, never a pie, never one of her delicious Sally Lunns.

She thought he began to look thinner and discouraged. Her heart ached to add something good to eat to his meagre purchase, but her courage failed at the act. She did not dare affront him. She knew the pride of artists.

Miss Martha took to wearing her blue-dotted silk waist behind the counter. In the back room she cooked a mysterious compound of 60 quince seeds and borax. Ever so many people use it for the complexion.

One day the customer came in as usual, laid his nickel on the show-

case, and called for his stale loaves. While Miss Martha was reaching
for them there was a great tooting and clanging, and a fire-engine came
lumbering past.

The customer hurried to the door to look, as anyone will. Suddenly
inspired, Miss Martha seized the opportunity.

On the bottom shelf behind the counter was a pound of fresh butter
that the dairyman had left ten minutes before. With a breadknife Miss
Martha made a deep slash in each of the stale loaves, inserted a   70
generous quantity of butter, and pressed the loaves tight again.

When the customer turned once more she was tying the paper
around them.

When he had gone, after an unusually pleasant little chat, Miss
Martha smiled to herself, but not without a slight fluttering of the heart.

Had she been too bold? Would he take offence? But surely not. There
was no language of edibles. Butter was no emblem of unmaidenly
forwardness.

For a long time that day her mind dwelt on the subject. She imagined
the scene when he should discover her little deception.   80

He would lay down his brushes and palette. There would stand his
easel with the picture he was painting in which the perspective was
beyond criticism.

He would prepare for his luncheon of dry bread and water. He
would slice into a loaf – ah!

Miss Martha blushed. Would he think of the hand that placed it there
as he ate? Would he ——

The front door bell jangled viciously. Somebody was coming in,
making a great deal of noise.

Miss Martha hurried to the front. Two men were there. One was a   90
young man smoking a pipe – a man she had never seen before. The
other was her artist.

His face was very red, his hat was on the back of his head, his hair
was wildly rumpled. He clinched his two fists and shook them
ferociously at Miss Martha. *At Miss Martha.*

'Dummkopf!' he shouted with extreme loudness; and then 'Tausen-
donfer!' or something like it, in German.

The young man tried to draw him away.

'I vill not go,' he said angrily, 'else I shall told her.'

He made a bass drum of Miss Martha's counter.   100

'You haf shpoilt me,' he cried, his blue eyes blazing behind his
spectacles. 'I vill tell you. You vas von *meddingsome* old cat!'

Miss Martha leaned weakly against the shelves and laid one hand on
her blue-dotted silk waist. The young man took his companion by the
collar.

'Come on,' he said, 'you've said enough.' He dragged the angry one
out at the door to the sidewalk, and then came back.

'Guess you ought to be told, ma'am,' he said, 'what the row is about.

25

That's Blumberger. He's an architectural draughtsman. I work in the same office with him.   110

'He's been working hard for three months drawing a plan for a new city hall. It was a prize competition. He finished inking the lines yesterday. You know, a draughtsman always makes his drawing in pencil first. When it's done he rubs out the pencil lines with handfuls of stale breadcrumbs. That's better than india-rubber.

'Blumberger's been buying the bread here. Well, to-day – well, you know, ma'am, that butter isn't – well, Blumberger's plan isn't good for anything now except to cut up into railroad sandwiches.'

Miss Martha went into the back room. She took off the blue-dotted silk waist and put on the old brown serge she used to wear. Then she   120 poured the quince seed and borax mixture out of the window into the ash can.

WITCHES' LOAVES O. Henry □

In the introduction to this passage it was said that the classic form of the short story deals with the telling of a single incident with a twist ending: *Witches' Loaves* falls into this category.

O. Henry's style of writing is very concise and crisp. He wastes few words and there is a precision about his story-telling that appeals to most readers. In the second paragraph of the story, he succinctly sums up Miss Martha's character:

> Miss Martha was forty, her bank-book showed a credit of two thousand dollars, and she possessed two false teeth and a sympathetic heart. Many people have married whose chances to do so were much inferior to Miss Martha's.

On the other hand those who do not admire O. Henry criticise him for writing corny stories with trite endings and for burdening the reader with unsophisticated, cracker-barrel philosophy.

1 O. Henry's style is usually considered to be economical and precise. In the light of this, discuss the length of sentences and paragraphs used in *Witches' Loaves*. In what sense could his narrative style be described as 'economical'?

2 'O. Henry's stories are the stories we tell one another. They are anecdotes, with a beginning, a middle and an end.' (William Trevor)

How does *Witches' Loaves* fit in with this analysis?

3 Readers' expectations were mentioned in the section dealing with the Tagore story (pages 19–23). How are these expectations met in *Witches' Loaves* if the readers are anticipating the classic type of short story?

4 Do you think O. Henry expected his readers to extract any kind of moral lesson from this story? If so, what is it?

● Write a short story that takes as its starting-point one of the following themes:

   revenge   mistaken identity   a well-meaning blunder   a court case

   Try to tell the story with pace, but add detail and dialogue where appropriate. You may
   wish to add a twist to the end of your story.

Generally, novels and stories are told either in first or third person narrative.
Obviously, within these categories of narrative, different approaches can be
taken. In first person narrative, the events of the story and the other characters
are seen through the eyes of the 'I', the narrator. Unlike novels written in the
third person where the omniscient author can intervene at any point, the first
person narrator can usually tell only of incidents that he or she has witnessed.

The next two passages are examples of first person narrative. The first comes
from *A Farewell to Arms* by Ernest Hemingway, an American novelist who
pioneered a terse, 'tough guy' kind of prose which reflected the masculine
world and values he generally explored in his writing. This style has been very
widely imitated.

The 'hero' of this novel, Henry, has been wounded during the First World War
and has married Catherine, the nurse who looked after him. She is expecting a
child but the pregnancy runs into problems and she is taken to hospital, where
she loses the baby.

■ Upstairs I met the nurse coming down the hall.
      'I just called you at the hotel,' she said. Something dropped inside
   me.
      'What is wrong?'
      'Mrs Henry has had a haemorrhage.'
      'Can I go in?'
      'No, not yet. The doctor is with her.'
      'Is it dangerous?'
      'It is very dangerous.' The nurse went into the room and shut the
   door. I sat outside in the hall. Everything was gone inside of me. I did   10
   not think. I could not think. I knew she was going to die and I prayed
   that she would not. Don't let her die. Oh, God, please don't let her die.
   I'll do anything for you if you won't let her die. Please, please, please,
   dear God, don't let her die. Dear God, don't let her die. Please, please,
   please don't let her die. God, please make her not die. I'll do anything
   you say if you don't let her die. You took the baby but don't let her die –
   that was all right but don't let her die. Please, please, dear God, don't
   let her die.
      The nurse opened the door and motioned with her finger for me to
   come. I followed her into the room. Catherine did not look up when I   20
   came in. I went over to the side of the bed. The doctor was standing by

the bed on the opposite side. Catherine looked at me and smiled. I bent down over the bed and started to cry.

'Poor darling,' Catherine said very softly. She looked grey.

'You're all right, Cat,' I said. 'You're going to be all right.'

'I'm going to die,' she said; then waited and said, 'I hate it.'

I took her hand.

'Don't touch me,' she said. I let go of her hand. She smiled. 'Poor darling. You touch me all you want.'

'You'll be all right, Cat. I know you'll be all right.'   30

'I meant to write you a letter to have if anything happened but I didn't do it.'

'Do you want me to get a priest or anyone to come and see you?'

'Just you,' she said. Then a little later, 'I'm not afraid. I just hate it.'

'You must not talk so much,' the doctor said.

'All right,' Catherine said.

'Do you want me to do anything, Cat? Can I get you anything?'

Catherine smiled. 'No.' Then a little later, 'You won't do our things with another girl, or say the same things will you?'

'Never.'   40

'I want you to have girls, though.'

'I don't want them.'

'You are talking too much,' the doctor said. 'You cannot talk. Mr Henry must go out. He can come back again later. You are not going to die. You must not be silly.'

'All right,' Catherine said. 'I'll come and stay with you nights,' she said. It was very hard for her to talk.

'Please go out of the room,' the doctor said. Catherine winked at me, her face grey. 'I'll be right outside,' I said.

'Don't worry, darling,' Catherine said. 'I'm not a bit afraid. It's just a   50
dirty trick.'

'You dear, brave sweet.'

I waited outside in the hall. I waited a long time. The nurse came to the door and came over to me. 'I'm afraid Mrs Henry is very ill,' she said. 'I'm afraid for her.'

'Is she dead?'

'No, but she is unconscious.'

It seems she had one haemorrhage after another. They couldn't stop it. I went into the room and stayed with Catherine until she died. She was unconscious all the time, and it did not take her very long to die.   60

Outside the room in the hall I spoke to the doctor. 'Is there anything I can do tonight?'

'No. There is nothing to do. Can I take you to your hotel?'

'No, thank you. I am going to stay here a while.'

'I know there is nothing to say. I cannot tell you –'

'No,' I said. 'There's nothing to say.'

'Good night,' he said. 'I cannot take you to your hotel?'
'No, thank you.'
'It was the only thing to do,' he said. 'The operation proved –'
'I do not want to talk about it,' I said.   70
'I would like to take you to your hotel.'
'No, thank you.'
He went down the hall. I went to the door of the room.
'You can't come in now,' one of the nurses said.
'Yes, I can,' I said.
'You can't come in yet.'
'You get out,' I said. 'The other one too.'
But after I had got them out and shut the door and turned off the
light it wasn't any good. It was like saying good-bye to a statue. After a
while I went out and left the hospital and walked back to the hotel in   80
the rain.

A FAREWELL TO ARMS *Ernest Hemingway* □

In this extract, the first person narrator, Henry, tells the story from his point of
view; he selects the details to be recounted, he expresses his emotional
response. In one passage (12–18), Hemingway uses the technique of interior
monologue, a device which allows the reader inside the narrator's mind to hear
his inner thoughts. However, behind Henry the narrator, is the creative hand
of Hemingway, the author; Henry is Hemingway's creation, so ultimately the
point of view of the story is his.

1 'Don't let her die. Oh, God, please don't let her die. . .' (12)

Read the rest of the passage of interior monologue. How effective is this technique in
this instance in communicating what the narrator is thinking and feeling?

2 'The nurse opened the door and motioned with her finger for me to come. I followed her
into the room. Catherine did not look up when I came in. I went over to the side of the
bed.' (19–21)

There are no long sentences in the whole extract. How would you describe the style of
the writing and how is it appropriate to the subject matter?

3 Read the last paragraph of the extract again. What feeling does it aim to convey and
what impact does it have on you, the reader?

4 In this extract we see through Henry's 'eyes' or consciousness. What effect does this
technique have?

The second example of first person narrative is from a novel called *Nausea* by
the twentieth-century French writer, Jean-Paul Sartre. Here the narrator is an
observer of the café life around him, almost detached from the world, except
when his life directly interlocks with the people he meets at the café.

■ It is half past one. I am at the Café Mably, eating a sandwich, and everything is more or less normal. In any case, everything is always normal in cafés and especially in the Café Mably, because of the manager, Monsieur Fasquelle, who has a vulgar expression in his eyes which is very straightforward and reassuring. It will soon be time for his afternoon nap and his eyes are already pink, but his manner is still lively and decisive. He is walking around among the tables and speaking confidentially to the customers:

'Is everything all right, Monsieur?'

I smile at seeing him so lively: when his establishment empties, his   10
head empties too. Between two and four the café is deserted, and then Monsieur Fasquelle takes a few dazed steps, the waiters turn out the lights, and he slips into unconsciousness: when this man is alone, he falls asleep.

There are still about a score of customers left, bachelors, small-time engineers, and office workers. They lunch hurriedly in boarding houses which they call their 'messes', and, since they need a little luxury, they come here after their meal, to drink a cup of coffee and play poker dice; they make a little noise, but a vague noise which doesn't bother me. In order to exist, they too have to join with others.   20

I for my part live alone, entirely alone. I never speak to anybody, I receive nothing, I give nothing. The Autodidact doesn't count. Admittedly there is Françoise, the woman who runs the Rendez-vous des Cheminots. But do I speak to her? Sometimes, after dinner, when she brings me a beer, I ask her:

'Have you got time this evening?'

She never says no and I follow her into one of the big bedrooms on the first floor, which she rents by the hour or by the day. I don't pay her: we make love on an *au pair* basis. She enjoys it (she has to have a man a day and she has many more besides me) and I purge myself in   30
this way of a certain melancholy whose cause I know only too well. But we barely exchange a few words. What would be the use? Every man for himself; besides, as far as she's concerned, I remain first and foremost a customer in her café. Taking off her dress, she says to me:

'I say, have you ever heard of an apéritif called Bricot? Because there are two customers who've asked for it this week. The girl didn't know it and she came to ask me. They were commercial travellers, and they must have drunk it in Paris. But I don't like to buy anything without knowing it. If you don't mind, I'll keep my stockings on.'

In the past – even long after she had left me – I used to think about   40
Anny. Now, I don't think about anybody any more; I don't even bother to look for words. It flows through me, more or less quickly, and I don't fix anything, I just let it go. Most of the time, because of their failure to fasten on to words, my thoughts remain misty and nebulous. They assume vague, amusing shapes and are then swallowed up: I promptly forget them.

These young people amaze me; drinking their coffee, they tell clear, plausible stories. If you ask them what they did yesterday, they don't get flustered; they tell you all about it in a few words. If I were in their place, I'd start stammering. It's true that for a long time now nobody 50 has bothered how I spend my time. When you live alone, you even forget what it is to tell a story: plausibility disappears at the same time as friends. You let events flow by too: you suddenly see people appear who speak and then go away; you plunge into stories of which you can't make head or tail: you'd make a terrible witness.

NAUSEA *Jean-Paul Sartre* □

In the extract above, the narrator seems incapable of real communication or emotional contact with the people around him. The tone and the style of the writing reflect that alienation:

I for my part live alone, entirely alone. I never speak to anybody, I receive nothing, I give nothing. (21–22)

The 'I' of the narrative observes the people and incidents and, although he takes part in some of the incidents described, there is a sense of his standing outside them even when he seems to be actively involved in them. There is a distance between the 'I' and the world he is describing; his real being, his emotional self, is detached from his surroundings and the people in them.

There is a contrast, then, between Hemingway's and Sartre's use of first person narrative in these two novels. The 'I' of the Hemingway extract is deeply involved with what is happening around him; the 'I' of the Sartre extract is somehow part of, and yet not part of, the world around him.

1 Most of the extract is written in the present tense. Try writing a paragraph of the extract in the past tense. Compare the past tense version with the original. What differences, if any, does the change of tense make to the impact of the extract on the reader?

2 How would you describe the tone of the extract? Is it joyful or sad, emotional or detached, optimistic or pessimistic, personal or impersonal? Discuss the tone of the extract in your own words, quoting briefly from the extract to back up what you have to say.

3 Show how the narrator uses his description of the people surrounding him and those with whom he has dealings to bring out a sense of his own isolation and to communicate his own feelings.

4 Both the Hemingway and Sartre extracts employ first person narrative. Compare the involvement shown by the narrator of the Sartre passage in people and events with that shown by the narrator of the Hemingway passage. Quote briefly from each extract in your answer.

● Write a short story in the first person in which the narrator is waiting for some bad news. As well as containing narrative, your story should allow the reader inside the narrator's thoughts.

● Write a short piece in which a first person narrator observes people and events in a public place, e.g. a railway station, a restaurant, a disco or a supermarket. None of the events should be very dramatic or out-of-the-ordinary. Allow your readers to enter the mind of the narrator.

Most novels and short stories employ a third person narrative. The use of the third person in fiction means that the novelist or short story writer becomes an unnamed presence in the telling of the story. However, this does not mean that the author's influence on the work is diminished. The author's voice is always there, however disguised, in the selection of standpoint, detail and language and in the way that the story is told.

Sometimes, that presence can be a very definite participation in the narrative, with comments in an author's voice on events and characters. Charles Dickens characteristically intervenes in his own narrative in this way. Below is the opening section of his famous story, *A Christmas Carol*.

■ Marley was dead, to begin with. There is no doubt whatever about that. The register of his burial was signed by the clergyman, the clerk, the undertaker, and the chief mourner. Scrooge signed it. And Scrooge's name was good upon 'Change for anything he chose to put his hand to.
   Old Marley was as dead as a door-nail.
   Mind! I don't mean to say that I know, of my own knowledge, what there is particularly dead about a door-nail. I might have been inclined, myself, to regard a coffin-nail as the deadest piece of ironmongery in the trade. But the wisdom of our ancestors is in the simile; and my unhallowed hands shall not disturb it, or the Country's done for. You   10
will therefore permit me to repeat, emphatically, that Marley was as dead as a door-nail.
   Scrooge knew he was dead? Of course he did. How could it be otherwise? Scrooge and he were partners for I don't know how many years. Scrooge was his sole executor, his sole administrator, his sole assign, his sole residuary legatee, his sole friend, and sole mourner. And even Scrooge was not so dreadfully cut up by the sad event, but that he was an excellent man of business on the very day of the funeral, and solemnised it with an undoubted bargain.
   The mention of Marley's funeral brings me back to the point I started   20
from. There is no doubt that Marley was dead. This must be distinctly understood, or nothing wonderful can come of the story I am going to relate. If we were not perfectly convinced that Hamlet's father died before the play began, there would be nothing more remarkable in his

taking a stroll at night, in an easterly wind, upon his own ramparts, than there would be in any other middle-aged gentleman rashly turning out after dark in a breezy spot – say Saint Paul's Churchyard for instance – literally to astonish his son's weak mind.

Scrooge never painted out Old Marley's name. There it stood, years afterwards, above the warehouse door: Scrooge and Marley. The firm 30 was known as Scrooge and Marley. Sometimes people new to the business called Scrooge Scrooge, and sometimes Marley, but he answered to both names. It was all the same to him.

Oh! but he was a tight-fisted hand at the grindstone. Scrooge! a squeezing, wrenching, grasping, scraping, clutching, covetous old sinner! Hard and sharp as flint, from which no steel had ever struck out generous fire; secret, and self-contained, and solitary as an oyster. The cold within him froze his old features, nipped his pointed nose, shrivelled his cheek, stiffened his gait; made his eyes red, his thin lips blue; and spoke out shrewdly in his grating voice. A frosty rime was on 40 his head, and on his eyebrows, and his wiry chin. He carried his own low temperature always about with him; he iced his office in the dog-days, and didn't thaw it one degree at Christmas.

External heat and cold had little influence on Scrooge. No warmth could warm, no wintry weather chill him. No wind that blew was bitterer than he, no falling snow was more intent upon its purpose, no pelting rain less open to entreaty. Foul weather didn't know where to have him. The heaviest rain, and snow, and hail, and sleet, could boast of the advantage over him in only one respect. They often 'came down' handsomely, and Scrooge never did. 50

Nobody ever stopped him in the street to say, with gladsome looks, 'My dear Scrooge, how are you? When will you come to see me?' No beggars implored him to bestow a trifle, no children asked him what it was o'clock, no man or woman ever once in all his life inquired the way to such and such a place, of Scrooge. Even the blind men's dogs appeared to know him; and when they saw him coming on, would tug their owners into doorways and up courts; and then would wag their tails as though they said, 'No eye at all is better than an evil eye, dark master!'

But what did Scrooge care! It was the very thing he liked. To edge his 60 way along the crowded paths of life, warning all human sympathy to keep its distance, was what the knowing ones call 'nuts' to Scrooge.

Once upon a time – of all the good days in the year, on Christmas Eve – old Scrooge sat busy in his counting-house. It was cold, bleak, biting weather: foggy withal: and he could hear the people in the court outside, go wheezing up and down, beating their hands upon their breasts, and stamping their feet upon the pavement stones to warm them. The city clocks had only just gone three, but it was quite dark already – it had not been light all day – and candles were flaring in the windows of the neighbouring offices, like ruddy smears upon the 70

palpable brown air. The fog came pouring in at every chink and keyhole, and was so dense without, that although the court was of the narrowest, the houses opposite were mere phantoms. To see the dingy cloud come dropping down, obscuring everything, one might have thought that Nature lived hard by, and was brewing on a large scale.

The door of Scrooge's counting-house was open that he might keep his eye upon his clerk, who in a dismal little cell beyond, a sort of tank, was copying letters. Scrooge had a very small fire, but the clerk's fire was so very much smaller that it looked like one coal. But he couldn't replenish it, for Scrooge kept the coal-box in his own room; and so surely as the clerk came in with the shovel, the master predicted that it would be necessary for them to part. Wherefore the clerk put on his white comforter, and tried to warm himself at the candle; in which effort, not being a man of a strong imagination, he failed.

80

A CHRISTMAS CAROL Charles Dickens □

Victorian novelists often intruded directly in their novels and the work of Charles Dickens is typical of this in the way he frequently comments on the actions of his characters to make some point about their psychology or to drive home some moral lesson to the reader. In *A Christmas Carol* he has chosen third person narrative as the means of telling his story, but he feels free to intervene as himself, the author, to comment directly on any matter of interest.

1 'This must be distinctly understood, or nothing wonderful can come of the story I am going to relate.' (21–23)

What role does this sentence clearly give to Dickens? Pick out other examples from the extract where Dickens assumes the same tone.

2 'Oh! but he was a tight-fisted hand at the grindstone...' (34)

Read the remainder of the analysis of the character of Scrooge. Does Dickens allow readers to make up their own minds about Scrooge's character or does he tell the reader what kind of man he is?

3 What details or images does Dickens use to underline the impression that Scrooge made on all who met him?

● Write a character description of any one of the following, making clear to the reader what your opinion of the character is:

    a conceited person   a miser   a male chauvinist   a pompous official

Often in third person narrative, the author does not intrude into the story in his or her own person at all and makes no direct comment or moral judgement on the action of the characters. The events of the story are communicated to the reader through an impersonal narrative and through the words, actions and consciousness of the characters. The author may use one main character through whose eyes the action of the story unfolds.

Below is an extract from Doris Lessing's *The Habit of Loving*: she uses George as her main character and it is through his reactions and from his standpoint that we see the events of the story and the other characters. However, whilst using this technique, Lessing also lets us know in subtle ways what she herself feels about George.

■ George asked his first wife to marry him again, and she was so startled that she let the sugar-tongs drop and crack a saucer. She asked what had happened to Myra, and George said: 'Well, dear, I think Myra forgot about me during those years in Australia. At any rate, she doesn't want me now.' When he heard his voice saying this it sounded pathetic, and he was frightened, for he could not remember ever having to appeal to a woman. Except to Myra.

His wife examined him and said briskly: 'You're lonely, George. Well, we're none of us getting any younger.'

'You don't think you'd be less lonely if you had me around?'   10

She got up from her chair in order that she could attend to something with her back to him, and she said that she intended to marry again quite soon. She was marrying a man considerably younger than herself, a doctor who was in the progressive minority at her hospital. From her voice George understood that she was both proud and ashamed of this marriage, and that was why she was hiding her face from him. He congratulated her, and asked her if there wasn't perhaps a chance for him yet? 'After all, dear, we were happy together, weren't we? I've never really understood why that marriage ever broke up? It was you who wanted to break it up.'   20

'I don't see any point in raking over that old business,' she said, with finality, and returned to her seat opposite him. He envied her very much, looking young with her pink and scarcely-lined face under that brave lock of deliberately-whitened hair.

'But dear, I wish you'd tell me. It doesn't do any harm now, does it? And I always wondered . . . I've often thought about it and wondered.' He could hear the pathetic note in his voice again, but he did not know how to alter it.

'You wondered,' she said, 'when you weren't occupied with Myra.'

'But I didn't know Myra when we got divorced.'   30

'You knew Phillipa and Georgina and Janet and lord knows who else.'

'But I didn't care about them.'

She sat with her competent hands in her lap and on her face a look he remembered seeing when she told him she would divorce him. It was bitter and full of hurt. 'You didn't care about me either,' she said.

'But we were happy. Well, I was happy ...' he tailed off, being pathetic against all his knowledge of women. For, as he sat there, his old rake's heart was telling him that if only he could find them, there must be the right words, the right tone. But whatever he said came out 40 in this hopeless, old-dog's voice, and he knew that this voice could never defeat the gallant and crusading young doctor. 'And I did care about you. Sometimes I think you were the only woman in my life.'

At this she laughed. 'Oh George, don't get maudlin now, please.'

'Well, dear, there was Myra. But when you threw me over there was bound to be Myra, wasn't there? There were two women, you and then Myra. And I've never never understood why you broke it all up when we seemed to be so happy.'

'You didn't care for me,' she said again. 'If you had, you would never have come home from Phillipa, Georgina, Janet et al and said calmly, 50 just as if it didn't matter to me in the least, that you had been with them in Brighton or wherever it was.'

'But if I had cared about them I would never have told you.'

She was regarding him incredulously, and her face was flushed. With what? Anger? George did not know.

'I remember being so proud,' he said pathetically, 'that we had solved this business of marriage and all that sort of thing. We had such a good marriage that it didn't matter, the little flirtations. And I always thought one should be able to tell the truth. I always told you the truth, didn't I?' 60

'Very romantic of you, dear George,' she said drily; and soon he got up, kissed her fondly on the cheek, and went away.

He walked for a long time through the parks, hands behind his erect back, and he could feel his heart swollen and painful in his side. When the gates shut, he walked through the lit streets he had lived in for fifty years of his life, and he was remembering Myra and Molly, as if they were one woman, merging into each other, a shape of warm easy intimacy, a shape of happiness walking beside him. He went into a little restaurant he knew well, and there was a girl sitting there who knew him because she had heard him lecture once on the state of the 70 British Theatre. He tried hard to see Myra and Molly in her face, but he failed; and he paid for her coffee and his own and went home by himself. But his flat was unbearably empty, and he left it and walked down by the Embankment for a couple of hours to tire himself, and there must have been a colder wind blowing than he knew, for next day he woke with a pain in his chest which he could not mistake for heartache.

THE HABIT OF LOVING Doris Lessing □

Look at the following section of the extract again:

> He walked for a long time through the parks, hands behind his erect
> back and he could feel his heart swollen and painful in his side. (63–64)

The first half of this sentence is straight narrative by the author. She tells us
what George did; 'he walked', but in the second half of the sentence she allows
us 'inside' George to learn how he is feeling; 'he could feel his heart swollen
and painful in his side.'

Sometimes, however, Lessing not only allows the reader inside her characters'
heads but also communicates her own feelings about them.

> ... he tailed off, being pathetic against all his knowledge of women.
> For, as he sat there, his old rake's heart was telling him... (37–39)

In this passage we are allowed to look into George's thoughts, but Lessing is
not neutral in her representation of them; the words 'pathetic' and 'old rake'
are not just George's judgement of himself – they are part of Lessing's own
judgement of her creation.

1 'I remember being so proud,' he said pathetically, 'that we had solved this business of
marriage and all that sort of thing.' (56–57)

Is it just the voice of George which is present here, or does the opinion of the author
intervene?

2 'From her voice George understood that she was both proud and ashamed of this
marriage, and that was why she was hiding her face from him. He congratulated her,
and asked her if there wasn't perhaps a chance for him yet?' (15–18)

Whose point of view does the narration in this section represent: is it that of George's
wife, the author, George himself, or is the narration from more than one point of view?

3 'He envied her very much, looking young with her pink and scarcely-lined face under
that brave lock of deliberately-whitened hair.' (22–24)

From whose standpoint do we see George's wife here?

4 In the introduction to this extract, it was seen that Doris Lessing combines straight
narrative with passages where the reader is allowed inside the thoughts of a character.
Analyse the final paragraph, saying which sections are straight narrative and which
sections are examples of Doris Lessing allowing us to enter George's mind.

5 Can you detect any attitude that the author takes to George, her character, from the
tone of the extract? Is she amused by him? Does he irritate her? Does an attitude of
superiority towards him emerge? Does she pity him? Quote briefly from the extract to
back up the answer you give.

George Eliot was a nineteenth-century female novelist who used a male pseudonym in an age when there was still great prejudice about the worth and seriousness of women writers. In *Middlemarch*, George Eliot wrote what many people consider to be one of the finest novels in English Literature.

Eliot uses third person narrative to concentrate on several main characters during the course of a very long novel. One of these is Dorothea Brooke, who as a young woman marries a much older man, Mr Casaubon, because she respects him as a scholar and a thinker; she also hopes that she will find purpose in her life by sharing and helping in his work.

In this extract from the novel, Dorothea and her husband have just returned from their honeymoon and already Dorothea is having doubts about the marriage and her role in it.

■ *1st Gent.*   All times are good to seek your wedded home
                     Bringing a mutual delight.
2nd Gent.   Why, true.
                     The Calendar hath not an evil day
                     For souls made one by love, and even death
                     Were sweetness, if it came like rolling waves
                     While they two clasped each other, and foresaw
                     No life apart.

Mr and Mrs Casaubon, returning from their wedding journey, arrived at Lowick Manor in the middle of January. A light snow was falling as 10 they descended at the door, and in the morning, when Dorothea passed from her dressing-room into the blue-green boudoir that we know of, she saw the long avenue of limes lifting their trunks from a white earth and spreading white branches against the dun and motionless sky. The distant flat shrank in uniform whiteness and low-hanging uniformity of cloud. The very furniture in the room seemed to have shrunk since she saw it before: the stag in the tapestry looked more like a ghost in his ghostly blue-green world; the volumes of polite literature in the bookcase looked more like immovable imitations of books. The bright fire of dry oak-boughs burning on the dogs seemed 20 an incongruous renewal of life and glow – like the figure of Dorothea herself as she entered carrying the red-leather cases containing the cameos for Celia.

    She was glowing from her morning toilette as only healthful youth can glow: there was gemlike brightness on her coiled hair and in her hazel eyes; there was warm red life in her lips; her throat had a breathing whiteness above the differing white of the fur which itself seemed to wind about her neck and cling down her blue-grey pelisse with a tenderness gathered from her own, a sentient commingled innocence which kept its loveliness against the crystalline purity of the 30 outdoor snow. As she laid the cameo-cases on the table in the bow-window, she unconsciously kept her hands on them, immediately absorbed in looking out on the still, white enclosure which made her visible world.

Mr Casaubon, who had risen early complaining of palpitation, was in the library giving audience to his curate, Mr Tucker. By and by Celia would come in her quality of bridesmaid as well as sister, and through the next weeks there would be wedding visits received and given, all in continuance of that transitional life understood to correspond with the excitement of bridal felicity and keeping up the sense of busy 40 ineffectiveness, as of a dream which the dreamer begins to suspect. The duties of her married life, contemplated as so great beforehand, seemed to be shrinking with the furniture and the white vapour-walled landscape. The clear heights where she expected to walk in full communion had become difficult to see even in her imagination; the delicious repose of the soul on a complete superior had been shaken into uneasy effort and alarmed with dim presentiment. When would the days begin of that active wifely devotion which was to strengthen her husband's life and exalt her own? Never perhaps, as she had preconceived them; but somehow – still somehow. In this solemnly 50 pledged union of her life, duty would present itself in some new form of inspiration and give a new meaning to wifely love.

Meanwhile there was the snow and the low arch of dun vapour – there was the stifling oppression of that gentlewoman's world, where everything was done for her and none asked for her aid – where the sense of connexion with a manifold pregnant existence had to be kept up painfully as an inward vision instead of coming from without in claims that would have shaped her energies. 'What shall I do?' 'Whatever you please, my dear.' That had been her brief history since she had left off learning morning lessons and practising silly rhythms 60 on the hated piano. Marriage, which was to bring guidance into worthy and imperative occupation, had not yet freed her from the gentle-woman's oppressive liberty; it had not even filled her leisure with the ruminant joy of unchecked tenderness. Her blooming, full-pulsed youth stood there in a moral imprisonment which made itself one with the chill, colourless, narrowed landscape, with the shrunken furniture, the never-read books, and the ghostly stag in a pale, fantastic world that seemed to be vanishing from the daylight.

MIDDLEMARCH *George Eliot* □

In the extract above, Dorothea's youthful thoughts and emotions and Eliot's mature analysis of her situation merge so that the joins between the two are not apparent. It is an example of how a novelist can present her view of the world, not through direct moral judgements, but by proxy, through the thoughts and emotions of her characters:

> Her blooming, full-pulsed youth stood there in a moral imprisonment which made itself one with the chill, colourless, narrowed landscape. . .
> (64–66)

There is usually a tone of moral seriousness in George Eliot's writing; her characters face moral and emotional dilemmas in the face of conflicting pressures from the society in which they live. Her writing is seldom less than warm and accessible to the reader, however, because, along with that moral seriousness, she has a sympathetic understanding of everyday human problems. This fusion of intellectual and emotional understanding marks her out as one of the great writers.

1 How does George Eliot use nature and the furniture in the room to reflect Dorothea's mood?

2 '. . . all in continuance of that transitional life understood to correspond with the excitement of bridal felicity and keeping up the sense of busy ineffectiveness, as of a dream which the dreamer begins to suspect.' (38–41)

    a How do the words 'understood' and 'keeping up the sense of busy ineffectiveness, as of a dream which the dreamer begins to suspect' help you to understand what attitude to the role of women within marriage George Eliot has in this extract?

    b Whose 'voice' is it here, Dorothea's or Eliot's, or a mixture of the two? Remember that Dorothea is a young, inexperienced woman in a new situation.

3 '. . . there was the stifling oppression of that gentlewoman's world, where everything was done for her and none asked for her aid'. (54–55)

In your opinion, are we following Dorothea's thoughts here or is this an example of an author intruding into the story and revealing her own attitudes about an issue? Give reasons for your answer.

4 How does the last sentence of the extract echo the first paragraph?

5 Comparing the Doris Lessing extract with the George Eliot passage, which author do you think is more sympathetic to her character and his/her problems?

The language of narrative prose in novels written by British writers is usually Standard English, even though the author may be portraying characters and communities that speak a dialect of English. Lewis Grassic Gibbon, however, was a Scottish writer who wrote in Scots dialect, not only in the dialogue his characters speak, but occasionally also in the narrative prose he uses to tell his story.

Below is an extract from Grassic Gibbon's novel *Sunset Song*; the setting is a Kincardineshire farming community. Chris, the young heroine of the novel, lives with her father and her brother, Will, on their farm.

■ But Will had unyoked and made off to Drumlithie, his usual gait, when Chris got home, and father was up on the moor with his gun, you heard the bang of the shots come now and then. Chris had a great baking to do that night, both father and Will would eat oatcakes and scones for a wager, bought bread from the vans soon scunnered them sore. Warm work it was when you'd heaped a great fire and the girdle glowed below, you'd nearly to strip in fine weather if you weren't to sweat yourself sick. Chris got out of most things but a vest and a petticoat, she was all alone and could do as she pleased, it was fine and free and she baked with a will. 10

She was lifting the last cake, browned and good and twice cross cut, when she knew that somebody watched her from the door of the kitchen, and she looked, it was Ewan Tavendale, him she hadn't seen since the day of the thresh at Peesie's Knapp. He was standing against the jamb, long and dark with his glowering eyes, but he reddened when she looked, not half as much as she did herself, she could feel the red warm blushing come through her skin from tip to toe; *such a look he's taking*, she thought, *it's a pity I'm wearing a thing and he can't study the blush to its end.*

But he just said *Hello, is Will about?* and Chris said *No, in Drumlithie I* 20 *think*, and they stood and glowered like a couple of gowks, Chris saw his eyes queer and soft and shy, the neck of his shirt had fallen apart, below it the skin was white as new milk, frothed white it looked, and a drop of sweat stood there where the brown of his tanning and the white of his real skin met. And then Chris suddenly knew *something* and blushed again, sharp and silly, she couldn't stop, she'd minded the night of the fire at Peesie's Knapp and the man that had kissed her on the homeward road, Ewan Tavendale it had been, no other, shameless and coarse.

He was blushing himself again by then, they looked at each other in a 30 white, queer daze, Chris wondered in a kind of a panic if he knew what she knew at last, half-praying she was he wouldn't speak of it when he began to move off from the door, still red, stepping softly, like father, like a limber, soft-stepping cat. *Well, I was hoping I'd see him in case he should leave us sudden-like.*

She stared at him all awake, that kissing on the winter road forgotten. *Leave? Who said Will was leaving? – Oh, I heard he was trying for a job in Aberdeen, maybe it's a lie. Tell him I called in about. Ta-ta.*

She called *Ta-ta, Ewan*, after him as he crossed the close, he half-turned round and smiled at her, quick and dark like a cat again, *Ta-ta*, 40 *Chris.* And she stood looking after him a long while, not thinking, smiling, till the smell of a burning cake roused her to run, just like the English creature Alfred.

And next morning she said to Will after breakfast, casual-like, but her heart in her throat, *Ewan Tavendale was down to see you last night, he thought you'd be leaving Blawearie soon.* And Will took it cool and quiet,

*Did he? God, they'd haver the breeks from a Highlandman's haunches, the
gossipers of Kinraddie. Tavendale down to see me? More likely he was down to
take a bit keek at you, Chris lass. So look after yourself, for he's Highland and
coarse.*   50

SUNSET SONG *Lewis Grassic Gibbon* □

Much of Grassic Gibbon's prose is Standard English, but he adapts it to the
rhythms and idiom of the Scottish community he is portraying. Other unusual
features are the unconventional manner in which the dialogue is printed and
the novel way in which the sentences are structured and the prose is
punctuated. These techniques give the prose a poetic and rhythmic quality
which helps to enhance the immediacy and vitality of the writing.

1 Consider the kind of language used in the narrative of the extract. Listen to the rhythm of
the prose. Read some of it aloud. What is different about it when compared to other
examples of narrative prose analysed in this chapter?

2 There are some dialect words used in the extract, not only in the dialogue but also in the
narrative prose:

'. . . they stood and glowered like a couple of gowks'. (21)

Do you find that the use of dialect adds to the realistic impact of the extract or is it a
barrier to understanding?

3 Chris and Ewan engage in rather mundane conversation, but there is considerable
tension in the scene. How does the author build up this tension for the reader?

4 Study the way the prose is punctuated and how the author employs unusual word-order
occasionally. What do you think his intention is in employing these techniques?

The device of interior monologue was used by Ernest Hemingway in *A Farewell
to Arms* to allow the reader into the thought processes of his character (pages
27–29). The stream of consciousness technique takes a further step towards the
actual reproduction of characters' thoughts. It was met earlier in the work of
B.S. Johnson (pages 15–16). We very often think in haphazard ways, jumping
from subject to subject, responding to immediate impressions and stimuli. The
interior monologue usually orders a person's thoughts in a more organized
way than might be the case in real life, whereas the stream of consciousness
technique is used to get closer to the way people really think. It appears less
ordered and selective, although what is finally written on paper depends still
on an author's selection of material.

The following extract is from J.P. Donleavy's *The Ginger Man*. In this passage, a
woman named Marion and her baby daughter Felicity are out for a walk in
Dublin.

45

■ Entering the park. Green, green grass, soft and sweet from the night rain. The flower beds. Circles and crosses and nice little fences. Pick that bench. Newly painted. If my father dies by Autumn I'll be very rich, golden udder. And sit on a park bench for the rest of my life. What a warm, lovely day. I'd like to take off my shirt and let a sup of sun to me chest but they'd be hounding me out of the place for indecency. Help my hairs to grow, give them a fashionable tinge of blond. Dear child, stop kicking me in the back. Here, now get on this blanket and play and I don't want any nonsense from you. Jesus, let go of the blanket, think I was going to kill you. Papa's got to study his law and   10
become a big K.C. and make lots of money. A great big golden udder. A tan on my chest means wealth and superiority. But I'm proud of my humility. And here, reading the dead language, my little book of Roman Law. For parricide, flung off the cliff in a bag with a viper. Fat ugliness writhing in the crotch. And little daughter, gurgling on the grass, have fun now. Because papa is finished. Getting it from all sides. Even in dreams. And last night I dreamt I was carrying a bundle of newspapers under my arm and climbed on a bus and went racing across the Curragh with massive horses galloping beside. In the bus, a man studying butterflies with a magnifying glass. And we were going   20
to the West. Then a bullock leaped from behind a hedge and the bus cut him up and left him hanging on a huge hook in front of a village butcher shop. Then suddenly I was in Cashel. Streets filled with goats and gutters brown with dried blood. And in the hot sun's stillness, a crowd of men and women in thick black overcoats walking down the middle of a winter road, summer's hesitating heat on every side. The funeral of the gombeen man. He caught her, lips bubbling, eyes spinning, sitting on the shop assistant on a crate from Chicago and he heard it collapse and was after them with a hatchet. And they conspired between hot wet lips, clutching at each other's clothes to put   30
poison in the tea, trembling hands to the till and each other's flesh, to wind a cocoon of sin between the pineapple and peaches. The box was closed. Summer. The long line shuffling. Through Cashel. A song:

> Shuffling through Cashel
> A box in the sun
> Through Cashel, through Cashel
> The gombeen man's dead.
> The gombeen man's dead
> In a box in the sun.
> The assistant got the wife   40
> And the gombeen man got done.
> Poor mercy on the gombeen man.
> There's a hand in the till.
> There's a box in the sun,
> God's mercy on the gombeen man.

THE GINGER MAN *J.P. Donleavy* □

The stream of consciousness technique may seem undisciplined and unstructured, but it involves the writer in just as much selection of detail and emphasis as any other form of writing. The 'stream' of thoughts does not just happen; the character is the creation of the author, who chooses what to write down as the thoughts passing through the character's mind. However realistic the end result of this technique may appear, the controlling hand of the author is just as present as in any other kind of narrative.

1 'Entering the park. Green, green grass, soft and sweet from the night rain. The flower beds.' (1–2)

Why do you think so much of the extract is written in short phrases like those above rather than fully-formed sentences?

2 'For parricide, flung off the cliff in a bag with a viper. Fat ugliness writhing in the crotch.' (14–15)

Are these examples of thoughts and images that might pass through a person's thoughts but would be unlikely to find expression in words? Explain what thought process the author is attempting to reflect in these words.

3 Marion's dream of the previous night is told in some detail. Is there any resemblance between the content of the dream and the stream of thoughts that come into Marion's mind as she sits on the park bench?

4 'And·they conspired between hot wet lips, clutching at each other's clothes to put poison in the tea, trembling hands to the till and each other's flesh, to wind a cocoon of sin between the pineapple and peaches.' (29–32)

What literary touches can you detect in the above – an author's hand rather than a realistic reproduction of the stream of consciousness of the character?

5 Compare this extract from Donleavy's novel with that of B.S. Johnson on pages 16–17. Which writer uses the stream of consciousness technique more effectively? Give reasons for your answer.

● Write a piece, using the stream of consciousness technique to communicate the thoughts and feelings of one of the following characters:

an old person sitting on a bench watching the world pass by

a teacher trying to teach a rowdy class

a young person feeling very shy at a social gathering.

Read the two extracts overleaf and then answer the questions on them. The first extract is from *Rain* by Somerset Maugham; the second is from *A Passage to India* by E.M. Forster.

■ Davidson's district consisted of a group of islands to the North of Samoa; they were widely separated and he had frequently to go long distances by canoe. At these times his wife remained at their headquarters and managed the mission. Dr Macphail felt his heart sink when he considered the efficiency with which she certainly managed it. She spoke of the depravity of the natives in a voice which nothing could hush, but with a vehemently unctuous horror. Her sense of delicacy was singular. Early in their acquaintance she had said to him:

'You know, their marriage customs when we first settled in the islands were so shocking that I couldn't possibly describe them to you. But I'll tell Mrs Macphail and she'll tell you.' 10

Then he had seen his wife and Mrs Davidson, their deck-chairs close together, in earnest conversation for about two hours. As he walked past them backwards and forwards for the sake of exercise, he had heard Mrs Davidson's agitated whisper, like the distant flow of a mountain torrent, and he saw by his wife's open mouth and pale face that she was enjoying an alarming experience. At night in their cabin she repeated to him with bated breath all she had heard.

'Well, what did I say to you?' cried Mrs Davidson, exultant next morning. 'Did you ever hear anything more dreadful? You don't 20 wonder that I couldn't tell you myself, do you? Even though you are a doctor.'

Mrs Davidson scanned his face. She had a dramatic eagerness to see that she had achieved the desired effect.

'Can you wonder that when we first went there our hearts sank? You'll hardly believe me when I tell you it was impossible to find a single good girl in any of the villages.'

She used the word *good* in a severely technical manner.

'Mr Davidson and I talked it over, and we made up our minds the first thing to do was put down the dancing. The natives were crazy 30 about dancing.'

'I was not averse to it myself when I was a young man,' said Dr Macphail.

'I guessed as much when I heard you ask Mrs Macphail to have a turn with you last night. I don't think there's any real harm if a man dances with his wife, but I was relieved that she wouldn't. Under the circumstances I thought it better that we should keep ourselves to ourselves.'

'Under what circumstances?'

Mrs Davidson gave him a quick look through her pince-nez, but did 40 not answer his question.

'But among white people it's not quite the same,' she went on, 'though I must say I agree with Mr Davidson, who says he can't understand how a husband can stand by and see his wife in another man's arms, and as far as I'm concerned I've never danced a step since I married. But the native dancing is quite another matter. It's not only immoral in itself, but it distinctly leads to immorality. However, I'm thankful to God that we stamped it out, and I don't think I'm wrong in saying that no one has danced in our district for eight years.'

RAIN *Somerset Maugham* □

■ He was an athletic little man, daintily put together, but really very strong. Nevertheless walking fatigued him, as it fatigues every one in India except the new-comer. There is something hostile in that soil. It either yields, and the foot sinks into a depression, or else it is unexpectedly rigid and sharp, pressing stones or crystals against the tread. A series of these little surprises exhausts; and he was wearing pumps, a poor preparation for any country. At the edge of the civil station he turned into a mosque to rest.

He had always liked this mosque. It was gracious, and the arrange-ment pleased him. The courtyard – entered through a ruined gate – 10 contained an ablution tank of fresh clear water, which was always in motion, being indeed part of a conduit that supplied the city. The courtyard was paved with broken slabs. The covered part of the mosque was deeper than is usual; its effect was that of an English parish church whose side has been taken out. Where he sat, he looked into three arcades whose darkness was illuminated by a small hanging lamp and by the moon. The front – in full moonlight – had the appearance of marble, and the ninety-nine names of God on the frieze stood out black, as the frieze stood out white against the sky. The contest between this dualism and the contention of shadows within 20 pleased Aziz, and he tried to symbolize the whole into some truth of religion or love. A mosque by winning his approval let loose his imagination. The temple of another creed, Hindu, Christian, or Greek, would have bored him and failed to awaken his sense of beauty. Here was Islam, his own country, more than a Faith, more than a battle-cry, more, much more . . . Islam, an attitude towards life both exquisite and durable, where his body and his thoughts found their home.

His seat was the low wall that bounded the courtyard on the left. The ground fell away beneath him towards the city, visible as a blur of trees, and in the stillness he heard many small sounds. On the right, over in 30 the club, the English community contributed an amateur orchestra. Elsewhere some Hindus were drumming – he knew they were Hindus, because the rhythm was uncongenial to him – and others were bewailing a corpse – he knew whose, having certified it in the afternoon. There were owls, the Punjab mail . . . and flowers smelt deliciously in the station master's garden. But the mosque – that alone signified, and he returned to it from the complex appeal of the night, and decked it with meanings the builder had never intended. Some day he too would build a mosque, smaller than this but in perfect taste, so that all who passed by should experience the happiness he felt now. 40

A PASSAGE TO INDIA *E.M. Forster* □

1 From whose standpoint do we see things in the two extracts? Is it through the consciousness of one person in each case, or is there more than one standpoint?

2 Compare the two extracts with regard to the authors' 'intrusion' on events.

3 Both extracts deal with aspects of religion: in the first passage, the Davidsons are missionaries; in the second the setting is a mosque. What contrasting religious feelings and thoughts are brought out by the writers of the two extracts?

4 Analyse the content of the passages in terms of the use of any of the following:

dialogue   description   straight narrative   characters' thoughts

5 How would you describe the mood created by the authors in the two extracts?

Chapter 3
Characterisation

It was stated at the beginning of Chapter 2 that a good story is what many people expect from novels. Another common criterion by which readers judge a book is whether it has interesting characters. What exactly makes for interesting characters in a novel is hard to define, but undoubtedly in order to be entertained by a book or aroused emotionally it is usually necessary to find the characters convincing and, to an extent, to identify with them.

The character portrayal does not have to be strictly realistic for us to be able to believe in the characters. For example, an author can take one main characteristic (e.g. greed, generosity, sadism) and focus almost exclusively on that. This yields a one-dimensional portrait of a character that may still have a credibility for the reader if the writing is sufficiently good.

Most novelists would claim to create many-faceted characters, especially in the case of the main protagonists of their novels. However, complexity of characterisation does not necessarily mean the characters will strike the reader as real or credible. Whether the characters assume a vitality of their own and are seen as more than mere puppets at the end of the author's string is perhaps the most appropriate criterion to apply in judging the success of a novel's characterisation.

Authors mainly reveal character through the action and dialogue of their stories, but they frequently fill in essential details about a character in an extended descriptive portrayal. In this way, the reader's understanding of the character's role in the events of a story is developed from what the author has already revealed about the person in this character description.

The extract below is from the American writer, Scott Fitzgerald's *The Beautiful and the Damned*, in which the author presents a character portrayal of his hero, Anthony, at the beginning of the novel. Fitzgerald's method is to give a chronological account of Anthony's life, picking out salient details and incidents that explain the kind of person he has developed into so that the reader has some idea of the influences and emotional experiences that have gone into the shaping of Anthony's personality.

■ At eleven he had a horror of death. Within six impressionable years his parents had died and his grandmother had faded off almost impercept- ibly, until, for the first time since her marriage, her person held for one day an unquestioned supremacy over her own drawing-room. So to

Anthony life was a struggle against death, that waited at every corner. It was as a concession to his hypochondriacal imagination that he formed the habit of reading in bed – it soothed him. He read until he was tired and often fell asleep with the lights still on.

His favourite diversion until he was fourteen was his stamp collection; enormous, as nearly exhaustive as a boy's could be – his   10 grandfather considered fatuously that it was teaching him geography. So Anthony kept up a correspondence with a half-dozen 'Stamp and Coin' companies and it was rare that the mail failed to bring him new stamp-books or packages of glittering approval sheets – there was a mysterious fascination in transferring his acquisitions interminably from one book to another. His stamps were his greatest happiness and he bestowed impatient frowns on any one who interrupted him at play with them; they devoured his allowance every month, and he lay awake at night musing untiringly on their variety and many-coloured splendour.   20

At sixteen he had lived almost entirely within himself, an inarticulate boy, thoroughly un-American, and politely bewildered by his contemporaries. The two preceding years had been spent in Europe with a private tutor, who persuaded him that Harvard was the thing; it would 'open doors', it would be a tremendous tonic, it would give him innumerable self-sacrificing and devoted friends. So he went to Harvard – there was no other logical thing to be done with him.

Oblivious to the social system, he lived for a while alone and unsought in a high room in Beck Hall – a slim dark boy of medium height with a shy sensitive mouth. His allowance was more than   30 liberal. He laid the foundations for a library by purchasing from a wandering bibliophile first editions of Swinburne, Meredith, and Hardy, and a yellowed illegible autograph letter of Keats's, finding later that he had been amazingly overcharged. He became an exquisite dandy, amassed a rather pathetic collection of silk pyjamas, brocaded dressing-gowns, and neckties too flamboyant to wear; in this secret finery he would parade before a mirror in his room or lie stretched in satin along his window-seat looking down on the yard and realizing dimly this clamour, breathless and immediate, in which it seemed he was never to have a part.   40

Curiously enough he found in senior year that he had acquired a position in his class. He learned that he was looked upon as a rather romantic figure, a scholar, a recluse, a tower of erudition. This amused him but secretly pleased him – he began going out, at first a little and then a great deal. He made the Pudding. He drank – quietly and in the proper tradition. It was said of him that had he not come to college so young he might have 'done extremely well'. In 1909, when he graduated, he was only twenty years old.

Then abroad again – to Rome this time, where he dallied with architecture and painting in turn, took up the violin, and wrote some   50 ghastly Italian sonnets, supposedly the ruminations of a thirteenth-century monk on the joys of the contemplative life. It became established among his Harvard intimates that he was in Rome, and those of them who were abroad that year looked him up and discovered with him, on many moonlight excursions, much in the city that was older than the Renaissance or indeed than the republic. Maury Noble, from Philadelphia, for instance, remained two months, and together they realised the peculiar charm of Latin women and had a delightful sense of being very young and free in a civilisation that was very old and free.   60

THE BEAUTIFUL AND THE DAMNED *F. Scott Fitzgerald* □

Authors do not always portray their characters from a disinterested standpoint. Some characters they clearly approve of and they want their readers to share that approval. Other characters they openly dislike or have mixed feelings about. There is a gently satirical edge to some details in Fitzgerald's portrayal of Anthony. For example, his collection of silk pyjamas is referred to as 'rather pathetic' and his drinking is described as being 'in the proper tradition'. With touches like these, Fitzgerald makes clear to the reader his own attitude to his character, Anthony. He is satirising or poking fun at him and the society he moved in.

1 Summarise the character traits that are revealed about Anthony in this portrait. Support what you say with evidence from the passage.

2 What does the physical description of Anthony given in the fourth paragraph of the extract add to our knowledge of him?

3 Describe in your own words how the other students saw Anthony.

4 What attitude does Fitzgerald take to his character in this portrayal? Does he wholly approve of him? Is it at all critical? Does he find him amusing or irritating? Pick out details from each paragraph which show what Fitzgerald's attitude to Anthony is.

● Write a piece about yourself, describing important events and influences in your past and bringing the portrait up to the present day. You can adopt a humorous or critical tone if you wish. If you prefer, write a character description of someone you know or of a fictional character.

In the previous passage it was seen that authors very often have attitudes towards their own characters; they are not neutral to their creations. Often their dislike or approval comes over strongly to the reader and this biased view of the character affects the reader's view.

Jane Austen, whose classic novels were published at the beginning of the last century, usually conveys her opinions of her own characters to the reader.

Frequently she does this by the use of irony, a technique for which she is famous. Irony is a way of saying one thing and meaning something quite different. When the reader senses that a writer is being ironical, then he or she should be looking for a layer of meaning below the surface meaning. Jane Austen often seems to adopt the silliness or prejudices of her characters only to make it clear that she is deriding their stupidity or narrowness. Austen was very skilful and delicate in her use of irony, often shredding her characters' pretensions with a few expert rapier slashes.

The following passage is from the opening to Jane Austen's novel *Persuasion*. Austen is introducing the reader to her characters.

■ Vanity was the beginning and the end of Sir Walter Elliot's character; vanity of person and of situation. He had been remarkably handsome in his youth; and, at fifty-four, was still a very fine man. Few women could think more of their personal appearance then he did; nor could the valet of any newmade lord be more delighted with the place he held in society. He considered the blessing of beauty as inferior only to the blessing of a baronetcy; and the Sir Walter Elliot, who united these gifts, was the constant object of his warmest respect and devotion.

His good looks and his rank had one fair claim on his attachment; since to them he must have owed a wife of very superior character to 10 any thing deserved by his own. Lady Elliot had been an excellent woman, sensible and amiable; whose judgement and conduct, if they might be pardoned the youthful infatuation which made her Lady Elliot, had never required indulgence afterwards. – She had humoured, or softened, or concealed his failings, and promoted his real respectability for seventeen years; and though not the very happiest being in the world herself, had found enough in her duties, her friends, and her children to attach her to life, and make it no matter of indifference to her when she was called on to quit them. – Three girls, the two eldest sixteen and fourteen, was an awful legacy for a mother to bequeath; an 20 awful charge rather, to confide to the authority and guidance of a conceited, silly father. She had, however, one very intimate friend, a sensible, deserving woman, who had been brought, by strong attachment to herself, to settle close by her, in the village of Kellynch; and on her kindness and advice, Lady Elliot mainly relied for the best help and maintenance of the good principles and instruction which she had been anxiously giving her daughters.

This friend, and Sir Walter, did *not* marry, whatever might have been anticipated on that head by their acquaintance. – Thirteen years had passed away since Lady Elliot's death, and they were still near 30 neighbours and intimate friends; and one remained a widower, the other a widow.

That Lady Russell, of steady age and character, and extremely well provided for, should have no thought of a second marriage, needs no

apology to the public, which is rather apt to be unreasonably discontented when a woman *does* marry again, than when she does *not*; but Sir Walter's continuing in singleness requires explanation. – Be it known, then, that Sir Walter, like a good father (having met with one or two private disappointments in very unreasonable application), prided himself on remaining single for his dear daughter's sake. For one 40
daughter, his eldest, he would really have given up anything, which he had not been very much tempted to do. Elizabeth had succeeded, at sixteen, to all that was possible, of her mother's rights and consequence; and being very handsome, and very like himself, her influence had always been great, and they had gone on together most happily. His two other children were of very inferior value. Mary had acquired a little artificial importance, by becoming Mrs Charles Musgrove; but Anne, with an elegance of mind and sweetness of character, which must have placed her high with any people of real understanding, was nobody with either father or sister: her word had no weight; her 50
convenience was always to give way – she was only Anne.

To Lady Russell, indeed, she was a most dear and highly valued goddaughter, favourite and friend. Lady Russell loved them all; but it was only in Anne that she could fancy the mother to revive again.

A few years before, Anne Elliot had been a very pretty girl, but her bloom had vanished early; and as even in its height, her father had found little to admire in her (so totally different were her delicate features and mild dark eyes from his own), there could be nothing in them, now that she was faded and thin, to excite his esteem. He had never indulged much hope, he had now none, of ever reading her 60
name in any other page of his favourite work. All equality of alliance must rest with Elizabeth: for Mary had merely connected herself with an old country family of respectability and large fortune, and had therefore *given* all the honour, and received none; Elizabeth would, one day or other, marry suitably.

PERSUASION Jane Austen □

Austen makes it very clear what she thinks of Sir Walter:

His good looks and his rank had one fair claim on his attachment; since to them he must have owed a wife of very superior character to any thing deserved by his own. (9–11)

This sentence is characteristic of Austen's ironical view of her characters: she refers to Sir Walter's good looks and his rank, seemingly approvingly, and then follows that by undermining his pretensions by saying that the only value of these qualities was that they had brought him a much better wife than his character really deserved. Even his good points are used by the author to detract further from his worth as a person. The technique of reversing an apparently favourable statement by following it immediately with a critical comment is a hallmark of Jane Austen's style.

1 ... the Sir Walter Elliot, who united these gifts, was the constant object of his warmest respect and devotion.' (7–8)

How does Austen undermine her character in this statement?

2 'His two other children were of very inferior value'. (46)

Do you think this is Austen's judgement of the two other daughters or Sir Walter's? Give reasons for your answer.

3 Select examples of irony from the extract and explain in each case how they add to our knowledge of the character concerned.

4 What does Lady Russell think of Anne and how could it be said that Austen's attitude to Anne is partly revealed through Lady Russell's view of her?

Comic writers, especially those with a satirical edge to their writing, often poke fun at their own characters. Fictional characters can represent social attitudes and hypocrisies, so by attacking them writers can expose society's ills. Evelyn Waugh wrote about the social mores of the first part of the twentieth century, taking a generally rather jaundiced view of his contemporaries.

In the extract below from his novel *Vile Bodies*, he reveals his talent for creating character through his use of dialogue, and also shows his ability to dissect a character in a few succinct phrases. A group of wealthy socialites are joining a liner for a cruise. The time is the 1920s.

■ Other prominent people were embarking, all very unhappy about the weather; to avert the terrors of sea-sickness they had indulged in every kind of civilized witchcraft, but they were lacking in faith.

Miss Runcible was there, and Miles Malpractice, and all the Younger Set. They had spent a jolly morning strapping each other's tummies with sticking plaster (how Miss Runcible had wriggled).

The Right Honourable Walter Outrage, M.P., last week's Prime Minister, was there. Before breakfast that morning (which had suffered in consequence) Mr Outrage had taken twice the maximum dose of a patent preparation of chloral, and losing heart later had finished the 10 bottle in the train. He moved in an uneasy trance, closely escorted by the most public-looking detective sergeants. These men had been with Mr Outrage in Paris, and what they did not know about his goings on was not worth knowing, at least from a novelist's point of view. (When they spoke about him to each other they called him 'the Right Honourable Rape', but that was more by way of being a pun about his name than a criticism of the conduct of his love affairs, in which, if the truth were known, he displayed a notable diffidence and the liability to panic.)

Lady Throbbing and Mrs Blackwater, those twin sisters whose portrait   20
by Millais auctioned recently at Christie's made a record in rock-bottom
prices, were sitting on one of the teak benches eating apples and
drinking what Lady Throbbing, with late Victorian *chic*, called 'a bottle
of pop', and Mrs Blackwater, more exotically, called *'champagne'*,
pronouncing it as though it were French.
   'Surely, Kitty, that is Mr Outrage, last week's Prime Minister.'
   'Nonsense, Fanny, where?'
   'Just in front of the two men with bowler hats, next to the
clergyman.'
   'It is certainly like his photographs. How strange he looks.'   30
   'Just like poor Throbbing ... all that last year.'
   '... And none of us even suspected ... until they found the bottles
under the board in his dressing-room ... and we all used to think it was
drink ...'
   'I don't think one finds *quite* the same class as Prime Minister
nowadays, do you think?'
   'They say that only *one* person *has* any influence with Mr Outrage ...'
   'At the Japanese Embassy ...'
   'Of course, dear, not so loud. But tell me, Fanny, seriously, do you
think really and truly Mr Outrage has ɪᴛ?'   40
   'He has a very nice figure for a man of his age.'
   'Yes, but *his* age, and the bull-like type is so often disappointing.
Another glass? You will be grateful for it when the ship begins to
move.'
   'I quite thought we *were* moving.'
   'How absurd you are, Fanny, and yet I can't help laughing.'
   So arm in arm and shaken by little giggles the two tipsy old ladies
went down to their cabin.
   Of the other passengers, some had filled their ears with cotton-wool,
others wore smoked glasses, while several ate dry captain's biscuits   50
from paper bags, as Red Indians are said to eat snake's flesh to make
them cunning. Mrs Hoop repeated feverishly over and over again a
formula she had learned from a yogi in New York City. A few 'good
sailors', whose luggage bore the labels of many voyages, strode
aggressively about smoking small, foul pipes and trying to get up a four
of bridge.

                                   VILE BODIES *Evelyn Waugh* □

A comic writer has to have a sense of the ridiculous and Evelyn Waugh had
that in abundance. Waugh's characterisation in the extract above veers
towards caricature. Caricature is taking certain outstanding traits of a character
and exaggerating them grossly for comic effect. It is obviously not a realistic
approach to characterisation; through caricature, however, an author can often
satirise general aspects of the society on which he or she is focusing.

1 Explain the use of irony in 'they were lacking in faith'. (3)

2 What attitude does the author take to the 'Younger Set' in the second paragraph of the extract?

3 Do you think the author disapproves at all of the two women characters or does he just want to portray them in an amusing way? Give reasons for your answer.

4 'Evelyn Waugh has a developed sense of how ridiculous human beings are'.

On the evidence of the extract, would you say that this statement was true? Quote briefly from the text to back up your answer.

5 Compare Evelyn Waugh's approach to comic characterisation with that of Jane Austen in the previous extract.

In Chapter 2 it was shown that standpoint is an important concept to grasp in considering a writer's narrative (story-telling) technique. Standpoint is just as important to keep in mind when looking at characterisation. From whose point of view are we seeing the characters of a story or novel? Does the author try to be neutral – or is this impossible? Do we see things and people through the consciousness of one or more characters?

Sometimes all the other characters in a novel are seen through the eyes of a first person narrator (the 'I' who tells the story). But it should be remembered that the narrator too is the creation of the writer. In the extract below from Graham Greene's novel, *The Quiet American*, the character of Pyle is presented to us through the eyes of Fowler, the first person narrator.

■ The morning Pyle arrived in the square by the Continental I had seen enough of my American colleagues of the Press, big, noisy, boyish and middle-aged, full of sour cracks against the French, who were, when all was said, fighting this war. Periodically, after an engagement had been tidily finished and the casualties removed from the scene, they would be summoned to Hanoi, nearly four hours' flight away, addressed by the Commander-in-Chief, lodged for one night in a Press Camp where they boasted that the barman was the best in Indo-China, flown over the late battlefield at a height of 3,000 feet (the limit of a heavy machine-gun's range) and then delivered safely and noisily back, like a school-   10 treat, to the Continental Hotel in Saigon.

Pyle was quiet, he seemed modest, sometimes that first day I had to lean forward to catch what he was saying. And he was very, very serious. Several times he seemed to shrink up within himself at the noise of the American Press on the terrace above – the terrace which was popularly believed to be safer from hand-grenades. But he criticised nobody.

'Have you read York Harding?' he asked.

'No. No, I don't think so. What did he write?'

He gazed at a milk-bar across the street and said dreamily, 'That 20 looks like a soda-fountain.' I wondered what depth of homesickness lay behind his odd choice of what to observe in a scene so unfamiliar. But hadn't I on my first walk up the rue Catinat noticed first the shop with the Guerlain perfume and comforted myself with the thought that, after all, Europe was only distant thirty hours? He looked reluctantly away from the milk-bar and said, 'York wrote a book called *The Advance of Red China*. It's a very profound book.'

'I haven't read it. Do you know him?'

He nodded solemnly and lapsed into silence. But he broke it again a moment later to modify the impression he had given. 'I don't know him 30 well,' he said. 'I guess I only met him twice.' I liked him for that – to consider it was boasting to claim acquaintance with – what was his name? York Harding. I was to learn later that he had an enormous respect for what he called serious writers. That term excluded novelists, poets and dramatists unless they had what he called a contemporary theme, and even then it was better to read the straight stuff as you got it from York.

I said, 'You know, if you live in a place for long you cease to read about it.'

'Of course I always like to know what the man on the spot has to 40 say,' he replied guardedly.

'And then check it with York?'

'Yes.' Perhaps he had noticed the irony, because he added with his habitual politeness, 'I'd take it as a very great privilege if you could find time to brief me on the main points. You see, York was here more than two years ago.'

I liked his loyalty to Harding – whoever Harding was. It was a change from the denigrations of the Pressmen and their immature cynicism. I said, 'Have another bottle of beer and I'll try to give you an idea of things.' 50

I began, while he watched me intently like a prize pupil, by explaining the situation in the North, in Tonkin, where the French in those days were hanging on to the delta of the Red River, which contained Hanoi and the only northern port, Haiphong. Here most of the rice was grown, and when the harvest was ready the annual battle for the rice always began.

'That's the North,' I said. 'The French may hold, poor devils, if the Chinese don't come to help the Vietminh. A war of jungle and mountain and marsh, paddy fields where you wade shoulder-high and 60 the enemy simply disappear, bury their arms, put on peasant dress. But you can rot comfortably in the damp in Hanoi. They don't throw bombs there. God knows why. You could call it a regular war.'

'And here in the South?'

'The French control the main roads until seven in the evening: they control the watch towers after that, and the towns – part of them. That doesn't mean you are safe, or there wouldn't be iron grilles in front of the restaurants.'

How often I had explained all this before. I was a record always turned on for the benefit of newcomers – the visiting Member of Parliament, the new British Minister. Sometimes I would wake up in 70 the night saying, 'Take the case of the Caodaists.' Or the Hoa-Haos or the Binh Xuyen, all the private armies who sold their services for money or revenge. Strangers found them picturesque, but there is nothing picturesque in treachery and distrust.

'And now,' I said, 'there's General Thé. He was Caodaist Chief of Staff, but he's taken to the hills to fight both sides, the French, the Communists. . . .'

'York,' Pyle said, 'wrote that what the East needed was a Third Force.' Perhaps I should have seen that fanatic gleam, the quick response to a phrase, the magic sound of figures: Fifth Column, Third 80 Force, Seventh Day. I might have saved all of us a lot of trouble, even Pyle, if I had realised the direction of that indefatigable young brain. But I left him with the arid bones of background and took my daily walk up and down the rue Catinat.

THE QUIET AMERICAN *Graham Greene* □

The narrator in this extract shapes our view of Pyle's character. Pyle does not exist for the reader, other than in the way his manner and statements are interpreted by Fowler, the narrator. To understand Pyle, then, it is necessary to understand Fowler's perspective on him. If Pyle were seen through the eyes of another person with a different view of him – one of the American reporters, for example – he would be portrayed in a different light.

Concealed behind the standpoint of the narrator, Fowler, is the author, who is responsible for the way that Fowler sees Pyle. If it suited his story, Greene, the author, could be deliberately making Fowler misjudge what Pyle is like or overlook some important feature of his character. It is the author, then, who is really responsible for the way that the characters are perceived.

1 How does the first paragraph prepare the way for the introduction of Pyle in the second?

2 What do we learn about Fowler's view of Pyle and how is that view communicated to the reader?

3 Is there any indication that Fowler fails fully to understand Pyle's character?

4 What sort of person does Greene portray Fowler as?

Frequently, an author will employ various viewpoints when describing a character. Thomas Hardy, one of the most famous novelists of the last century, looks at his characters from the standpoint of other characters, from that of the fictional community in which the character lives and from the author's own point of view. The author may also use physical description of a character's face, body and dress to imply certain things about that character's personality. Thomas Hardy's novel *Far from the Madding Crowd* begins with a detailed description of Gabriel Oak, one of the leading characters of the novel.

■ When Farmer Oak smiled, the corners of his mouth spread till they were within an unimportant distance of his ears, his eyes were reduced to chinks, and diverging wrinkles appeared round them, extending upon his countenance like the rays of a rudimentary sketch of the rising sun.

His Christian name was Gabriel, and on working days he was a young man of sound judgement, easy motions, proper dress, and general good character. On Sundays he was a man of misty views, rather given to postponing, and hampered by his best clothes and umbrella: upon the whole, one who felt himself to occupy morally that 10 vast middle space of Laodicean neutrality which lay between the Communion people of the parish and the drunken section – that is, he went to church, but yawned privately by the time the congregation reached the Nicene creed, and thought of what there would be for dinner when he meant to be listening to the sermon. Or, to state his character as it stood in the scale of public opinion, when his friends and critics were in tantrums, he was considered rather a bad man; when they were pleased, he was rather a good man; when they were neither, he was a man whose moral colour was a kind of pepper-and-salt mixture. 20

Since he lived six times as many working-days as Sundays, Oak's appearance in his old clothes was most peculiarly his own – the mental picture formed by his neighbours in imagining him being always dressed in that way. He wore a low-crowned felt hat, spread out at the base by tight jamming upon the head for security in high winds, and a coat like Dr Johnson's; his lower extremities being encased in ordinary leather leggings and boots emphatically large, affording to each foot a roomy apartment so constructed that any wearer might stand in a river all day long and know nothing of damp – their maker being a conscientious man who endeavoured to compensate for any weakness 30 in his cut by unstinted dimensions and solidity.

Mr Oak carried about him, by way of watch, what may be called a small silver clock; in other words, it was a watch as to shape and intention, and a small clock as to size. This instrument being several years older than Oak's grandfather, had the peculiarity of going either too fast or not at all. The smaller of its hands, too, occasionally slipped round on the pivot, and thus, though the minutes were told with precision, nobody could be quite certain of the hour they belonged to. The stopping peculiarity of his watch Oak remedied by thumps and shakes, and he escaped any evil consequences from the other two 40 defects by constant comparisons with and observations of the sun and stars, and by pressing his face close to the glass of his neighbours' windows, till he could discern the hour marked by the green-faced timekeepers within. It may be mentioned that Oak's fob being difficult of access, by reason of its somewhat high situation in the waistband of his trousers (which also lay at a remote height under his waistcoat), the watch was as a necessity pulled out by throwing the body to one side, compressing the mouth and face to a mere mass of ruddy flesh on account of the exertion, and drawing up the watch by its chain, like a bucket from a well. 50

But some thoughtful persons, who had seen him walking across one of his fields on a certain December morning – sunny and exceedingly mild – might have regarded Gabriel Oak in other aspects than these. In his face one might notice that many of the hues and curves of youth had tarried on to manhood: there even remained in his remoter crannies some relics of the boy. His height and breadth would have been sufficient to make his presence imposing, had they been exhibited with due consideration. But there is a way some men have, rural and urban alike, for which the mind is more responsible than flesh and sinew: it is a way of curtailing their dimensions by their manner of 60 showing them. And from a quiet modesty that would have become a vestal, which seemed continually to impress upon him that he had no great claim on the world's room, Oak walked unassumingly, and with a faintly perceptible bend, yet distinct from a bowing of the shoulders. This may be said to be a defect in an individual if he depends for his valuation more upon his appearance than upon his capacity to wear well, which Oak did not.

He had just reached the time of life at which 'young' is ceasing to be the prefix of 'man' in speaking of one. He was at the brightest period of masculine growth, for his intellect and his emotions were clearly 70 separated: he had passed the time during which the influence of youth indiscriminately mingles them in the character of impulse, and he had not yet arrived at the stage wherein they become united again, in the character of prejudice, by the influence of a wife and family. In short, he was twenty-eight, and a bachelor.

FAR FROM THE MADDING CROWD *Thomas Hardy* ☐

Much of Hardy's portrayal of Oak is devoted to physical description, but it is not merely detail for the sake of detail. Each feature of the description adds to our impression of Oak's personality.

Hardy also adds a wider perspective to the view of Oak presented in this portrayal by telling us the community's opinion of him:

> . . . to state his character as it stood in the scale of public opinion . . . (15–16)

He adds a realistic touch by showing that different people have different views of the same person and that some are more perceptive than others:

> But some thoughtful persons . . . might have regarded Gabriel Oak in other aspects than these. (51–53)

By looking at Oak from these different viewpoints, Hardy gives life to his character and creates interest in him. But he also subtly allies his own views about Oak with those of the 'thoughtful persons'.

1 What impression does the first paragraph give of Oak's personality?

2 What do the other details of Oak's physical appearance add to our impression of him as a man? Is that impression entirely favourable?

3 Is Hardy successful in presenting Oak as a well-known figure in the community?

4 How does Hardy show that there is more to Oak's character than a casual observer would notice?

One of the most common ways of portraying character used by novelists is to dramatise an incident by placing characters in a situation and showing aspects of their personalities by dialogue and actions. Novels are not plays, but at times they can employ dialogue to dramatise situations in a very similar way to stage plays.

The extract below from Paul Bailey's novel, *Trespasses*, consists entirely of dialogue; it could be acted on stage more or less as it is written. Paul Bailey uses the dialogue to reveal the attitudes of his characters. Mrs Chivers has come to visit her daughter, Ellie and Ralph (the 'I' of the extract), the man with whom Ellie is living in the flat.

■ 'The word has gone right out of my mind,' said Mrs Chivers. 'It's most annoying. It was used to describe artists starving in garrets.'
  'Bohemian,' I suggested.
  'Yes. Yes, I think that's the word that best describes this place.'
  'Are you intending a compliment, Mummy, or the reverse?'
  'Well, dear, in all truth, it isn't as bad as I was expecting. I mean no offence to Ralph' – she swallowed on my name – 'but I was rather dreading coming here today. I know what a rare capacity you have for martyrdom and I seriously thought you'd deposited yourself in some slum. Did you put wine vinegar in this vinaigrette?'   10

'Yes.'

'It tastes just a little too sharp, that's why I asked. No, there's nothing wrong with this room that some fresh paint and a few decent pieces wouldn't put right. If you *have* to be so modern, if you *must* insist on living together before marriage, I suppose here is as good as anywhere else to stay. It's all right as a stop-gap.'

'It's no stop-gap, Mummy. We intend living here after we're married. Don't we, Ralph?'

'Yes, Ellie. We do.'

'Surely not, Elspeth' – I stood corrected, Ellie's name was most   20
definitely Elspeth – 'surely not. Not in this room. It's large, I grant you, but it's still a room. It isn't a flat.'

'It appeals to us. The light. The view.'

'What view? Roof-tops, pigeons, chimneys? Television aerials? They don't constitute any view *I* could bear to look at for long.'

'You won't be living with us, Mummy. Think of me for once; of what I want. I want Ralph. He doesn't have a rosy complexion and he doesn't come from your mythical good family. His bloody blood isn't of the bluest. I want him and I want to live here with him in this room – that is what I want. Can you hear? Oh, Mummy, why can't you open   30
yourself to me? There's nothing and no one in your way. Why, please, can't you?'

'That avocado was very nice. It could have been riper but I enjoyed it, even so. Can I help you in any way with the next course?'

Ellie got up and gathered the dishes together without replying.

We looked into our wine as she went into the kitchen.

'Do you think she *can* manage?'

'Yes.'

'I *did* offer.'   TRESPASSES *Paul Bailey* □

The tone of the dialogue is very important. If the reader is to detect all the nuances of meaning and emphasis, an understanding of the tone is absolutely necessary. If the dialogue from the extract were to be performed by three actors on a stage, then the actors would provide the differences of tone in the manner of their delivery. The reader of a novel has to interpret the tone from the printed page; a skilled writer, such as Paul Bailey, can suggest tone to the reader and thus portray character through dialogue.

1 'I know what a rare capacity you have for martyrdom and I seriously thought you'd deposited yourself in some slum.' (8–10)

The vocabulary used by Mrs Chivers and the tone of the sentence reveal something about her character and attitudes. What can you deduce about her from this sentence?

3 / Passages to Compare

2 'It tastes just a little too sharp, that's why I asked.' (12)

If you were the actress playing Mrs Chivers in a dramatised version of this scene, what tone would you use in saying the line above?

3 'That avocado was very nice. It could have been riper but I enjoyed it, even so.' (33–34)

Why do you think Mrs Chivers chooses this moment to discuss the ripeness of her avocado?

4 Discuss the contrasting attitudes which Mrs Chivers and Ellie have to Ellie's living in the flat with Ralph.

● Write a short piece of dialogue, taking *The Visit* as your title. Use a situation of your own choice and try to make the dialogue revealing of character and attitudes. Intersperse the dialogue with description of actions or comments on the events.

In the two extracts below, Iris Murdoch and Joyce Carol Oates introduce the leading characters of their respective novels to the reader. As you read the passages, consider how the two authors build up their characters.

■ Dora Greenfield left her husband because she was afraid of him. She decided six months later to return to him for the same reason. The absent Paul, haunting her with letters and telephone bells and imagined footsteps on the stairs had begun to be the greater torment. Dora suffered from guilt, and with guilt came fear. She decided at last that the persecution of his presence was to be preferred to the persecution of his absence.

Dora was still very young, though she vaguely thought of herself as past her prime. She came of a lower middle-class London family. Her father had died when she was nine years old, and her mother, with 10 whom she had never got on very well, had married again. When Dora was eighteen she entered the Slade school of art with a scholarship, and had been there two years when she encountered Paul. The rôle of an art student suited Dora. It was indeed the only rôle she had ever been able whole-heartedly to play. She had been an ugly and wretched schoolgirl. As a student she grew plump and peach-like and had a little pocket money of her own, which she spent on big multi-coloured skirts and jazz records and sandals. At that time, which although it was only three years ago now seemed unimaginably remote, she had been happy. Dora, who had so lately discovered in herself a talent for happiness, 20 was the more dismayed to find that she could be happy neither with her husband nor without him.

Paul Greenfield, who was thirteen years older than his wife, was an art historian connected with the Courtauld Institute. He came of an old

66

family of German bankers and had money of his own. He had been born in England and attended an English public school, and preferred not to remember the distinction of his ancestors. Although his assets were never idle, he did not speak of stocks and shares. He first met Dora when he came to lecture on mediaeval wood-carving at the Slade. Dora had accepted his proposal of marriage without hesitation and 30 for a great many reasons. She married him for his good taste and his flat in Knightsbridge. She married him for a certain integrity and nobility of character which she saw in him. She married him because he was so wonderfully more grown-up than her thin neurotic art-student friends. She married him a little for his money. She admired him and was extremely flattered by his attentions. She hoped, by making what her mother (who was bursting with envy) called a 'good marriage', to be able to get inside society and learn how to behave; although this was something she did not put clearly to herself at the time. She married, finally, because of the demonic intensity of Paul's desire for her. He 40 was a passionate and poetic suitor, and something exotic in him touched Dora's imagination, starved throughout her meagre education, and unsatisfied still amid the rather childish and provincial gaieties of her student life. Dora, though insufficiently reflective to suffer from strong inferiority feelings, had never valued herself highly. She was amazed that Paul should notice her at all, and she passed quickly from this amazement to the luxurious pleasure of being able so easily to delight this subtle and sophisticated person. She never doubted that she was in love.

THE BELL *Iris Murdoch* ☐

■ One warm evening in August 1937 a girl in love stood before a mirror. Her name was Loretta. It was her reflection in the mirror she loved, and out of this dreamy, pleasing love there arose a sense of excitement that was restless and blind – which way would it move, what would happen? Her name was Loretta; she was pleased with that name too, though Loretta Botsford pleased her less. Her last name dragged down on her, it had no melody. She stood squinting into the plastic-rimmed mirror on her bureau, trying to get the best of the light, seeing inside her rather high-colored, healthy, ordinary prettiness a hint of some-thing daring and dangerous. Looking into the mirror was like looking 10 into the future; everything was there, waiting. It was not just that face she loved. She loved other things. During the week she worked at Ajax Laundry and Dry Cleaners, and she was very lucky to have that job, and during the week the steamy, rushed langour of her work built up in her a sense of excitement. What was going to happen? Today was Saturday.

Her face was rather full, and there was a slight mischievous puffiness about her cheeks that made her look younger than she was – she was

sixteen – and her eyes were blue, a mindless, bland blue, not very
sharp. Her lips were painted a deep scarlet, exactly the style of the day.   20
Her eyebrows were plucked in exactly the style of the day. Did she not
dream over the Sunday supplement features, and did she not linger on
her way to work before the Trinity Theater in order to stare at the
pictures? She wore a navy-blue dress pulled in tight at the waist. Her
waist was surprisingly narrow, her shoulders a little broad, almost
masculine; she was a strong girl. Upon her competent shoulders sat
this fluttery, dreamy head, blond hair puffed out and falling down in
coquettish curls past her ears, past her collar, down onto her back, so
that when she ran along the sidewalk it blew out behind her and men
stopped to stare at her; never did she bother to glance back at these   30
men – they were like men in movies who do not appear in the
foreground but only focus interest, show which way interest should be
directed. She was in love with the thought of this. Behind her good
clear skin was a universe of skin, all of it healthy. She loved this, she
was in love with the fact of girls like her having come into existence,
though she could not have expressed her feelings exactly. She said to
her friend Rita, 'Sometimes I feel so happy over nothing I must be
crazy.' Dragging around in the morning, trying to get her father up and
trying to get her brother Brock fed and out before somebody started a
fight, still she felt a peculiar sense of joy, of prickly excitement, that   40
nothing could beat down. What was going to happen? 'Oh, you're not
crazy,' Rita said thoughtfully, 'you just haven't been through it yet.'

She combed her hair with a heavy pink brush. It worried her to see
her curls so listless – that was because of the heat. From the apartment
across the way, through the open window, she could hear a radio
playing music that meant Saturday night, and her heart began to
pound with anticipation of the long hours ahead during which
anything might happen. Her father, who had been out of work for
almost ten years and who couldn't do a thing, liked to lie in bed and
drink and smoke, not caring that so many hours rushed by he'd never   50
be able to get back – but Loretta felt that time was passing too quickly. It
made her nervous. She scratched at her bare arm with the brush in a
gentle, unconscious, caressing gesture, and felt the dreaminess of the
late summer afternoon rise in her. In the kitchen someone sat down
heavily, as if answering her, in response to her wondering.

THEM *Joyce Carol Oates* □

1 Compare the two extracts from the point of view of what we learn about the two
characters, Dora and Loretta.

2 Discuss and compare how the writers create an impression of the two people.

In the final two passages of the chapter, taken from two novels which are very different in style, Joseph Heller and William Faulkner present contrasting pictures of the characters they portray.

■ Hungry Joe was crazy, and no one knew it better then Yossarian, who did everything he could to help him. Hungry Joe just wouldn't listen to Yossarian. Hungry Joe just wouldn't listen because he thought Yossarian was crazy.

'Why should he listen to you?' Doc Daneeka inquired of Yossarian without looking up.

'Because he's got troubles.'

Doc Daneeka snorted scornfully. 'He thinks he's got troubles? What about me?' Doc Daneeka continued slowly with a gloomy sneer. 'Oh, I'm not complaining. I know there's a war on. I know a lot of people are 10 going to have to suffer for us to win it. But why must I be one of them? Why don't they draft some of these old doctors who keep shooting their kissers off in public about what big sacrifices the medical game stands ready to make? I don't want to make sacrifices. I want to make dough.'

Doc Daneeka was a very neat, clean man whose idea of a good time was to sulk. He had a dark complexion and a small, wise, saturnine face with mournful pouches under both eyes. He brooded over his health continually and went almost daily to the medical tent to have his temperature taken by one of the two enlisted men there who ran things 20 for him practically on their own, and ran it so efficiently that he was left with little else to do but sit in the sunlight with his stuffed nose and wonder what other people were so worried about. Their names were Gus and Wes and they had succeeded in elevating medicine to an exact science. All men reporting on sick call with temperatures above 102 were rushed to the hospital. All those except Yossarian reporting on sick call with temperatures below 102 had their gums and toes painted with gentian violet solution and were given a laxative to throw away into the bushes. All those reporting on a sick call with temperatures of exactly 102 were asked to return in an hour to have their temperatures 30 taken again. Yossarian, with his temperature of 101, could go to the hospital whenever he wanted to because he was not afraid of them.

The system worked just fine for everybody, especially for Doc Daneeka, who found himself with all the time he needed to watch old Major —— de Coverley pitching horsehoes in his private horseshoe-pitching pit, still wearing the transparent eye patch Doc Daneeka had fashioned for him from the strip of celluloid stolen from Major Major's orderly room window months before when Major —— de Coverley had returned from Rome with an injured cornea after renting two apartments there for the officers and enlisted men to use on their rest leaves. 40 The only time Doc Daneeka ever went to the medical tent was the time he began to feel he was a very sick man each day and stopped in just to have Gus and Wes look him over. They could never find anything wrong with him. His temperature was always 96.8, which was perfectly all right with them, as long as he didn't mind. Doc Daneeka did mind. He was beginning to lose confidence in Gus and Wes and was thinking of having them both transferred back to the motor pool and replaced by someone who *could* find something wrong.

CATCH 22 *Joseph Heller* ☐

■ From beyond the screen of bushes which surrounded the spring, Popeye watched a man drinking. A faint path led from the road to the spring. Popeye watched the man – a tall, thin man, hatless, in worn gray flannel trousers and carrying a tweed coat over his arm – emerge from the path and kneel to drink from the spring.

The spring welled up at the root of a beech tree and flowed away upon a bottom of whorled and waved sand. It was surrounded by a thick growth of cane and brier, of cypress and gum in which broken sunlight lay sourceless. Somewhere, hidden and secret yet nearby, a bird sang three notes and ceased. 10

In the spring the drinking man leaned his face to the broken and myriad reflection of his own drinking. When he rose up he saw among them the shattered reflection of Popeye's straw hat, though he had heard no sound.

He saw, facing him across the spring, a man of under size, his hands in his coat pockets, a cigarette slanted from his chin. His suit was black, with a tight, high-waisted coat. His trousers were rolled once and caked with mud above mud-caked shoes. His face had a queer, bloodless color, as though seen by electric light; against the sunny silence, in his slanted straw hat and his slightly akimbo arms, he had that vicious 20 depthless quality of stamped tin.

Behind him the bird sang again, three bars in monotonous repetition: a sound meaningless and profound out of a suspirant and peaceful following silence which seemed to isolate the spot, and out of which a moment later came the sound of an automobile passing along a road and dying away.

The drinking man knelt beside the spring. 'You've got a pistol in that pocket, I suppose,' he said.

Across the spring Popeye appeared to contemplate him with two knobs of soft black rubber. 'I'm asking you,' Popeye said. 'What's that 30 in your pocket?'

The other man's coat was still across his arm. He lifted his other hand toward the coat, out of one pocket of which protruded a crushed felt hat, from the other a book. 'Which pocket?' he said.

'Don't show me,' Popeye said. 'Tell me.'

The other man stopped his hand. 'It's a book.'

'What book?' Popeye said.

'Just a book. The kind that people read. Some people do.'

'Do you read books?' Popeye said.

The other man's hand was frozen above the coat. Across the spring   40
they looked at one another. The cigarette wreathed its faint plume
across Popeye's face, one side of his face squinted against the smoke
like a mask carved into two simultaneous expressions.

SANCTUARY *William Faulkner* □

1 What methods do Heller and Faulkner use to portray Doc Daneeka and Popeye: how
does each use dialogue, physical description, description of incidents involving the
character and direct author's analysis?

2 Compare the contribution made by the personalities of Popeye and Doc Daneeka to the
tone and atmosphere of the two extracts.

3 Discuss the authors' attitudes to their respective characters. Do you sense, for instance,
that the authors like or dislike, approve or disapprove of, their characters? Refer to
evidence from both extracts in answering.

Chapter 4
Diaries, Essays and Autobiography

This chapter looks at more personal types of literature, in which writers reveal something of themselves and express their own opinions more openly than is done in other types of prose. This has the effect of bringing them into a closer, more direct relationship with their readers.

People keep diaries for a number of different reasons: to record the daily events of their lives, to give private expression to their emotions or to analyse their own lives and the society in which they live. However, diaries may also be written with a potential reader in mind and this will affect both the content and the style of the diary. Very often, too, the need to keep a diary is a sign that a person wants to write. The first step in the career of many professional writers has been to keep a diary and this has developed later into other forms of expression.

Autobiographies written by both the famous and the unknown present a fascinating insight into the minds of other people. Personal writing of this kind enables readers to share the experience of the writer; they are able to make connections between their own lives and that of the autobiographer in a way that is subtly different to the feeling of empathy produced by the lives of fictional characters.

The essay used to be an established literary form, a genre in which many important and famous writers specialized. The form gave writers the opportunity to write in a wide range of styles which reflected the variety of their standpoints, ranging from the gentle and contemplative to those expressing trenchant views on serious moral issues. In the twentieth century, the decline of the journal – the publishing outlet which succoured the essay – has meant the loss of the expert craft of the essayist. Only occasionally now is a well-known writer or journalist allowed the space in a publication to write a piece which is at all like that once illustrious genre.

Diaries kept by important historical figures are naturally of great interest both because of the light they shed on important events and because of what they reveal about the individuals themselves. The extract which follows is from the diaries of Josef Goebbels. Goebbels was the person who was chiefly responsible for creating the myth of the all-powerful Führer, Adolf Hitler. In the 1930s and 1940s, Goebbels used the mass media to distort information; the mass of the German people and the world at large were fed an image of Hitler that was vastly different to the evil reality. Goebbels committed suicide in 1945 in the Berlin bunker where Hitler himself met death by his own hand.

Goebbels' diaries for those last months were recently found. Below is an extract from the entry for 27 February 1945, less than two months before his death and the end of the war. Göring, mentioned in the extract, was in charge of the Luftwaffe, the German Air Force.

■ The discussion which I had with the Führer over this, in my view, completely fundamental problem of our war leadership was very dramatic and heated. But the Führer agreed with me on every point. I feel in fact that he is annoyed that things should have gone so far, not that I spoke so bluntly and frankly. On the contrary he complimented me on it, took my side openly and unreservedly and expressed his pleasure that I for one made no bones about my views. I told him that I had recently been reading Carlyle's book on Frederick the Great. The Führer knows the book very well himself. I repeated certain passages from the book to him and they affected him very deeply. That is how 10 we must be and that is how we will be. If someone like Göring dances totally out of line, then he must be called to order. Bemedalled idiots and vain perfumed coxcombs have no place in our war leadership. Either they must mend their ways or be eliminated. I shall not rest or repose until the Führer has put this in order. He must change Göring both inside and outside or show him the door. For instance it is simply grossly bad style for the senior officer of the Reich, in the present wartime situation, to strut round in a silver-grey uniform. What effeminate behaviour in face of present developments! It is to be hoped that the Führer will succeed in turning Göring into a man again. The 20 Führer is glad that Göring's wife has now moved to the Obersalzberg because she was a bad influence on him. Anyway Göring's whole entourage is not worth a row of beans. It encouraged instead of

restraining his tendency to effeminacy and pleasure-seeking. By
contrast the Führer had high praise for the simplicity and purity of my
family life. This is the only way to meet the demands of the present
times.

I have the very definite impression that this discussion with the
Führer made a real impact. It was necessary and the timing was entirely
right. We argued so loudly that the aides outside could hear what we   30
said through the door. They were extremely pleased. These splendid
young men are interested solely in seeing the Party led back to its true
essence and nature since only in this way can the fortunes of this war
be turned. All these young people are on my side and look upon me as
their mouthpiece since I can say to the Führer point-blank what has to
be said. Round the dinner-table in the Reich Chancellery there sits a
worn-out collection of officers. I barely say 'good evening' to them.
These people are as foreign to me as men can be.

Back at home I have a mountain of work to deal with. But I can now
get on with it very quickly and energetically since I have got a real   40
burden off my chest.

In the evening we have the regulation Mosquito raid on Berlin once
more.

The situation in the West causes me great anxiety. What will happen
if the enemy really makes a break-through here? But we will not
assume the worst. The great thing is that I have at last succeeded in
hacking my way through this fundamental question of our war
leadership.

During the night the cursed Englishmen return to Berlin with their
Mosquitos and deprive one of the few hours' sleep which one needs   50
more than ever these days.

THE GOEBBELS DIARIES □

The making of history is not only about great events and decision-making; it is
also concerned with the interaction of personalities and with the ambitions and
follies of individuals:

... only in this way can the fortunes of this war be turned. (33–34)

This is Goebbels' opinion, but it is open to the reader to question whether his
squabble with Göring was really of such fundamental importance. Historical
diaries are for this reason doubly revealing: as well as examining what light the
diarist sheds on famous events, we can look at how the writer presents his or
her own rôle in those events.

Another interesting question, which is especially worth asking in the light of
Goebbels' career as a propagandist and manipulator of the media, is whether
the diaries are self-revealing – an expression of inner anxieties – or whether the
public persona of the politician persists, so that the diary becomes a kind of
private self-justification.

1 'Bemedalled idiots and vain perfumed coxcombs have no place in our war leadership.'
(12–13).

Goebbels is describing Göring here. How does this description contrast with the way
Goebbels sees himself and what light does it throw on 'this fundamental question of our
war leadership' (47–48)?

2 What evidence is there from the extract that Goebbels needed Hitler's approval and that
he believed himself to be a major influence on Hitler's thinking?

3 What does the diary entry reveal about Goebbels' personality?

4 How would you describe the tone of the diary extract – is it formal, informal or a mixture
of both? Illustrate your answer with evidence from the passage.

5 On the evidence of this extract, what does Goebbels use his diaries for: unburdening
himself of his anxieties, recording events, analysing the situation rationally, expressing
his enthusiasms and prejudices, or a mixture of all these? Quote from the text to back up
your analysis.

As a contrast to the extract from Goebbels' diaries, read the extract below
which is taken from the diary of a young British soldier caught up in the
horrendous trench warfare of the First World War. This soldier managed to
write his diary entries under the severest of conditions. He did not survive the
war, but his diaries were first published in 1923.

■ *July 14.*   Informed that the Division on our right are doing a raid to-
night, but working parties are to go out as usual! If I were sentimental I
should have to write a last letter home every night – then I would
certainly be killed.
      Started work on a strong point in front of the hill, and shortly
afterwards our barrage started in conjunction with the raid. It was very
fierce, and the S.O.S. lights went up at once over the German lines. We
were watching the pretty colours when their protective barrage came
down, just like a sudden thunderstorm, and I realised to my horror that
we were working dead on their barrage line. Before I saw exactly what   10
had happened two men were knocked to pieces and the remainder
were running all over the place looking for cover. There were the ruins
of a farm on our left, and I was trying to get the men together into the
holes around this. We got about fifteen into this and several wounded,
and then they shortened range. A salvo came bang on top of us, there
was a great lurid flash and a roar by my feet and I thought I was done
for. I went clean off my feet and was blown several yards, but got up
and found I was untouched but nearly blind and awfully dizzy. I heard
some one calling, and found McDougall. He had been knocked over by
the same shell and was quite blind. We crawled into a hole together and   20
waited to get our breath. The shells were coming just round us in solid

masses so close that we could feel the earth heaving, and once or twice
we were half buried. I had lost my bearings completely, and McDougall
was still blind and apparently dazed, for he wouldn't answer when I
shouted in his ear. Then I felt alone and I thought I would go mad –
there were rats in the same hole with us, screaming with terror, and all
the time those blasted shells, crash, crash, crash. I felt I must do
something, so I looked over into the next shell-hole and saw that it was
part of an old trench. I shoved McDougall over and together we
flopped down into it and felt much safer, as it was deeper than the one   30
we had left. Then I started to crawl along the trench, and to my great
delight we found some of the men.

For three-quarters of an hour we lay in that ditch with the earth
jumping and falling all round us – at times the whole trench seemed to
move three or four feet. A ration party out on the mule track hadn't got
such good cover, and we could hear the poor devils moaning and
screaming as some of the others tried to drag them back to the aid post.
Some of the kids in our trench began to cry, and I felt like it myself. We
were all choking, and the valley was so full of smoke and dust that I
couldn't even see the Verey lights which were less than 300 yards away   40
– only the great red splashes of fire where the shells burst.

It seemed to last for hours; the steady crashing of the bursts, the
whine of the flying pieces and all around the screaming of shattered
men who had once been strong. And then the smell which, if a man has
known it once, will haunt him to the end of time, the most sickly
nauseating stench in the world – the combined smell of moist earth,
high explosive, and warm human blood.

God, in Thy mercy, let me never again hear any one speak of the
Glory of War!

About 1.30 the noise stopped almost as suddenly as it had begun, but   50
he put down two more barrages, one at 2.0 a.m. and one at 2.30. Had
an awful headache when I got to bed.

A SOLDIER'S DIARY □

The extract from *A Soldier's Diary* raises the question of whom a diarist writes
for. Do diarists write only for themselves or do they secretly consider the
possibility that someone else will eventually read their innermost thoughts?
Some diaries do seem to be written with one eye on posterity. There is perhaps
a literary flavour to the writing of the soldier's diary, as though the writer was
conscious that what he wrote was likely to be read by someone at a later date
and so paid attention to the style and content of what he wrote.

1 a Compare the tone of the soldier's diary entry with the tone of Goebbels' diary.

   b How do the two diarists differ in their attitudes to war?

2 'Had an awful headache when I got to bed.' (51–52)

   How could this be considered an incongruous last sentence for the day's diary entry?

3 On the evidence of the passage, has the soldier's anticipation of a future readership
   affected the way he has written the diary?

The Diary of a Nobody was first published in 1892; it was written by George and
Weedon Grossmith. They invented Mr Pooter, a lower middle-class clerk, who
is meant to be the keeper of the diary. Mr Pooter's account of his day-to-day life
acquires a representative quality so that a picture of the snobbery and pettiness
of suburban life in late Victorian times emerges from its pages.

■ *April 14.* Spent the whole of the afternoon in the garden, having this
morning picked up at a bookstall for fivepence a capital little book, in
good condition, on *Gardening*. I procured and sowed some half-hardy
annuals in what I fancy will be a warm, sunny border. I thought of a
joke, and called out Carrie. Carrie came out rather testy, I thought. I
said: 'I have just discovered we have got a lodging-house.' She replied:
'How do you mean?' I said: 'Look at the *boarders*.' Carrie said: 'Is that all
you wanted me for?' I said: 'Any other time you would have laughed at
my little pleasantry.' Carrie said: 'Certainly – *at any other time*, but not
when I am busy in the house.' The stairs look very nice. Gowing called,   10
and said the stairs looked *all right*, but it made the banisters look *all
wrong*, and suggested a coat of paint on them also, which Carrie quite

77

agreed with. I walked round to Putley, and fortunately he was out, so I
had a good excuse to let the banisters slide. By-the-by, that is rather
funny.

April 15, Sunday. At three o'clock Cummings and Gowing called for a
good long walk over Hampstead and Finchley, and brought with them
a friend named Stillbrook. We walked and chatted together, except
Stillbrook, who was always a few yards behind us staring at the ground
and cutting at the grass with his stick.   20

As it was getting on for five, we four held a consultation, and
Gowing suggested that we should make for 'The Cow and Hedge' and
get some tea. Stillbrook said: 'A brandy-and-soda was good enough for
him.' I reminded them that all public-houses were closed till six o'clock.
Stillbrook said, 'That's all right – *bona-fide* travellers.'

We arrived; and as I was trying to pass, the man in charge of the gate
said: 'Where from?' I replied: 'Holloway.' He immediately put up his
arm, and declined to let me pass. I turned back for a moment, when I
saw Stillbrook, closely followed by Cummings and Gowing, make for
the entrance. I watched them, and thought I would have a good laugh   30
at their expense. I heard the porter say: 'Where from?' When, to my
surprise, in fact disgust, Stillbrook replied: 'Blackheath,' and the three
were immediately admitted.

Gowing called to me across the gate, and said: 'We shan't be a
minute.' I waited for them the best part of an hour. When they
appeared they were all in most excellent spirits, and the only one who
made an effort to apologise was Mr Stillbrook, who said to me: 'It was
very rough on you to be kept waiting, but we had another spin for S.
and B.'s.' I walked home in silence; I couldn't speak to them. I felt very
dull all the evening, but deemed it advisable *not* to say anything to   40
Carrie about the matter.

April 16. After business, set to work in the garden. When it got dark I
wrote to Cummings and Gowing (who neither called, for a wonder;
perhaps they were ashamed of themselves) about yesterday's adventure at 'The Cow and Hedge.' Afterwards made up my mind not to
write *yet*.

April 17. Thought I would write a kind little note to Gowing and
Cummings about last Sunday, and warning them against Mr Stillbrook.
Afterwards, thinking the matter over, tore up the letter and determined
not to *write* at all, but to *speak* quietly to them. Dumbfounded at   50
receiving a sharp letter from Cummings, saying that both he and
Gowing had been waiting for an explanation of *my* (mind you, MY)
extraordinary conduct coming home on Sunday. At last I wrote: 'I
thought I was the aggrieved party; but as I freely forgive you, you –
feeling yourself aggrieved – should bestow forgiveness on me.' I have

copied this *verbatim* in the diary, because I think it is one of the most perfect and thoughtful sentences I have ever written. I posted the letter, but in my own heart I felt I was actually apologising for having been insulted.

THE DIARY OF A NOBODY *George and Weedon Grossmith* □

Here we are dealing with a fictional diary, however realistic the entries may seem. Two authors have created the diarist and his diary. They are manipulating their creations for a satirical end. The success of the book with readers will largely depend on how appropriate the diary entries seem for the kind of person Pooter is and how much of a real person Pooter becomes. Through Pooter's diary, the authors intend to satirise a whole stratum of pretentious, lower middle-class society.

1 Judging from the first entry, how would you describe Pooter's sense of humour?

2 What methods do the real authors of the diaries employ to allow Pooter to reveal himself as small-minded and pompous?

3 How would you describe the content and tone of these diary entries?

4 Goebbels' diary is obviously important because he was an important historical figure. The soldier's diary makes fascinating reading because of the circumstances in which it was written. Mr Pooter's fictional diary has been of equal interest to many people since it was first published in 1892. Explain why you think Mr Pooter's diary could be of interest almost a century later.

● Write one or more entries for the diary of any one of the following:

a snob   a housewife   a prisoner   a rock star   a contemporary nobody

In autobiography, a person writes about his or her own life and aims to share their experience of life with the reader. The best autobiographies touch upon veins of common feeling so that many people can relate to the writer's experience and compare it with their own lives.

Simone de Beauvoir is a French novelist and philosopher who has a reputation for looking very honestly and rationally at events and people. In her book *A Very Easy Death*, she describes the last months of her mother's life. During that time her mother was suffering from an incurable cancer and was a patient in a private clinic.

In this extract, de Beauvoir analyses the rights and wrongs of having extended her mother's life through medical treatment, the effects of the last months on the writer herself and the kind of death her mother had.

■ What would have happened if Maman's doctor had detected the cancer as early as the first symptoms? No doubt it would have been treated with rays and Maman would have lived two or three years longer. But she would have known or at least suspected the nature of her disease, and she would have passed the end of her life in a state of dread. What we bitterly regretted was that the doctor's mistake had deceived us; otherwise Maman's happiness would have become our chief concern. The difficulties that prevented Jeanne and Poupette from having her in the summer would not have counted. I should have seen more of her: I should have invented things to please her.   10

And is one to be sorry that the doctors brought her back to life and operated, or not? She, who did not want to lose a single day, 'won' thirty: they brought her joys; but they also brought her anxiety and suffering. Since she did escape from the martyrdom that I sometimes thought was hanging over her, I cannot decide for her. For my sister, losing Maman the very day she saw her again would have been a shock from which she would scarcely have recovered. And as for me? Those four weeks have left me pictures, nightmares, sadness that I should never have known if Maman had died that Wednesday morning. But I cannot measure the disturbance that I should have felt since my sorrow   20 broke out in a way that I had not foreseen. We did derive an undoubted good from this respite: it saved us, or almost saved us, from remorse. When someone you love dies you pay for the sin of outliving her with a thousand piercing regrets. Her death brings to light her unique quality; she grows as vast as the world that her absence annihilates for her and whose whole existence was caused by her being there; you feel that she should have had more room in your life – all the room, if need be. You snatch yourself away from this wildness: she was only one among many. But since you never do all you might for anyone – not even within the arguable limits that you have set yourself – you have plenty   30 of room left for self-reproach. With regard to Maman we were above all guilty, these last years, of carelessness, omission and abstention. We felt that we atoned for this by the days that we gave up to her, by the peace that our being there gave her, and by the victories gained over fear and pain. Without our obstinate watchfulness she would have suffered far more:

For indeed, comparatively speaking, her death was an easy one. 'Don't leave me in the power of the brutes.' I thought of all those who have no one to make that appeal to: what agony it must be to feel oneself a defenceless thing, utterly at the mercy of indifferent doctors   40 and overworked nurses. No hand on the forehead when terror seizes them; no sedative as soon as pain begins to tear them; no lying prattle to fill the silence of the void. 'She aged forty years in twenty-four hours.' That phrase too had obsessed my mind. Even today – why? – there are horrible agonizing deaths. And then in the public wards, when the last hour is coming near, they put a screen round the dying

man's bed: he has seen this screen round other beds that were empty
the next day: he knows. I pictured Maman, blinded for hours by the
black sun that no one can look at directly: the horror of her staring eyes
with their dilated pupils. She had a very easy death; an upper-class   50
death.

A VERY EASY DEATH *Simone de Beauvoir* ☐

Although in *A Very Easy Death*, Simone de Beauvoir is describing her mother's
last illness, the book is a segment of autobiography because it is essentially
about the effect the death, and the manner of it, has on the author herself.

To write about the prolonged last illness of one's own mother may seem to be
in doubtful taste to many people; the justification for it may lie in the honesty
of the self-observation and the perceptiveness with which de Beauvoir reveals
the nature of death, guilt and grief. She seems to be able to distance herself
from events and analyse the situation and her own involvement in it from an
objective standpoint.

1 The first and second paragraphs follow a similar construction. What is this construction
and why do you think the author uses it?

2 'Don't leave me in the power of the brutes'. (38)

Simone de Beauvoir's mother is begging not to be left alone. Why do you think de
Beauvoir chooses to include the actual words of her mother here? How do this sentence
and the rest of the paragraph fit into the structure of the passage?

3 Do you think it is brave and honest for the author to analyse her feelings publicly about
such a personal matter, or do you think that this is in bad taste? Why do you think de
Beauvoir chose to write such a book?

4 The extract is written in the first person and, if you hadn't been told it was
autobiographical, you might have thought it was an extract from a novel written in the
first person. What elements in the extract could lead you to think it was from a novel?

The periodical essay probably reached its peak as a literary form in the
eighteenth century. Educated people of this time considered that they were
living in the Age of Reason and the contemplative essay reflected their concern
for a philosophical analysis of social issues and the eternal questions about life
and morality. It was, for the wealthy, a leisured age, where much time was
spent by gentlemen of reason and intellect in discussion in clubs and coffee-
houses.

Periodicals such as *The Tatler* and *The Spectator* reflected and nurtured these
strivings towards rationality. In these journals, writers like Richard Steele were
given free rein to comment on contemporary society and its concerns. The
extract below is from an essay about the education of women written by Steele
for *The Spectator*.

■ The general Mistake among us in Educating our Children, is, That
in our Daughters we take Care of their Persons and neglect their Minds;
in our Sons, we are so intent upon adorning their Minds, that we
wholly neglect their Bodies. It is from this that you shall see a young
Lady celebrated and admired in all the Assemblies about Town; when
her elder Brother is afraid to come into a Room. From this ill
Management it arises, That we frequently observe a Man's Life is half
spent before he is taken Notice of; and a Woman in the Prime of her
Years is out of Fashion and neglected. The Boy I shall consider upon
some other Occasion, and at present stick to the Girl: And I am the   10
more inclined to this, because I have several Letters which complain to
me that my Female Readers have not understood me for some Days last
past, and take themselves to be unconcerned in the present Turn of my
Writings. When a Girl is safely brought from her Nurse, before she is
capable of forming one simple Notion of any thing in Life, she is
delivered to the Hands of her Dancing-Master; and with a Collar round
her Neck, the pretty wild Thing is taught a fantastical Gravity of
Behaviour, and forced to a particular Way of holding her Head, heaving
her Breast, and moving with her whole Body; and all this under Pain of
never having an Husband, if she steps, looks, or moves awry. This   20
gives the young Lady wonderful Workings of Imagination, what is to
pass between her and her Husband, that she is every Moment told of,
and for whom she seems to be educated. Thus her Fancy is engaged to
turn all her Endeavours to the Ornament of her Person, as what must
determine her Good and Ill in this Life; and she naturally thinks, if she
is tall enough, she is wise enough for any thing for which her Education
makes her think she is designed. To make her an agreeable Person is
the main Purpose of her Parents; to that is all their Cost, to that all their
Care directed; and from this general Folly of Parents we owe our
present numerous Race of Coquets. These Reflections puzzle me, when   30
I think of giving my Advice on the Subject of managing the wild Thing
mentioned in the Letter of my Correspondent. But sure there is a
middle Way to be followed; the Management of a young Lady's Person
is not to be overlooked, but the Erudition of her Mind is much more to
be regarded. According as this is managed, you will see the Mind
follow the Appetites of the Body, or the Body express the Virtues of the
Mind.

ESSAY ON THE EDUCATION OF WOMEN *Richard Steele* □

The final sentence of the essay succinctly expresses the balance between nature
and reason that eighteenth-century rationalists cultivated:

According as this is managed, you will see the Mind follow the
Appetites of the Body, or the Body express the Virtues of the Mind.
(35–7)

Steele's style reflects this quest for balance. Nothing is overstated or over-emphasised, although in this essay Steele is obviously strongly committed to the point of view he is expressing. This view is reflected in the balanced sentences he writes:

> But sure there is a middle Way to be followed; the Management of a young Lady's Person is not to be overlooked, but the Erudition of her Mind is much more to be regarded. (32–35)

It is possible, nevertheless, that the technique of using balanced sentences lends an appeal to his arguments which comes from their rhetorical effectiveness and is quite separate from the merit of what he is saying.

1 According to Steele, what is the main purpose behind the education of a young woman of the eighteenth century? How does this differ from the approach that Steele recommends?

2 The last sentence of the extract is an example of a balanced sentence. Pick out other sentences from the extract that have a similar construction and balance. Do you find that the balanced approach lends a force to what Steele says which is independent of his actual arguments?

3 This type of essay is often described as contemplative; this means that the writer has taken the opportunity to analyse some philosophical idea or social issue in a rational, analytical manner. How effective is this approach in dealing with this particular issue? Does the writer, in your opinion, present a convincing argument?

● Write an essay entitled, 'Should educational opportunities be the same for both sexes?'

Adopt a rational, unemotional tone in your writing, although you may well want to make some forceful points in the course of your essay.

Essayists sometimes use an ostensibly rational, unemotional approach to their subject as a satirical method of exposing grotesque injustices and hypocrisies. This was the technique favoured by Dean Swift, who was a contemporary of Steele. However, Swift's essays are usually much more committed and trenchant than the gently satirical writings of Steele.

Swift was very concerned about Britain's policy to Ireland, which in the eighteenth century resulted in widespread starvation among the Irish people. Instead of attacking English politicians and absentee landlords directly, he chose in an essay called *A Modest Proposal for preventing the Children of Ireland from being a Burden to their Parents or Country* to use a business-like tone in the manner of politicians and civil servants in putting forward a solution to some of the problems. His purpose was to ridicule the English government and to show how utterly contemptible its policy towards Ireland was.

■ I shall now therefore humbly propose my own Thoughts, which I hope will not be liable to the least Objection.

I have been assured by a very knowing American of my acquaintance in London, that a young healthy Child well Nursed is at a year Old a most delicious nourishing and wholesome Food, whether Stewed, Roasted, Baked, or Boiled; and I make no doubt that it will equally serve in a Fricasie, or a Ragoust.

I do therefore humbly offer it to publick consideration, that of the Hundred and twenty thousand Children, already computed, twenty thousand may be reserved for Breed, whereof only one fourth part to 10 be Males; which is more than we allow to Sheep, black Cattle, or Swine, and my Reason is, that these Children are seldom the Fruits of Marriage, a Circumstance not much regarded by our Savages, therefore, one Male will be sufficient to serve four Females. That the remaining Hundred thousand may at a year Old be offered in Sale to the Persons of Quality and Fortune, through the Kingdom, always advising the Mother to let them Suck plentifully in the last Month, so as to render them Plump, and Fat for a good Table. A Child will make two Dishes at an Entertainment for Friends, and when the Family dines alone, the fore or hind Quarter will make a reasonable Dish, and 20 seasoned with a little Pepper or Salt will be very good Boiled on the fourth Day, especially in Winter.

I have reckoned upon a Medium, that a Child just born will weigh 12 pounds, and in a solar Year, if tolerably nursed, encreaseth to 28 Pounds.

I grant this food will be somewhat dear, and therefore very proper for Landlords, who, as they have already devoured most of the Parents seem to have the best Title to the Children.

Infant's flesh will be in Season throughout the Year, but more plentiful in March, and a little before and after; for we are told by a 30 grave Author an eminent French Physician, that Fish being a prolifick Dyet, there are more Children born in Roman Catholick Countries about nine Months after Lent, than at any other Season; therefore reckoning a Year after Lent, the Markets will be more glutted than usual, because the Number of Popish Infants, is at least three to one in this Kingdom, and therefore it will have one other Collateral advantage, by lessening the Number of Papists among us.

I have already computed the Charge of nursing a Begger's Child (in which List I reckon all Cottagers, Labourers, and four fifths of the Farmers) to be about two Shillings per Annum, Rags included; and I 40 believe no Gentleman would repine to give Ten Shillings for the Carcass of a good fat Child, which, as I have said will make four Dishes of excellent Nutritive Meat, when he hath only some particular Friend, or his own Family to dine with him. Thus the Squire will learn to be a good Landlord, and grow popular among his Tenants, the Mother will have Eight Shillings neat Profit, and be fit for Work till she produces another Child.

Those who are more thrifty (as I must confess the Times require) may flay the Carcass; the Skin of which, Artificially dressed, will make admirable Gloves for Ladies, and Summer Boots for fine Gentlemen. 50 As to our City of Dublin, Shambles may be appointed for this purpose, in the most convenient parts of it, and Butchers we may be assured will not be wanting; although I rather recommend buying the Children alive, and dressing them hot from the Knife, as we do roasting Pigs.

A MODEST PROPOSAL *Jonathan Swift* □

Irony, when it is used by writers such as Jane Austen (as was seen in Chapter 3), can be subtle and biting, but in the hands of Swift it becomes a savage weapon which mercilessly unmasks the hypocrisies and heartlessness of the people he is attacking. Swift uses a rational tone to present his *Modest Proposal*, but beneath the rational tone there is deep anger:

I grant this food will be somewhat dear, and therefore very proper for Landlords, who, as they have already devoured most of the Parents seem to have the best Title to the Children. (26–28)

In the lines above it can be seen that this anger is transmuted into satire through the use of irony.

1 'I shall now therefore humbly propose my own Thoughts, which I hope will not be liable to the least Objection.' (1–2)
What is Swift's satirical intention in prefacing his proposal with these words?

2 Swift not only makes his proposals for cooking children in great detail, but also sets out at length the advantages of his plan. What do these features contribute to the effect of his satire?

3 Explain the irony Swift uses in the seventh paragraph of the extract. (38–47)

4 In his references to gloves and summer boots, do you think it is Swift's intention to shock his readers? If so, does he succeed with you? Give reasons for your answer and discuss Swift's intention in including details like these.

5 Analyse in your own words the discrepancy between the tone of the writing and the proposals Swift is making.

William Hazlitt (1778–1830) brought a quality of honest directness to his essays: there is a passion in his writing that communicates itself forcibly to readers. It is as if he thinks aloud and transfers his thoughts white-hot to the page. He writes in such a way that the reader feels immediately drawn into and involved with the subject matter. The extract which follows is from Hazlitt's essay *On the Pleasure of Hating*.

■ Nature seems (the more we look into it) made up of antipathies: without something to hate, we should lose the very spring of thought and action. Life would turn to a stagnant pool, were it not ruffled by the jarring interests, the unruly passions, of men. The white streak in our own fortunes is brightened (or just rendered visible) by making all around it as dark as possible; so the rainbow paints its form upon the cloud. Is it pride? Is it envy? Is it the force of contrast? Is it weakness or malice? But so it is, that there is a secret affinity with, a *hankering* after, evil in the human mind, and that it takes a perverse, but a fortunate delight in mischief, since it is a never-failing source of satisfaction. Pure 10
good soon grows insipid, wants variety and spirit. Pain is a bitter-sweet, which never surfeits. Love turns, with a little indulgence, to indifference or disgust: hatred alone is immortal. Do we not see this principle at work everywhere? Animals torment and worry one another without mercy: children kill flies for sport: every one reads the accidents and offences in a newspaper as the cream of the jest: a whole town runs to be present at a fire, and the spectator by no means exults to see it extinguished. It is better to have it so, but it diminishes the interest; and our feelings take part with our passions rather than with our understandings. Men assemble in crowds, with eager enthusiasm, 20
to witness a tragedy: but if there were an execution going forward in the next street, as Mr Burke observes, the theatre would be left empty. A strange cur in a village, an idiot, a crazy woman, are set upon and baited by the whole community. Public nuisances are in the nature of public benefits. How long did the Pope, the Bourbons, and the Inquisition keep the people of England in breath, and supply them with nicknames to vent their spleen upon! Had they done us any harm of late? No: but we have always a quantity of superfluous bile upon the stomach, and we wanted an object to let it out upon. How loth were we to give up our pious belief in ghosts and witches, because we liked to 30
persecute the one, and frighten ourselves to death with the other! It is not the quality so much as the quantity of excitement that we are anxious about: we cannot bear a state of indifference and *ennui*: the mind seems to abhor a *vacuum* as much as ever nature was supposed to do. Even when the spirit of the age (that is, the progress of intellectual refinement, warring with our natural infirmities) no longer allows us to carry our vindictive and head-strong humours into effect, we try to revive them in description, and keep up the old bugbears, the phantoms of our terror and our hate, in imagination. We burn Guy Fawx in effigy, and the hooting and buffeting and maltreating that poor 40
tattered figure of rags and straw makes a festival in every village in England once a year.

ON THE PLEASURE OF HATING *William Hazlitt* □

An important criterion for judging the worth of a reflective essay must be how thought-provoking it is. To provoke a response from the reader within the brevity of an essay, the writer is usually obliged to discuss the subject in generalities. Hazlitt makes several sweeping statements in his essay, but he has the sense to back these up with particular examples of what he is referring to.

This balance between the general and the specific is one of the characteristics of good essay writing; Hazlitt arouses our interest in his initial premise:

> ... without something to hate, we should lose the very spring of thought and action. (2–3)

He then gives us very specific examples to back up his argument.

One of the stylistic methods Hazlitt employs is the use of the rhetorical question. When he writes:

> Is it pride? Is it envy? Is it the force of contrast? (7)

Hazlitt is not genuinely asking readers to make up their own minds, he is using the form of a question mainly for the effect it creates.

1 'Love turns, with a little indulgence, to indifference or disgust: hatred alone is immortal.' (12–13)

   This sentence is a good example of the tone of the essay. How would you describe this tone?

2 'Life would turn to a stagnant pool...' (3)
   'The white streak in our own fortunes...' (4–5)

   What does the use of these images contribute to the writing?

3 Why do you think Hazlitt uses so many rhetorical questions?

4 'Hazlitt makes generalisations about life and then follows these up by quoting particular instances'.

   How is this statement borne out by the extract?

5 Hazlitt's style is often described as conversational. Do you agree with this description of his style, judging by the extract above?

The extracts below present pictures of warfare seen from three different standpoints, revealing the points of view of three people involved in different ways: an officer in the front line, a civilian in a city under siege and a war correspondent. The first extract is from Robert Graves's *Goodbye to all that* and is about the First World War; the second is an extract from a Soviet woman's diary kept during the long siege of Leningrad (1941–44); the third was written by a journalist about the Vietnam war.

■ At this point the Royal Welch Fusiliers came up Maison Rouge Alley. The Germans were shelling it with five-nines (called 'Jack Johnsons' because of their black smoke) and lachrymatory shells. This caused a continual scramble backwards and forwards, to cries of: 'Come on!' 'Get back you bastards!' 'Gas turning on us!' 'Keep your heads, you men!' 'Back like hell, boys!' 'Whose orders?' 'What's happening?' 'Gas!' 'Back!' 'Come on!' 'Gas!' 'Back!' Wounded men and stretcher-bearers kept trying to squeeze past. We were alternately putting on and taking off our gas-helmets, which made things worse. In many places the trench had caved in, obliging us to scramble over the top. Childe- 10 Freeman reached the front line with only fifty men of 'B' Company; the rest had lost their way in some abandoned trenches half-way up.

The adjutant met him in the support line. 'Ready to go over, Freeman?' he asked.

Freeman had to admit that he had lost most of his company. He felt this disgrace keenly; it was the first time that he had commanded a company in battle. Deciding to go over with his fifty men in support of the Middlesex, he blew his whistle and the company charged. They were stopped by machine-gun fire before they had got through our own entanglements. Freeman himself died – oddly enough, of heart- 20 failure – as he stood on the parapet.

A few minutes later, Captain Samson, with 'C' Company and the remainder of 'B', reached our front line. Finding the gas-cylinders still whistling and the trench full of dying men, he decided to go over too – he could not have it said that the Royal Welch had let down the Middlesex. A strong, comradely feeling bound the Middlesex and the Royal Welch, intensified by the accident that the other three battalions in the brigade were Scottish, and that our Scottish brigadier was, unjustly no doubt, accused of favouring them. Our adjutant voiced the extreme non-Scottish view: 'The Jocks are all the same; both the 30 trousered kind and the bare-arsed kind: they're dirty in trenches, they skite too much, and they charge like hell – both ways.' The First Middlesex, who were the original 'Diehards', had more than once, with the Royal Welch, considered themselves let down by the Jocks. So Samson charged with 'C' and the remainder of 'B' Company.

One of 'C' officers told me later what happened. It had been agreed to advance by platoon rushes with supporting fire. When his platoon had gone about twenty yards, he signalled them to lie down and open covering fire. The din was tremendous. He saw the platoon on his left flopping down too, so he whistled the advance again. Nobody seemed 40 to hear. He jumped up from his shell-hole, waved and signalled 'Forward!'

Nobody stirred.

He shouted: 'You bloody cowards, are you leaving me to go on alone?'

His platoon-sergeant, groaning with a broken shoulder, gasped: 'Not cowards, sir. Willing enough. But they're all f—ing dead.' The Pope's Nose machine-gun, traversing, had caught them as they rose to the whistle.

'A' Company, too, had become separated by the shelling. I was with 50 the leading platoon. The Surrey-man got a touch of gas and went coughing back. The Actor accused him of scrimshanking. This I thought was unfair; the Surrey-man looked properly sick. I don't know what happened to him, but I heard that the gas-poisoning was not serious and that he managed, a few months later, to get back to his own regiment in France.

GOODBYE TO ALL THAT *Robert Graves* ☐

■ *2nd January, 1942* Most of the people admitted to the hospital die in Casualty. Long trenches are dug in the cemetery, in which the bodies are laid. The cemetery guards only dig separate graves if they are bribed with bread.

There are many coffins to be seen in the streets. They are transported on sleighs. If the coffin is empty it moves easily from side to side, it skids. Once such a coffin hit my legs. A coffin with a body is usually pulled by two women. The ropes cut deeply into their shoulders, but not because the coffin is heavy; rather because the women are weak.

Recently I saw a body without a coffin. It had on the chest, under the 10 twisted shroud, some wood shavings, apparently as a mark of dignity. One felt a professional not an amateur hand. This technical touch was more macabre than anything. It could well be that this had to be paid for by bread.

Another time, two sleighs caught by their runners. On one sleigh a spade and a crowbar were neatly tied to the lid of the coffin. The other sleigh carried logs. Truly a meeting of life and death.

Living people are frequently carried on sleighs as well. I saw two women pulling a sleigh with some difficulty. A third woman sat on it. She was holding a dead child wrapped in a small blanket. This was by 20 the Anichkov Bridge, where Klodt's bronze horses used to be, before they were removed to a safer place.

The other day I saw an emaciated, though still young, woman having trouble with her sleigh. For on it she had put a large so-called 'modern' wardrobe from a Commission shop, and this was to be converted into a coffin.

One Sunday we walked from our gate to the Leo Tolstoy Square, and on this small stretch we met eight coffins, large and small, and a few bodies which were carried wrapped in blankets. At the same time two women were leading a third to our hospital, she being at the start of her 30 labour. There were dark bags under her eyes – sure sign of scurvy. She was as thin as a skeleton and was hardly able to drag one foot after other.

On another occasion I saw two women who looked like teachers or librarians pulling an old man along on a sleigh. He wore spectacles, an overcoat and a fur hat, and he lay uncomfortably on the small sleigh, leaning on his elbow, his legs dragging on the ground. 'Be careful! Do be careful!' he cried at every pothole. And those women were sweating profusely, in spite of forty degrees of frost.

LENINGRAD DIARY □

■ Once your body was safe your problems weren't exactly over. There was the terrible possibility that a search for information there could become so exhausting that the exhaustion itself became the information. Overload was such a real danger, not as obvious as shrapnel or blunt like a 2,000-foot drop, maybe it couldn't kill you or smash you, but it could bend your aerial for you and land you on your hip. Levels of information were levels of dread, once it's out it won't go back in, you can't just blink it away or run the film backward out of consciousness. How many of those levels did you really want to hump yourself through, which plateau would you reach before you shorted   10 out and started sending the messages back unopened?

Cover the war, what a gig to frame for yourself, going out after one kind of information and getting another, totally other, to lock your eyes open, drop your blood temperature down under the 0, dry your mouth out so a full swig of water disappeared in there before you could swallow, turn your breath fouler than corpse gas. There were times when your fear would take directions so wild that you had to stop and watch the spin. Forget the Cong, the *trees* would kill you, the elephant grass grew up homicidal, the ground you were walking over possessed malignant intelligence, your whole environment was a bath. Even so,   20 considering where you were and what was happening to so many people, it was a privilege just to be able to feel afraid.

So you learned about fear, it was hard to know what you really learned about courage. How many times did somebody have to run in front of a machine gun before it became an act of cowardice? What about those acts that didn't require courage to perform, but made you a coward if you didn't? It was hard to know at the moment, easy to make a mistake when it came, like the mistake of thinking that all you needed to perform a witness act were your eyes. A lot of what people called courage was only undifferentiated energy cut loose by the intensity of   30 the moment, mind loss that sent the actor on an incredible run; if he survived it he had the chance later to decide whether he'd really been brave or just overcome with life, even ecstasy. A lot of people found the guts to just call it all off and refuse to ever go out any more, they'turned and submitted to the penalty end of the system or they just split. A lot of reporters, too, I had friends in the press corps who went out once or twice and then never again. Sometimes I thought that they were the sanest, most serious people of all, although to be honest I never said so until my time there was almost over.

DISPATCHES *Michael Herr* ☐

1 Two of the extracts deal explicitly with the subject of courage. Briefly summarise what each extract says about courage and discuss what attitude is taken, if any, by the respective writers to this subject.

2 Compare the three extracts from the point of view of how the experience of war is presented to the reader.

3 The language, style and tone of the three extracts are quite dissimilar. Compare the three extracts and show how these differences reflect the different standpoints of the writers to their subjects.

Compare the two contrasting diary entries below. The first is from Samuel Pepys's famous diary which was written in the latter half of the seventeenth century. The second is from the diary of Evelyn Waugh, one of the most important twentieth-century British novelists (an extract from one of his novels can be found on page 56).

■ *14th August* (Thanksgiving day). After dinner with my wife and Mercer to the Beare-garden, where I have not been, I think, of many years, and saw some good sport of the bull's tossing of the dogs, one into the very boxes. But it is a very rude and nasty pleasure. We had a great many hectors in the same box with us (and one very fine went into the pit and played his dog for a wager, which was a strange sport for a gentleman), where they drank wine, and drank Mercer's health first, which I pledged with my hat off; and who should be in the house but Mr Pierce the surgeon, who saw us and spoke to us. Thence home, well enough satisfied however with the variety of this afternoon's   10 exercise; and so I to my chamber, till in the evening our company come to supper. We had invited to a venison pasty Mr Batelier and his sister Mary, Mrs Mercer, her daughter Anne, Mr Le Brun and W. Hewer; and so we supped, and very merry. And then about nine o'clock to Mrs Mercer's gate, where the fire and boys expected us, and her son had provided abundance of serpents and rockets; and there mighty merry (my Lady Pen and Pegg going thither with us, and Nan Wright), till about twelve at night, flinging our fireworks, and burning one another and the people over the way. And at last our businesses being most spent, we into Mrs Mercer's, and there mighty merry, smutting one   20 another with candle grease and soot, till most of us were like devils. And that being done, then we broke up, and to my house, and there I made them drink; and upstairs we went, and then fell into dancing (W. Batelier dancing well) and dressing, him and I and one Mr Banister (who with his wife come over also with us) like women; and Mercer put on a suit of Tom's, like a boy, and mighty mirth we had, and Mercer danced a jigg; and Nan Wright and my wife and Pegg Pen put on periwigs. Thus we spent till three or four in the morning, mighty merry; and then parted, and to bed.

DIARY OF SAMUEL PEPYS ☐

■ *Tuesday 9 September 1924* There has arrived in the house one Emma Raban, a half-sister to my mother, who makes life very heavy for me. I cannot write, think or eat, I hate her so.

Yesterday the importunance of my mother induced me to suffer the degrading ordeal of being photographed. A place in New Bond Street called Swaine had offered to do it free. I think it must be the worst shop in London. I waited half-an-hour in a drawing-room furnished with enormous photographs of the Royal Family. Then I was taken up to the 'studio' where a repulsive little man attempted to be genial while two other men worked a camera. I am confident that it will be an 10 abominable photograph.

I dined with Dudley Carew at his expense at the Previtali and went with him to the gallery at Covent Garden to see the first night of Pavlova's season. The seats were most discomfortable, and to see at all well we were forced to stand up. The theatre was inexpressibly hot. Mme Pavlova herself was of course enchanting but the big ballet Don Quixote did not seem to me to be very remarkable. I gained most pleasure from a tiny Chinese dance by two people whose names I have forgotten.

The audience was most curious. I think I have never seen so many 20 repulsive people in so short a space of time as I saw in the gallery bar.

DIARY OF EVELYN WAUGH ☐

1 Compare the sort of detail which the writers choose to comment on.

2 Do the extracts differ greatly in tone? What do they reveal about the personalities of the two writers?

Chapter 5
The Prose of Persuasion

One of the most important uses to which prose is put is in attempting to influence people's opinions, choices and actions. The rôle of persuasive prose in people's lives is often taken for granted, yet its power is formidable. It can be used for a whole range of purposes: at one end of the scale this may be something comparatively trivial, such as motivating people to change to a different brand of chocolate, but persuasive prose can equally well be employed to induce someone to take an important decision such as changing their career or their political or moral beliefs.

More insidiously, language that is subtly, and sometimes not so subtly, biased and emotionally charged is often used in what is supposedly objective reporting of news in the media. What is essentially opinion or one person's view of events masquerades as objective reporting. At the same time, the importance of the mass media in our lives is immense. When these two facts are appreciated, it can be seen that there has never been a greater need for the close analysis of meaning in any article or report that has the overt purpose of informing, but which really is out to persuade.

The purpose of this chapter is to take a close look at some of the different types of prose that are written to persuade, and to see how they work.

The first examples of persuasive prose come from the world of advertising, perhaps the most common contemporary user of persuasive prose. The purpose of advertising is usually to sell a product or a service; the first advertisement, from a popular film magazine of the 1950s, has been written to try to persuade people to buy a holiday guide. The second example (overleaf) uses a human interest approach to attempt to persuade people to take up a certain career.

DIZZY'S CORNER

Of course, I'm the absolute *terminus* when it comes to anything *brainy*, like mending fuses and things. But with *holidays* I'm really jolly sensible. (*Hearty laughter from Mike, the pig!*) After all, those two precious weeks have got to see me through the other fifty, and I've just got to be choosy. Honestly, pets, do *you* pick your hotel with a pin? Don't like that – do what Dizzy does! Each year I send to Torquay for a wonderful wee book called the Little Guide to Village Inns, Hotels, Farms and Guesthouses, and I pick my holiday spot from there. I've found some winners too – a castle in Ireland, a chateau in Worcestershire, a cottage in Cornwall and a wonderful farm in Somerset. There's lots of other lovely places too, all recommended and most *fetchingly* described, with all the gen on the bedrooms, garages, dancing and games facilities, and terms (which seem to suit all cheque-books). Everything is there, pets, practically down to the names of the maids, and whether it's for a holiday or a honeymoon (*lucky you!*) in a grand and glossy hotel or a tumbledown pub, you need this Little Guide. It's handbag-size and costs 3/6, postage 2d., direct from P.G. Hilton, 45 Fleet Street, Torquay.

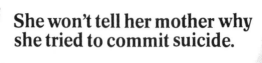

She won't tell her mother why she tried to commit suicide.

Could you persuade her to tell you?

Unrequited love is particularly hard to take the first time around. In Jan's case, it coincided with exams and the final break-up of her parents' unhappy marriage. Convinced that life wasn't worth living, Jan slashed her wrists.

Fortunately, she received prompt hospital treatment and survived.

Even more fortunately, she was then assigned a community psychiatric nurse she could relate to.

The nurse's first job, of course, was to stop Jan making a second attempt.

And the only way to do that was to help Jan come to terms with her life and herself.

Not an easy undertaking. But then, community psychiatric nursing is not a career for anyone looking for a cushy number.

It involves three years' hospital based training for the Registered Mental Nurse qualification, a spell as a Staff Nurse, then further experience in the community.

Something all psychiatric nurses learn is how to think on their feet.

How to respond positively to what are often very fluid situations.

And how to cope with the emotional demands that the close one-to-one relationships inevitably give rise to.

Frankly, there are times when this job could try the patience of a saint.

But when you succeed, it's heady stuff.

There's just no describing how you feel when someone as desperate as Jan shows the first glimmer of optimism.

And it's no exaggeration to claim that, in certain circumstances, good psychiatric nursing can literally save lives.

If you think you can handle that sort of responsibility, get your fingers round your pen.

To find out how you could qualify as a Registered Mental Nurse, write to the Chief Nursing Officer, Department of Health and Social Security (I/SC2), P.O. Box 702, London SW20 8SZ.

Nursing.
Make a career out of caring.

Reproduced with the permission of the Controller, Her Majesty's Stationery Office

94

The words of both advertisements have been chosen carefully, with their potential customers in mind, although many women nowadays would find the tone of *Dizzy's Corner* insulting because of the image of women it projects. The attitudes and values which both advertisements seek to appeal to are clearly reflected in the language and tone they employ.

1 What kind of person do you think each of the two advertisements is aimed at?

2 Compare the approach that is adopted in each case to attract the reader; for this you should analyse the style of each advertisement, including a discussion of the tone used and of any key words selected by the advertiser to appeal to the reader.

Journalese is the term often used to describes the clichés or exaggerated language employed by journalists in newspaper reports and articles. Below is an article about rock music from the magazine *Time* which has often been accused of, or congratulated for, rewriting the English language. Though the subject is popular music, the writer still has a definite standpoint and is seeking to persuade the reader that his analysis is valid.

Most artistic fields create their own jargon or special terms which some aficionados and critics use like a badge of entry to show they are 'in the know'. Not only does rock music have its own jargon, but commentators and writers on the rock 'scene' seem compelled to use a 'hip' style in speech and writing. The adoption of such a style may have as one of its aims the distancing of the world of rock music from the more staid world of the established arts as well as acting as a kind of guarantee of the authority of the writer. How far this in itself leads to the writing of new clichés and the creation of a new journalese is a matter of individual opinion.

To create its effect, the writing leans heavily on well-known and rather conventional literary devices such as alliteration (the placing of words with the same initial consonant in close proximity to one another): 'Big bucks', 'dazzling diversity' and 'factionalized and fractionalized' are all examples of alliteration.

The use of techniques such as alliteration, together with the use of jargon and clichés, creates a knowing style which puts writer and reader on familiar terms so that the reader more readily accepts the writer's point of view. The rapid succession of examples which are given in evidence of the decline of pop music also serves to increase this effect; the reader is deluged with a stream of 'facts' which the writer seems to assume everyone is so familiar with, that merely mentioning them confirms the truth of his assertion.

Rock Hits the Hard Place

Is there hope? This week, the J. Geils Band has settled itself onto the sunny, snowy peak of the *Billboard* chart. Score one for the good guys. J. Geils has managed to nudge off Foreigner, which on and off occupied the top slot for eleven weeks. Score eleven for the bad guys. And these days, in rock and in the record business, the bad guys are winning.

Big bucks, much media attention and even some good reviews go to a 598-page biography of Elvis Presley that is like a game of mumblety-peg played on a corpse. REO Speedwagon has moved more than 6 million copies of its latest record, thereby making *Hi InFidelity* the second largest selling album in the history of CBS Records. *Rolling Stone*, a magazine that was once the most prominent and articulate forum for rock culture, divests itself of much of its music coverage and aims for a more general readership. Record companies have cut back on corporate extravagances and are making a little money, mostly by kicking up prices. Punk is dead, New Wave is over, disco moved out when your older sister left home. The Clash can't swing a major hit single, so its albums don't get high on the charts; and does anyone know there's a great new record by a great new group called the Blasters? Is anyone listening? Does anyone care?

Wrote a song for ev'ryone,
Wrote a song for truth.
Wrote a song for ev'ryone
And I couldn't even talk to you.
John Fogerty

Those days are over: days when a rocker had a right to expect that the music he made – like Fogerty and his peerless band, Creedence Clearwater Revival – could reach a large as well as a knowing audience; when the radio played a dazzling diversity of music, not a range as thin as the air between two stations. For the first time, under the regency of radio programmers and the tyranny of marketing studies and demographics, rock 'n' roll has been successfully factionalized and fractionalized, smashed into a mass of splinters with few sharp edges. A song for everyone? If it has no specific gravity to unite factions of the audience, then it has a shot. □

1 Read the second paragraph of the article again. Analyse its content and show how it is constructed to lead up to the questions at the end.

2 What do you consider to be the key or topic sentence in the last paragraph of the article, the sentence that more or less states what the rest of the paragraph is about? Give reasons for your choice.

3 How would you describe the quality of the tone and language of the article – is it formal or colloquial, solemn or witty, literary or very direct? Quote from the article to back up your answer.

4 Does the writer of the article seek to convince readers of the truth of his ideas by a well-structured argument or does he rely on other means?

Charles Dickens, as well as writing many novels, was a prolific journalist. Below is the opening passage of the chapter entitled *Slavery* from Dickens' *American Notes*, which are a series of journalistic impressions of his travels through America in 1842. In this piece, he shows his commitment to the abolition of slavery.

■ The upholders of slavery in America – of the atrocities of which system, I shall not write one word for which I have not had ample proof and warrant – may be divided into three great classes.

The first, are those more moderate and rational owners of human cattle, who have come into the possession of them as so many coins in their trading capital, but who admit the frightful nature of the Institution in the abstract, and perceive the dangers to society with which it is fraught: dangers which however distant they may be, or howsoever tardy in their coming on, are as certain to fall upon its guilty head, as is the Day of Judgement.   10

The second, consists of all those owners, breeders, users, buyers and sellers of slaves, who will, until the bloody chapter has a bloody end, own, breed, use, buy, and sell them at all hazards; who dogged, deny the horrors of the system in the teeth of such a mass of evidence as never was brought to bear on any other subject, and to which the experience of every day contributes its immense amount; who would at this or any other moment, gladly involve America in a war, civil or foreign, provided that it had for its sole end and object the assertion of their right to perpetuate slavery, and to whip and work and torture slaves, unquestioned by any human authority, and unassailed by any   20
human power; who, when they speak of Freedom, mean the Freedom to oppress their own kind, and to be savage, merciless, and cruel; and of whom every man on his own ground, in republican America, is a more exacting and a sterner, and a less responsible despot than the Caliph Haroun Alraschid in his angry robe of scarlet.

The third, and not the least numerous or influential, is composed of all that delicate gentility which cannot bear a superior, and cannot brook an equal; of that class whose Republicanism means 'I will not tolerate a man above me: and of those below, none must approach too near'; whose pride, in a land where voluntary servitude is shunned as a   30
disgrace, must be ministered to by slaves; and whose inalienable rights can only have their growth in negro wrongs.

It has sometimes been urged that, in the unavailing efforts which have been made to advance the cause of Human Freedom in the republic of America (strange cause for History to treat of!), sufficient regard has not been had to the existence of the first class of persons; and it has been contended that they are hardly used, in being confounded with the second. This is, no doubt, the case; noble instances of pecuniary and personal sacrifice have already had their

growth among them; and it is much to be regretted that the gulf 40
between them and the advocates of emancipation should have been
widened and deepened by any means: the rather, as there are, beyond
dispute, among these slave-owners, many kind masters who are tender
in the exercise of their unnatural power. Still, it is feared that this justice
is inseparable from the state of things with which humanity and truth
are called upon to deal. Slavery is not a whit the more endurable
because some hearts are to be found which can partially resist its
hardening influences; nor can the indignant tide of honest wrath stand
still, because in its onward course it overwhelms a few who are
comparatively innocent among a host of guilty.   50

The ground most commonly taken by these better men among the
advocates of slavery, is this: 'It is a bad system; and for myself I would
willingly get rid of it, if I could; most willingly. But it is not so bad, as
you in England take it to be. You are deceived by the representations of
the emancipationists. The greater part of my slaves are much attached
to me. You will say I do not allow them to be severely treated; but I will
put it to you whether you believe that it can be a general practice to
treat them inhumanly, when it would impair their value, and would
obviously be against the interests of their masters.'

Is it the interest of any man to steal, to game, to waste his health and 60
mental faculties by drunkenness, to lie, forswear himself, indulge
hatred, seek desperate revenge, or do murder? No. All these are roads
to ruin. And why, then, do men tread them? Because such inclinations
are among the vicious qualities of mankind. Blot out, ye friends of
slavery, from the catalogue of human passions, brutal lust, cruelty, and
the abuse of irresponsible power (of all earthly temptations the most
difficult to be resisted), and when ye have done so, and not before, we
will enquire whether it be the interest of a master to lash and maim the
slaves, over whose lives and limbs he has an absolute control!

AMERICAN NOTES *Charles Dickens* □

When you have been asked to write essays expressing your own opinion, the
necessity of writing balanced essays by dealing with the arguments of those
who hold the opposing view may have been explained to you. To a certain
extent, Dickens follows this structure; he does deal with the slavers' point of
view, but he does so with such indignation and caustic scorn that a balanced
view is not really present in the essay. Dickens speaks of the kinder slave
owners as:

> ... those more moderate and rational owners of human cattle, who
> have come into the possession of them as so many coins in their trading
> capital ... (4–6)

By using emotive phrases such as 'human cattle' and 'coins in their trading
capital', Dickens prejudges the issues. He appeals to the reader's emotions
without allowing a genuine consideration of both points of view to take place.

For the same reason, the language which Dickens uses is often repetitive, rhythmical and colourful:

> . . . all those owners, breeders, users, buyers and sellers of slaves, who will, until the bloody chapter has a bloody end . . . (11–12)

Dickens' words are impressive because of their rhetorical qualities as much as because of the soundness of the content of what he is saying.

However, considering the subject, perhaps Dickens' eloquent indignation is a much more appropriate weapon than a cooler, more dispassionate appraisal of slavery. Dickens sets up the opposing arguments only to brush them aside. The balanced view is not really Dickens' aim in this essay. He manages to sweep the reader along with his indignation.

1 Briefly summarise the three categories of slave owners as perceived by Dickens.

2 What arguments does Dickens use in the final paragraph of the extract to contradict the arguments put forward in the previous paragraph?

3 How is Dickens' condemnation reflected in the tone and language of the essay? Show how he uses rhetorical and exaggerated language to reinforce his point of view.

4 How do you react to Dickens' impassioned style? In your opinion, would a more restrained, reflective style have been more effective as a means of persuading readers?

● Write an article intended for publication in your school magazine which takes a committed attitude to a social or political issue. Present evidence for your case, but also deal with arguments put forward by the opposing side.

George Orwell (1903–1945) is considered to be one of the greatest journalists Britain has produced. He is perhaps best known as the author of *Nineteen Eighty-four* and *Animal Farm*, although he also wrote many occasional articles for periodicals and newspapers. Below is an extract from a piece called *England at First Glance*.

■ In peace time, it is unusual for foreign visitors to this country to notice the existence of the English people. Even the accent referred to by Americans as 'the English accent' is not in fact common to more than a quarter of the population. In cartoons in continental papers England is personified by an aristocrat with a monocle, a sinister capitalist in a top-hat, or a spinster in a Burberry. Hostile or friendly, nearly all the generalizations that are made about England base themselves on the property-owning class and ignore the other forty-five million.
But the chances of war brought to England, either as soldiers or as refu- gees, hundreds of thousands of foreigners who would not normally   10

have come here, and forced them into intimate contact with ordinary people. Czechs, Poles, Germans, and Frenchmen to whom 'England' meant Piccadilly and the Derby found themselves quartered in sleepy East Anglian villages, in northern mining towns, or in the vast working-class areas of London whose names the world had never heard until they were blitzed. Those of them who had the gift of observation will have seen for themselves that the real England is not the England of the guide books. Blackpool is more typical than Ascot, the top-hat is a moth-eaten rarity, the language of the B.B.C. is barely intelligible to the masses. Even the prevailing physical type does not 20 agree with the caricatures, for the tall, lanky physique which is traditionally English is almost confined to the upper classes: the working classes, as a rule, are rather small, with short limbs and brisk movements, and with a tendency among the women to grow dumpy in early middle life.

It is worth trying for a moment to put oneself in the position of a foreign observer, new to England, but unprejudiced, and able because of his work to keep in touch with ordinary, useful, unspectacular people. Some of his generalizations would be wrong, because he would not make enough allowance for the temporary dislocations resulting 30 from war. Never having seen England in normal times, he might underrate the power of class distinctions, or think English agriculture healthier than it is, or be too much impressed by the dinginess of the London streets or the prevalence of drunkenness. But with this fresh eye he would see a great deal that a native observer misses, and his probable impressions are worth tabulating. Almost certainly he would find the salient characteristics of the English common people to be artistic insensibility, gentleness, respect for legality, suspicion of foreigners, sentimentality about animals, hypocrisy, exaggerated class distinctions, and an obsession with sport. 40

As for our artistic insensibility, ever-growing stretches of beautiful countryside are ruined by planless building, the heavy industries are allowed to convert whole counties into blackened deserts, ancient monuments are wantonly pulled down or swamped by seas of yellow brick, attractive vistas are blocked by hideous statues to nonentities – and all this without any *popular* protest whatever. When England's housing problem is discussed, its aesthetic aspect simply does not enter the mind of the average man. Nor is there any widespread interest in any of the arts, except perhaps music. Poetry, the art in which above all others England has excelled, has for more than a century had no appeal 50 whatever for the common people. It is only acceptable when – as in some popular songs and mnemonic rhymes – it is masquerading as something else. Indeed the very word 'poetry' arouses either derision or embarrassment in ninety-eight people out of a hundred.

Our imaginary foreign observer would certainly be struck by our gentleness: by the orderly behaviour of English crowds, the lack of pushing and quarrelling, the willingness to form queues, the good temper of harassed, overworked people like bus conductors. The manners of the English working class are not always very graceful, but they are extremely considerate. Great care is taken in showing a 60 stranger the way, blind people can travel across London with the certainty that they will be helped on and off every bus and across every street. In war-time a few of the policemen carry revolvers, but England has nothing corresponding to the *gendarmerie*, the semi-military police living in barracks and armed with rifles (sometimes even with tanks and aeroplanes), who are the guardians of society all the way from Calais to Tokyo. And except for certain well-defined areas in half a dozen big towns there is very little crime or violence. The average of honesty is lower in the big towns than in the country, but even in London the news-vendor can safely leave his pile of pennies on the 70 pavement while he goes for a drink. The prevailing gentleness of manners is a recent thing, however. Well within living memory it was impossible for a smartly dressed person to walk down Ratcliff Highway without being assaulted, and an eminent jurist, asked to name a typically English crime, could answer: 'Kicking your wife to death.'

There is no revolutionary tradition in England, and even in extremist political parties, it is only the middle-class membership that thinks in revolutionary terms. The masses still more or less assume that 'against the law' is a synonym for 'wrong'. It is known that the criminal law is harsh and full of anomalies and that litigation is so expensive as always 80 to favour the rich against the poor: but there is a general feeling that the law, such as it is, will be scrupulously administered, that a judge or magistrate cannot be bribed, that no one will be punished without trial. An Englishman does not believe in his bones, as a Spanish or Italian peasant does, that the law is simply a racket. It is precisely this general confidence in the law that has allowed a good deal of recent tampering with Habeas Corpus to escape public notice. But it also causes some ugly situations to end peacefully. During the worst of the London blitz the authorities tried to prevent the public from using the Tube stations as shelters. The people did not reply by storming the gates, they simply 90 bought themselves penny-halfpenny tickets: they thus had legal status as passengers, and there was no thought of turning them out again.

ENGLAND AT FIRST GLANCE *George Orwell* □

Orwell's intention in this essay is quite different from that of Dickens in his piece on slavery. The tone of the writing reflects this intention: it is gentler, more reflective and more analytical.

The analytical approach, however, is couched in accessible terms. There is no turgid phraseology in Orwell's writing; his English is very readable and almost everyday in its vocabulary. Orwell argued in other essays for a simple, clear style of written English. His own writing has a clarity and a conciseness that communicate to the reader in an undemonstrative, unemphatic manner.

It is not only the language, but also the structure of his writing which is clear and simple. Orwell's practice in this passage is to make a general statement and then back it up with examples.

1 In the second paragraph, Orwell says that 'the real England is not the England of the guide books' and then goes on to mention 'Ascot', 'the top-hat' and 'the language of the B.B.C.'. How are these linked to the main argument he is putting forward in the second paragraph?

2 According to Orwell, how would wartime conditions give unprejudiced foreign visitors an unbalanced picture of England?

3 '...he would find the salient characteristics of the English common people to be artistic insensibility, gentleness, respect for legality...' (36–38)

Relate this general statement to the structure of the rest of the essay.

4 Compare the tone and standpoint used by Orwell in his essay on England with the tone and standpoint of the Dickens article on America. What are the differences?

● Write a short piece giving your analysis of the quality of life in your particular area. Describe the kind of people who live there, their general attitudes to life, their customs and manners. Try to use a balanced tone and style in the piece.

Norman Mailer is a well-known contemporary American novelist and journalist. The subject matter of much of Mailer's writing is himself and his reactions to the things that have happened to him in life. In the article below, he uses an incident in his life to draw some conclusions about the misuse of the mass media.

■ HOW TO COMMIT MURDER IN THE MASS-MEDIA

A few months ago, I was approached by a man who had started to do a broadcast for the Canadian Broadcasting System on the Beat Generation. He had been collecting taped interviews from various people who might be considered figures in the ferment, and on the basis of 'The White Negro' he wished to interview me as well. I tried to refuse; I offered the excuse that usually I avoided interviews because there was a tendency to talk away too many new ideas. In that case, he asked, would I merely read some passages from 'The White Negro'. I said yes.

He came over to my apartment one evening with his tape recorder, 10 and after ten or fifteen minutes of passing conversation, I read a few pages of my words into his microphone. He told me that once the various tapes were put together into a master tape, he would invite me to a party where he would play it.

About a month later, the party took place. I went with my wife and my friend Mickey Knox to a cold-water pad, south of the village, and the scene had three beards to every chin, a lot of wine, some beer, and no whisky. We were late, and the tape (which was more than an hour long) was already in the middle. What I heard of it was good, candid, even informative for a broadcast. On the other hand, it was tendentious. The man who had interviewed me was the narrator, and he was not sympathetic to the Beat, his tacit attitude was closer to his presumably Square Canadian audience than to the men and women he interviewed.

When my voice came on, I had a shock. It is rarely good to hear one's own voice, but I had lived through that years ago, and I was familiar with the sound now, I was even able to listen to myself with a cool ear. What I was hearing now at this party was not my own voice, however. It was high-pitched, shrill, very rapid, and with a clipped staccato beat – I sounded like Hitler. Then the narrator came on: a warm masculine voice. His natural speech had been good, but it was not this good.

It took something to keep silent. As the broadcast went on, I noticed that this contrast of voices continued. All the hipsters and Beatniks were shrill, feminine, nervous and quick – the narrator was the rich radio voice of North America. I knew something had been done to the tape, and the moment the machine was turned off, I went over to the narrator and asked him if the voice on the tape sounded very much like my voice. He looked uneasy. No, it didn't seem the same, he said. I asked the narrator if he had turned up the treble for the others, and the bass for himself, and he seemed honest in his answer that he had only an English field machine which had no such controls.

Finally a girl whispered to me, 'Probably his batteries were weak, and he didn't have money to buy new ones.' Looking at him through the filter of such small detail, I knew that was part of the explanation, for weak batteries slow the speed of the tape. When such a tape is played at normal speed, the voices turn quick and shrill, like a record on an old-fashioned gramophone whose turntable revolves too quickly. Of course, the narrator had had the leisure to re-record his own voice at the studio, which was why he had sounded good, and now felt guilty. The tape had expressed a sad comedy of vanity and worn-out tools.

I tell this bit of story because it gives a hint of what is done on every broadcast and telecast. On a major network, only subtle improvements or flaws are added by sound engineers to the voice, but since millions are listening, it is fair to assume that a few hundred thousand people are shifted from an instinctive dislike to a small appreciation of the performer. If the super-state of the future arrives, this technique has its obvious uses for brain-washing the populace out of one ideological corral and into another: by good make-up or bad, by bass or by treble,

by a camera closing in at bad times, and dollying backward at moments
of climax, a man with ideas unhappy for the State may be shuffled to 60
the rear of a debate, and never know how much of him was lost in the
adjusted mirror of a television screen. The present-tense will be altered
at the instant it comes into being.

Even worse, the history of the past may be warped at the root, by the
judgment of our senses. If a new sympathy for Nazism should arise in
America, who knows but that the unforgettable voice of Adolph Hitler
will be relayed to the ear of a future people, so modified, made so
attractive and so *American* that the Fuehrer's tone will be heard in the
Twenty-First Century as the Big Daddy voice of all virile and velvety
broadcasters.   70

Norman Mailer □

Some writers feed directly off their own experiences and life for the material of
their writing. Others distil their experience to such an extent that the original
incident is barely discernible in the finished piece of writing. Norman Mailer is
very much a writer who puts himself in the forefront of his writing. The essay
above is a very personal piece. Mailer has elevated a comparatively
unimportant event in his life to a level from which he can give portentous
warnings about the manipulation of the mass media; he even manages to bring
in Hitler as the ultimate example of how the media can create an image. The
question is: is the experience Mailer had with the radio interview serious
enough to justify the grave warnings he hands out in the latter half of the
essay?

1 'I tell this bit of story. . .' (51)

The first six paragraphs of the extract take the form of a story (narrative) written in the
first person. How do the tone and form of this narrative help Mailer in his aim of
persuading the audience of the dangers of the power of the media?

2 'The tape had expressed a sad comedy of vanity and worn-out tools.' (50)

How would you describe the tone and language of this sentence? Why do you think
Mailer ends his story with this sentence?

3 In what ways is the content of the last two paragraphs different from the rest of the
article? How does Mailer link the two parts of the article together?

● Write a first person account of something interesting or disturbing that has happened to
you. You could use something that happened to you at school, in public or any unusual
incident in which you have been involved. Draw some general conclusions from your
experience in the same way that Mailer makes some general points about the mass
media which are drawn from his experience with the radio interview. You should link the
two sections of your piece – the first-hand account and the general conclusions you
draw.

Most newspapers and journals make their political opinions and attitudes to social issues evident not only in their editorials but also in their news reporting. Read the following article entitled *High Noon at the Nuclear Corral*; it is from the magazine *Vole*. The article discusses the Israeli attack on an Iraqi nuclear reactor, the President of the United States' reaction to the news and the wider implications of this kind of military action for the world as a whole.

Even in the reporting of news items, there has to be a selection of detail by the reporter involved. The emphasis a reporter gives to a report will affect the readers' response to the news. It may be doubted whether there is such a thing as an objective news report since all news reports are the products of an individual's viewpoint; the reporter must select which details to include at the very least, so it is difficult to see how a reporter can present a completely neutral viewpoint on any issue. Selection of detail, and indeed selection of language, almost inevitably implies a point of view on the writer's part; where there is a point of view, then there is the potential for persuasion.

1 Why do you think the second paragraph of the article consists of only one sentence?

2 The writer uses numerous rhetorical questions in the article. Why do you think he does this? Do you think he overuses the device?

3 Comment on the last sentence of the fourth paragraph with regard to its content and position in relation to the whole paragraph.

4 The subject of this article is clearly a very serious issue and yet the writer allows himself some humorous touches and uses an informal style at times.
 a Pick out humorous touches in the article and examples of an informal, even colloquial style.
 b In your opinion, what does the humour and the occasional use of an informal style contribute to the article? Give reasons for your answer.

5 The writer goes well beyond the bare facts of the Israeli attack in his article. How does he use the attack to persuade us of his own views? Whom does he blame?

High Noon at the Nuclear Corral

Lawrence McGinty

He stood there like a boy scout who had been asked to tie a really difficult knot. He admitted that he didn't know that Israel had not signed the Non-proliferation Treaty. He said he would have to think about the implications of this new and startling fact. The grin never left his face – it was meant to be disarming, but was in fact dreadfully disturbing. If he had been a sixth former in a general studies class, teacher might well have reproached him for his ignorance. But he wasn't. He was the president of the United States at his first press conference after Israel had taken out the Iraqis' nuclear reactor at Tuwaitha. The fact that the leader of the world's most powerful nation is either an ignoramus or a brilliant actor (on the evidence, he isn't) is, in many ways, even more disturbing than the stark facts of Israel's adventure in Iraq.

For the significance of that terrorist attack (how else can it be described?) is far greater than its immediate repercussions for the politics of the tinderbox that is the Middle East.

First, the attack shows that the guarantees against the proliferation of nuclear weapons embodied in the 1968 Non-proliferation Treaty and enforced by the United Nations' Mickey Mouse outfit in Vienna (the International Atomic Energy Agency) are at best unconvincing and at worst worthless. Israel, for one, was so unimpressed by the fact that Iraq had signed the treaty that it was willing to take fearsome military action to prevent Iraq building nuclear weapons. And there seems little doubt that Israel was right in its assessment of Iraq's real intentions in building up its nuclear abilities. Iraq's pattern of shopping in the nuclear supermarket seems inexplicable unless it wanted nuclear weapons. Why else would it buy – from the Italians – a 'hot cell' to extract plutonium? Why else did it refuse low enriched uranium fuel – from France, where it bought its 'research' reactor – and insist on weapons grade uranium? Iraq has played by the rules but has still managed to collect enough nuclear expertise and equipment to make its own bombs (unlike Israel which has not played by the rules and deliberately keeps the Arab world guessing about the nuclear weapons that it undoubtedly has).

But Israel and Iraq are by no means the only ones. India, with its 'peaceful nuclear device', Pakistan, with its secret uranium-enrichment plant, Canada, West Germany, Japan, South Africa, Argentina, and a dozen or so other states are on the brink of being able to join the nuclear club, if they wanted to (and some of them do want to join). The nuclear superpowers' bargain with the rest of the world – that we will renounce some nuclear weapons if you forego them altogether – looks increasingly dubious. And why not? Why should non-nuclear states deny themselves when the superpowers – East and West – are armed to the teeth and show little inclination to hand their sixshooters to the sheriff while in town? The inescapable conclusion is that the arrogant North cannot keep the nuclear genie in the bottle.

But even more worrying than all this – and largely ignored by the press – is the answer to the following question: would Israel have attacked if the reactor had been working and fuelled up? If it had, there is no doubt but that radioactive fall-out would have devastated the area. But Israel's aggression and macho (clearly appreciated by the B-movie cowboy in the White House) leaves me, for one, believing that the Israelis would succumb to the argument 'better the fall-out should be on Baghdad than on Jerusalem'. Or if you don't believe that Israel could go so far, how about the Russians? Would they attack China's nuclear facilities? Or how about Pakistan's dictator, Zia ul-Haq? Would he attack India's Tarapur reactor if he thought it militarily sensible? Sooner or later, someone somewhere will attack a nuclear power station – the uncontrollable proliferation of nuclear technology makes it inevitable.

And the consequences will be terrifying. The Political Ecology Research Group (a group that has won a surprising amount of credibility outside the environmentalists' world) has just finished a frightening study of these consequences for the Ecology Party. Its report says that the relatively large amounts of long-lived radioactive elements in the core of a reactor would, even in the event of a conventional attack, be released over large areas of land – leading to a 'peacetime catastrophe'. If the reactor were hit by a nuclear weapon, the fall-out originating from the reactor would be more significant than the bomb's fall-out after a month (because it contains more of the long-lived radioisotopes). Most frightening of all would be an attack on Windscale, which stores the same amount of long-lived radioactive elements as do 200 reactor cores. A direct hit by a 1 megaton bomb would vapourise these elements. People as far away as Algeria and Finland would be exposed to the fall-out. Out of every thousand people exposed to the fall-out, between one and ten would develop cancer as a result.

The greater accuracy of the nuclear weapons that the superpowers now want to deploy makes an attack on nuclear targets all the more likely. The nuclear club has let the genie out of the bottle. The argument that nuclear attacks (or conventional attacks on nuclear targets) are not the responsibility of those who sold the nuclear technology in the first place is as convincing as the plea that 'I didn't gas the Jews, I only built the gas ovens'. ☐

Below are two newspaper articles about a civil war in El Salvador. Read them both carefully, comparing their content, tone and language. The first article is an editorial from *The Sunday Times*; the second is from *Labour Weekly*.

The tragedy of El Salvador

BRITAIN has decided to send two observers to the elections in El Salvador next month. Every other EEC country has refused or is refusing. They are right. The elections will be a farce, observers cannot make them less so.

El Salvador is in the middle of a horrible civil war. In 1979 a long established landowning oligarchy was ousted by a group of disgruntled army officers with the blessing of the Roman Catholic church and a programme of moderate reforms. A civilian-military junta with Jose Napoleon Duarte as president took over. Superficially it is still in power. In reality, however, it has been transformed. The reforms have not been introduced and President Duarte is the prisoner of a ruthless resurgent right which murdered Archbishop Romero of San Salvador in 1980 and the next year slaughtered something like 20,000 Salvadorans, old and young, male and female. The left has retaliated with equivalent brutality.

Elections next month will cure none of this. Left wing parties are refusing to take part since their leaders have been killed or gaoled. Left wing guerrillas will make voting impossible in some areas. Observers will be able to observe next to nothing but, seeing no flagrant malpractices, will be likely to give the regime a spurious bill of health and popular legitimacy. In any case the purpose of the elections has little to do with parliamentary democracy. It is to give Duarte a veneer of international approval. For President Reagan El Salvador is part of a global crisis.

After a long history of right wing misgovernment Central America is swinging left. In Nicaragua, the largest country in the area, the long reign of the Somaza family was ended three years ago by the Sandinista broad front, but this coalition quickly fell apart and its more left-wing components have gained control. Washington now sees Nicaragua as lost to world Communism. Hence the importance of little El Salvador as the place where somebody has got to put a finger in the dyke.

The United States is in a dilemma whenever it becomes convinced that its own defences against Soviet Communism require it to support an evil regime in another country. Doing so wins vocal hard-line approval but alienates many American allies and weakens American protests against Soviet interventions elsewhere. The alternative is to leave the Salvadorans to slog it out on their own. But this fails to meet the argument that abstention simply hands the country over to Castro and Moscow.

There is a third possibility: to use the existing international machinery. Venezuela has proposed intervention by the Organisation of American States. This would take the form of a mediatory mission of, say, three states with the object of getting the junta's army and the guerrillas to cease fire, as a prelude to free elections. It should be tried.

The oligarchies of Central America are coming to their end. They are challenged by a bourgeoisie of shopkeepers and professional people who, when it comes to a clash, are supported by the peasantry, much of the clergy and – initially at least – a distinct militant left. It will be a tragedy for the peoples if the activities of the militants lead to a reinstatement of the oligarchs. And it is certainly not Britain's business to get into a position where it may have to endorse such a tragedy. □

US extends aid to army in Salvador

In January, the massacre of 1,000 women, old people and children by the army was finally reported in Britain. An all party delegation of Irish MPs was refused entry to El Salvador.

The US Administration announced that the junta had met with US Congressional human rights conditions and would therefore receive not just aid already programmed but probably increased amounts.

The 1,000 civilians died during the December army manoeuvres which intended to dislodge guerrillas from the north east province of Morazan. The troops were unable to catch up with the guerrillas and so they killed those they could find – the unarmed peasants.

The Irish MPs arrived in mid-January on a fact finding mission. They were refused entry in San Salvador on the grounds that visa requirements had been changed.

In 1981, US aid to El Salvador totalled US$144 million. The US administration is now worried that the regime could collapse under military and economic pressure. Aid for 1982 is likely to reach US$250 million although some US officials suggest figures of US$400 or even US$700 million.

The US government has also announced a training programme for 1,500 Salvadorean soldiers in the US and this week announced it will send $55 million worth of replacement helicopters and planes.

This week, too, it was reported 100 people were killed during fighting around the town of Nueva Trinidad near the border with Honduras.

Outside, the country is in ruins. Power lines and stations, 20 bridges and 30 communication posts have been destroyed by guerrillas in recent months. Normal economic activity has been brought to a standstill.

In December, the United Nations voted 68–22 in favour of a resolution presented by France, Denmark, Greece and the Netherlands calling on the Salvadorean junta to negotiate with the guerrillas and urging an end to all military aid to El Salvador. The US delegation voted against and turned its attention to more military aid and the March elections.

In Britain, an early day motion tabled by Dafydd Thomas backs the UN initiative and spells out the impossibility of holding elections in El Salvador with no electoral rolls, no up to date census, 620,000 refugees, participation of only right wing parties, martial law and suppression of basic rights under a new legal code.   JANE McINTOSH ☐

---

1 In the second article, what is the effect of following up the details given in the first paragraph with the facts contained in the second paragraph?

2 Do *The Sunday Times* and *Labour Weekly* differ in their assessment of American involvement in El Salvador and in their apportioning of the blame for the brutality?

3 Point to any sections in either of the articles where the opinions of the writers are clearly stated.

4 Each of the articles attempts to persuade readers of several different things. What are they and how have the writers of the articles gone about the task of persuasion?

5 Which of the two articles seems to you to be the more objective in its tone or approach, or are they in their different ways equally committed to a point of view?

The relationship between parents and children is the subject of the two passages which follow. The first is by Francis Bacon, the sixteenth-century essayist, the second is by Keith Waterhouse, a contemporary columnist.

■ The joys of parents are secret, and so are their griefs and fears: they cannot utter the one, nor they will not utter the other. Children sweeten labours, but they make misfortunes more bitter: they increase the cares of life, but they mitigate the remembrance of death. The perpetuity by generation is common to beasts; but memory, merit and noble works are proper to men: and surely a man shall see the noblest works and foundations have proceeded from childless men, which have sought to express the images of their minds, where those of their bodies have failed: so the care of posterity is most in them that have no posterity. They that are the first raisers of their houses are most 10 indulgent towards their children; beholding them as the continuance not only of their kind but of their work; and so both children and creatures.

The illiberality of parents in allowance towards their children is an harmful error; makes them base; acquaints them with shifts; makes them sort with mean company; and makes them surfeit more when they come to plenty: and therefore the proof is best, when men keep their authority towards their children, but not their purse. Men have a foolish manner (both parents and schoolmasters and servants) in creating and breeding an emulation between brothers during child- 20 hood, which many times sorteth to discord when they are men and disturbeth families.

Let parents choose betimes the vocations and courses they mean their children should take; for then they are most flexible; and let them not too much apply themselves to the disposition of their children, as thinking they will take best to that which they have most mind to. It is true, that if the affection or aptness of the children be extraordinary, then it is good not to cross it.

                    OF PARENTS AND CHILDREN *Francis Bacon* □

■ But, dear children, has it ever occurred to you that parents have their rights too? I would be very surprised if this revolutionary thought has ever entered your heads, and for that reason, I have drafted, for your consideration, a Charter of Parents' Rights.

1. Parents have the right to their sleep. If you've promised to be in by 10.30 they have no wish to be counting the flowers on the wallpaper at one in the morning.

2. Parents have the right to freedom from unnecessary worry. If it takes you three hours to nip out and buy an iced lolly it will not occur to your parents that halfway down the road you decided to go to a pop 10

concert instead. They will conclude that you have been raped, kidnapped or murdered, or a grisly combination of all three.

3. A parent's personal appearance is his own concern. He does not want to be told that his hair is too short or that turn-ups are out of fashion. Nor does he require a psychedelic kipper tie on Father's Day.

4. Parents have the right to be human beings. That is to say, they have the right to fall into irrational rages, to contradict themselves, to change their minds without reason, to be stubborn, dogmatic and bloody-minded, and in general to behave occasionally like children, who as you well know are the salt of the earth.   20

5. No parent shall be scoffed at, sneered at or in any way discriminated against for his opinions.

6. Parents have the right to freedom from political indoctrination. It may well be the case that the world would be perfect if all money were distributed equally, the police force abolished, pot legalised, and the factories turned into communes, but your parents are not necessarily shambling morons if they prefer to go on voting Co-op Labour.

7. Parents shall have the right to make complaints about their children without fear of reprisal. The expression 'reprisal' includes sulking, screaming, slamming doors, making a motion with the hand   30 as if winding up a gramophone, and threatening to throw yourself in the river.

8. Parents have the right to be parents.

THE PARENTS' CHARTER *Keith Waterhouse* □

1 Compare the kind of language and style the two writers employ to make their points.

2. What attitude does each writer take to his subject?

Chapter 6
Style

The style of a piece of writing should emerge from its content and tone and from the author's intention in writing; content and style are inextricably linked. Style that is inappropriate for the content, or false in some way, is obtrusive and grating. Some writers feel they have to graft a style on to their writing, as though it is a kind of embellishment. When a writer parades a self-consciously ornate, inflated or witty style in front of readers, usually the piece of writing is merely an exercise in style and little else. In writing of significance and substance, style emerges from the content and is not welded on.

Some famous writers have denied having a style of their own at all. William Hazlitt, who is often referred to as a stylist, denied that he had an individual style. Hazlitt, however, wrote eloquent prose which is clear and cogently-expressed – all admirable stylistic qualities (an example of his writing can be found on page 86). When he denied having a style, he meant he did not consciously sit down and think of style when he was writing. His style emerged from the content of and intention behind his writing.

There are no definitions of what good style is. Bear that in mind as you look at the extracts in this chapter.

Jonathan Swift (1667–1745), was one of the great masters of English prose. A passage of his writing in which he satirises Britain's treatment of Ireland is included in Chapter 4. Swift aimed to use satire 'to mend the world' by exposing the moral defects and prejudices of the society in which he lived.

When discussing Swift's style, as with every writer, it is impossible to divorce the manner – the style, in which he wrote – from the context of his writing. His aims as a writer (to ridicule contemporary follies and dishonesty), the content (usually in the form of an allegory or an account of an imaginary voyage) and the style of his writing are all intertwined.

The extract below is from *Gulliver's Travels*, the voyage to the Houhyhnhnms section, in which Gulliver has supposedly made a journey to a civilisation populated by two contrasting types of creature; there are the Houhyhnhnms, who are superior, rational beings and have the form of horses; and there are the Yahoos, who are repellent, gross creatures, in appearance a parody of human beings. In this extract, Gulliver is explaining English law to his master, a Houhyhnhnm.

■ I assured his Honour, that *Law* was a Science wherein I had not much conversed, further than by employing Advocates, in vain, upon some Injustices that had been done me. However, I would give him all the Satisfaction I was able.

I said there was a Society of Men among us, bred up from their Youth in the Art of proving by Words multiplied for the Purpose, that *White is Black*, and *Black is White*, according as they are paid. To this Society all the rest of the People are Slaves.

For Example. If my Neighbour hath a mind to my *Cow*, he hires a Lawyer to prove that he ought to have my *Cow* from me. I must then 10 hire another to defend my Right; it being against all Rules of *Law* that any Man should be allowed to speak for himself. Now in this Case, I who am the true Owner lie under two great Disadvantages. First, my Lawyer being practiced almost from his Cradle in defending Falshood; is quite out of his Element when he would be an Advocate for Justice, which as an Office unnatural, he always attempts with great Awkwardness, if not with Ill-will. The second Disadvantage is, that my Lawyer must proceed with great Caution: Or else he will be reprimanded by the Judges, and abhorred by his Brethren, as one who would lessen the Practice of the Law. And therefore I have but two Methods to preserve 20 my *Cow*. The first is, to gain over my Adversary's Lawyer with a double Fee; who will then betray his Client, by insinuating that he hath Justice on his Side. The second way is for my Lawyer to make my Cause appear as unjust as he can; by allowing the *Cow* to belong to my Adversary; and this if it be skilfully done, will certainly bespeak the Favour of the Bench.

Now, your Honour is to know, that these Judges are Persons appointed to decide all Controversies of Property, as well as for the Tryal of Criminals; and picked out from the most dextrous Lawyers who are grown old or lazy: And having been byassed all their Lives 30 against Truth and Equity, are under such a fatal Necessity of favouring Fraud, Perjury and Oppression; that I have known some of them to have refused a large Bribe from the Side where Justice lay, rather than injure the *Faculty*, by doing any thing unbecoming their Nature or their Office.

It is a Maxim among these Lawyers, that whatever hath been done before, may legally be done again: And therefore they take special Care to record all the Decisions formerly made against common Justice and the general Reason of Mankind. These, under the Name of *Precedents*, they produce as Authorities to justify the most iniquitous Opinions; 40 and the Judges never fail of decreeing accordingly.

In pleading, they studiously avoid entering into the *Merits* of the Cause; but are loud, violent and tedious in dwelling upon all *Circumstances* which are not to the Purpose. For Instance, in the Case already mentioned: They never desire to know what Claim or Title my Adversary hath to my *Cow*; but whether the said *Cow* were Red or

Black; her Horns long or short; whether the Field I graze her in be round or square; whether she were milked at home or abroad; what Diseases she is subject to, and the like. After which they consult *Precedents*, adjourn the Cause, from Time to Time, and in Ten, Twenty, 50 or Thirty Years come to an Issue.

It is likewise to be observed, that this Society hath a peculiar Cant and Jargon of their own, that no other Mortal can understand, and wherein all their Laws are written, which they take special Care to multiply; whereby they have wholly confounded the very Essence of Truth and Falshood, of Right and Wrong; so that it will take Thirty Years to decide whether the Field, left me by my Ancestors for six Generations, belong to me, or to a Stranger three Hundred Miles off.

In the Tryal of Persons accused for Crimes against the State, the Method is much more short and commendable: The Judge first sends to 60 sound the Disposition of those in Power; after which he can easily hang or save the Criminal, strictly preserving all the Forms of Law.

Here my Master interposing, said it was a Pity, that Creatures endowed with such prodigious Abilities of Mind as these Lawyers, by the Description I gave of them must certainly be, were not encouraged to be Instructors of others in Wisdom and Knowledge. In Answer to which, I assured his Honour, that in all Points out of their own Trade, they were usually the most ignorant and stupid Generation among us, the most despicable in common Conversation, avowed Enemies to all Knowledge and Learning; and equally disposed to pervert the general 70 Reason of Mankind, in every other Subject of Discourse, as in that of their own Profession.

GULLIVER'S TRAVELS *Jonathan Swift* □

Swift uses Gulliver's explanation of English law as an opportunity to satirise the legal profession. He makes us take a fresh look at common legal practices by adopting the stance that all lawyers are corrupt and self-seeking and that the law itself is seldom interested in natural justice.

From this critical standpoint, the style of the piece emerges. Swift adopts the pompous, rather long-winded style of the legal profession to make satirical points about English law:

It is a Maxim among these Lawyers, that whatever hath been done before, may legally be done again: And therefore they take special Care to record all the Decisions formerly made against common Justice and the General Reason of Mankind. (36–39)

The pomposity and moral laxity of the legal world is reflected in Swift's choice of style.

1 Read the second paragraph of the extract again. Swift packs several satirical points about lawyers into two sentences. What are these satirical points?

2 '... that I have known some of them to have refused a large Bribe from the side where Justice lay ...' (32–33)

Swift, in describing how judges operate, uses irony to make his satirical point. Explain the irony involved in this section about the morality of judges.

3 Swift parodies the legal style to reinforce his points. Pick out examples of Swift's use of legalistic language and concepts and show how this contributes to his denunciation of lawyers.

4 Does Swift employ a very savage tone in his attack on lawyers or is it a more gently satirical tone? Is he more or less hard-hitting here than in his *Modest Proposal* on page 84? Give reasons for your answer, quoting briefly from the two passages.

● Imagine that a being from another planet or civilisation asks you to explain how the following practise their professions:

    school teachers   bus conductors   traffic wardens

    the police   members of parliament

Explain to this being some of the attitudes, beliefs and practices of one of these professions, but make your piece satirical in tone.

The writing of Henry Fielding (1707–1754) provides an interesting contrast to that of Jonathan Swift. Fielding's humour is rumbustious and extravert, rather than subtle like Swift's. This is reflected in his style; his humour is often broad and slapstick with one-dimensional characters caught up in gross comic situations.

In this extract from Fielding's novel *Tom Jones*, the hero, Tom, arrives at an inn with a half-naked woman whom he has rescued from an attack by a soldier. Tom orders a room for the woman then leaves her to find her some clothes.

■ Mr Jones and his companion no sooner entered the town; than they went directly to that inn which in their eyes presented the fairest appearance to the street. Here Jones, having ordered a servant to show a room above stairs, was ascending, when the dishevelled fair, hastily following, was laid hold on by the master of the house, who cried, 'Heydey, where is that beggar-wench going? stay below stairs, I desire you.' But Jones at that instant thundered from above, 'Let the lady come up,' in so authoritative a voice, that the good man instantly withdrew his hands, and the lady made the best of her way to the chamber.   10

    Here Jones wished her joy of her safe arrival, and then departed, in order, as he promised, to send the landlady up with some clothes. The poor woman thanked him heartily for all his kindness, and said, she hoped she should see him again soon to thank him a thousand times more. During this short conversation, she covered her white bosom as well as she could possibly with her arms; for Jones could not avoid stealing a sly peep or two, though he took all imaginable care to avoid giving any offence.

Our travellers had happened to take up their residence at a house of exceeding good repute, whither Irish ladies of strict virtue, and many 20 Northern lasses of the same predicament, were accustomed to resort in their way to Bath. The landlady, therefore, would by no means have admitted any conversation of a disreputable kind to pass under her roof. Indeed, so foul and contagious are all such proceedings, that they contaminate the very innocent scenes where they are committed, and give the name of a bad house, or of a house of ill repute, to all those where they are suffered to be carried on.

Not that I would intimate, that such strict chastity as was preserved in the temple of Vesta, can possibly be maintained at a public inn. My good landlady did not hope for such a blessing, nor would any of the 30 ladies I have spoken of, or, indeed, any of the others of the most rigid note, have expected or insisted on any such thing. But to exclude all vulgar concubinage, and to drive all whores in rags from within the walls, is within the power of every one. This my landlady very strictly adhered to, and this her virtuous guests, who did not travel in rags, would very reasonably have expected of her.

Now it required no very blameable degree of suspicion, to imagine that Mr Jones and his ragged companion had certain purposes in their intention, which, though tolerated in some Christian countries, connived at in others, and practised in all, are however as expressly 40 forbidden as murder, or any other horrid vice, by that religion which is universally believed in those countries. The landlady, therefore, had no sooner received an intimation of the entrance of the abovesaid persons, than she began to meditate the most expeditious means for their expulsion. In order to this, she had provided herself with a long and deadly instrument, with which, in times of peace, the chambermaid was wont to demolish the labours of the industrious spider. In vulgar phrase, she had taken up the broomstick, and was just about to sally from the kitchen, when Jones accosted her with a demand of a gown and other vestments, to cover the half-naked woman above stairs. 50

Nothing can be more provoking to the human temper, nor more dangerous to that cardinal virtue, patience, than solicitations of extraordinary offices of kindness on behalf of those very persons with whom we are highly incensed. For this reason Shakespeare hath artfully introduced his Desdemona soliciting favours for Cassio of her husband, as the means of inflaming not only his jealousy, but his rage, to the highest pitch of madness; and we find the unfortunate Moor less able to command his passion on this occasion, than even when he beheld his valued present to his wife in the hands of his supposed rival. In fact, we regard these efforts as insults on our understanding, and to 60 such the pride of man is very difficultly brought to submit.

My landlady, though a very good-tempered woman, had, I suppose, some of this pride in her composition; for Jones had scarce ended his request, when she fell upon him with a certain weapon, which, though it be neither long, nor sharp, nor hard, nor indeed threatens from its appearance with either death or wound, hath been however held in great dread and abhorrence by many wise men, nay, by many brave ones; insomuch that some who have dared to look into the mouth of a loaded cannon, have not dared to look into a mouth where this weapon was brandished; and rather than run the hazard of its execution, have 70 contented themselves with making a most pitiful, and sneaking figure in the eyes of all their acquaintance.

To confess the truth, I am afraid Mr Jones was one of these; for though he was attacked, and violently belaboured with the aforesaid weapon, he could not be provoked to make any resistance; but in a most cowardly manner applied, with many entreaties, to his antagonist to desist from pursuing her blows; in plain English, he only begged her with the utmost earnestness to hear him; but before he could obtain his request, my landlord himself entered into the fray, and embraced that side of the cause which seemed to stand very little in need of assistance. 80

TOM JONES *Henry Fielding* □

Fielding's use of irony is less subtle than Swift's or Austin's but this reflects the fact that his whole approach is bluffer and more extravert. His subject-matter has much to do with sensual appetites of one kind or another and with the hypocrisies and indiscretions of society. These he shows up with irony:

> ... her virtuous guests, who did not travel in rags ... (35)

In these words, Fielding suggests that society judges virtue by the wrong criteria, by outward respectability rather than by genuine qualities.

Fielding links a clever turn of phrase with a pointed contrast of style to puncture people's pretensions:

> But to exclude all vulgar concubinage, and to drive all whores in rags from within the walls ... (32–34)

In the first part of the sentence we hear the pompous tones of polite society; in the second we see a more honest portrayal of reality. The sentence is also typical of Fielding's use of exaggerated language for comic effect.

The incidents Fielding dramatises in his novels are usually vulgar and noisy involving chases and violence, such as the episode of the broomstick in this extract. His use of comic exaggeration is an appropriate style of writing with which to handle this kind of subject-matter.

6 / A Comic Vision

1   Look at the sentence beginning 'Indeed, so foul and contagious . . .' (24)
    Do you think Fielding intends any irony here or does he really mean what he seems to
    be saying?

2   '. . . which, though tolerated in some Christian countries, connived at in others, and
    practised in all . . .' (39–40)

    What is Fielding's satirical point in this sentence?

3   Fielding uses comic exaggeration in the fifth and seventh paragraphs to explain the
    terrors of the broomstick. Explain how he exaggerates to achieve his comic effect.

4   Both Swift (in the previous extract) and Fielding aim to satirise human folly and
    hypocrisy. They are very different writers as far as style is concerned. Discuss the
    differences in style and tone that you can detect between the two extracts.

The style of comic writing practised by Swift and Fielding reflects the societies
and the times they wrote in. It is unlikely that a contemporary writer would
write in a style similar to either of those two writers because each age has its
own comic vision.

Fay Weldon is a contemporary writer who often adopts a partly serious and
partly humorous standpoint to the eccentricities of human behaviour. In the
extract below from her novel *Praxis*, Patricia (Pattie) and Hilda are at boarding
school and Hilda has become Head Girl. The period is the Second World War.

■ Pupils, it is true, certainly fell silent when Hilda approached. She
seldom smiled: her eyes glittered: the black braid with its embossed
metal bars now hung almost to her waist, and clanked against the
buckle of her money-belt: Head Girl, House Captain, the engravings
read: and descending, Hockey, Latin, English, French, Geography,
Religious Knowledge, Deportment – there seemed no end to Hilda's
accomplishments. She meted out punishment liberally if erratically.
She might give twenty lines or 2000 for the same offence: she invented
crimes. She had designated the second peg to the left of the cloakroom
door as one which for some reason must be kept free of hats and coats,   10
and would give a detention to anyone who used it: and once compelled
a third year girl, a certain Audrey Denver, to stand on her head in the
playground until she fainted for the sin of having brown laces in black
shoes. Then she kept the entire third year in after school until whoever
had done it owned up. But done what? Nobody was quite sure: nobody
owned up: and Hilda went home in the middle of the detention
anyway. The staff seemed unaware of their head girl's eccentricity: on
the contrary, the head-mistress enthused about her capacity for
keeping order, and the general lack of silliness in the school since her
appointment. It was as if a certain implicit insanity in the school,   20
dressing its burgeoning female adolescents in collars, ties, boaters and
blazers; having them learn classics while the walls around them

collapsed, and play netball on playgrounds increasingly pitted by falling shrapnel, had become explicit in Hilda.

Since her appointment as head girl, Hilda had been unusually pale, and her eyes dark, shiny and troubled. But she had been more talkative and confiding than usual: she would keep Pattie up until the early hours, talking about the third year girls, remarking on how like rats they were, scuttling here and there, carrying diseases, secretly watching Hilda and sending each other messages concerning her. Hilda went 30 over and over the same ground: it was as if some gramophone record in her head had stuck. Pattie almost came to believe her. Audrey Denver certainly had a sharp little face, and red eyes due (she said) to chronic conjunctivitis: it was perfectly possible that the one black shoe lace and one brown was a signal of some kind and that standing her on her head would cross the connections and scramble the lines between the rat armies, before worse befall; and all was known.

Anything, Pattie thought increasingly, was possible.

PRAXIS *Fay Weldon* ☐

The subject of the passage is Hilda's 'eccentricity' (17) which, in fact, is nearer to insanity. This is disguised, however, by the 'implicit insanity in the school' (20). Fay Weldon's comic vision is of a slightly crazy institution that unleashes Hilda's madness and gives it official status by making her Head Girl. The author uses Pattie as a symbol of relative sanity within a mad world.

1 Whose view does it seem to be that the school is insane – Pattie's or the author's?

2 What is comic about Hilda's obsession about the third year girls (and Audrey Denver in particular), and Pattie's thoughts about the matter?

3 'Fay Weldon uses considerable concrete detail in her writing to get across her comic vision of the world'.

Relate the above statement to the extract, showing how the author's use of detail adds to the effectiveness of the writing.

4 Fay Weldon's comic style of writing has been called 'succinct' and 'devastatingly witty, undermining the pomposities of the people in the society she portrays'. Are these comments appropriate to the style of writing she adopts here?

Realism is a term used to describe an approach taken by novelists (films and plays are often described as being realistic as well). What does taking a realistic approach mean in terms of novel-writing? Realistic novelists deal with the everyday world: the physical environment, the ordinary concerns of people, ordinary people themselves. Realistic content is reflected in an unpretentious style in which literary adornment is mainly absent.

Arnold Bennett (1867–1931) is usually seen as belonging to the realist school of
novelists. In the following extract from *Hilda Lessways*, Bennett describes the
area where his heroine lives. After reading this extract compare it with the next
one which comes from a novel by Alan Sharp called *A Green Tree in Gedde*.
Sharp, by contrast with Bennett, aims to write on a more elevated, poetic
plane. In the passage below, he describes a cemetery in the town of Greenock,
Scotland.

■ Mr Skellorn did not come; he was most definitely late.

From the window of her bedroom, at the front of the house, Hilda
looked westwards up toward the slopes of Chatterley Wood, where as
a child she used to go with other children to pick the sparse bluebells
that thrived on smoke. The bailiwick of Turnhill lay behind her; and all
the murky district of the Five Towns, of which Turnhill is the northern
outpost, lay to the south. At the foot of Chatterley Wood the canal
wound in large curves on its way towards the undefiled plains of
Cheshire and the sea. On the canal-side, exactly opposite to Hilda's
window, was a flour-mill, that sometimes made nearly as much smoke   10
as the kilns and chimneys closing the prospect on either hand. From
the flour-mill a bricked path, which separated a considerable row of
new cottages from their appurtenant gardens, led straight into Lessways Street, in front of Mrs Lessways' house. By this path Mr Skellorn
should have arrived, for he inhabited the farthest of the cottages.

Hilda held Mr Skellorn in disdain, as she held the row of cottages in
disdain. It seemed to her that Mr Skellorn and the cottages mysteriously
resembled each other in their primness, their smugness, their detest-
able self-complacency. Yet those cottages, perhaps thirty in all, had
stood for a great deal until Hilda, glancing at them, shattered them with   20
her scorn. The row was called Freehold Villas: a consciously proud
name in a district where much of the land was copyhold and could only
change owners subject to the payment of 'fines' and to the feudal
consent of a 'court' presided over by the agent of a lord of the manor.
Most of the dwellings were owned by their occupiers, who, each an
absolute monarch of the soil, niggled in his sooty garden of an evening
amid the flutter of drying shirts and towels. Freehold Villas symbolized
the final triumph of Victorian economics, the apotheosis of the prudent
and industrious artisan. It corresponded with a Building Society
Secretary's dream of paradise. And indeed it was a very real achieve-   30
ment. Nevertheless Hilda's irrational contempt would not admit this.
She saw in Freehold Villas nothing but narrowness (what long narrow
strips of gardens, and what narrow homes all flattened together!), and
uniformity, and brickiness, and polished brassiness, and righteous-
ness, and an eternal laundry.

From the upper floor of her own home she gazed destructively down
upon all that, and into the chill, crimson eye of the descending sun. Her

own home was not ideal, but it was better than all that. It was one of
the two middle houses of a detached terrace of four houses built by her
grandfather Lessways, the teapot manufacturer; it was the chief of the   40
four, obviously the habitation of the proprietor of the terrace. One of
the corner houses comprised a grocer's shop, and this house had been
robbed of its just proportion of garden so that the seigneurial garden-
plot might be triflingly larger than the others. The terrace was not a
terrace of cottages, but of houses rated at from twenty-six to thirty-six
pounds a year; beyond the means of artisans and petty insurance
agents and rent-collectors. And further, it was well built, generously
built; and its architecture, though debased, showed some faint traces of
Georgian amenity. It was admittedly the best row of houses in that
newly settled quarter of the town. In coming to it out of Freehold Villas   50
Mr Skellorn obviously came to something superior, wider, more liberal.

HILDA LESSWAYS *Arnold Bennett* ☐

■ The old cemetery on Inverkip Street is now kept as a kind of public
gardens. The turf is shaved close and there is a small tree in the centre
that is trained over into a kind of canopy. There are seats where people
may sit. Not many use it, old men in the summer come and look
around at the tombstones and smoke pipes and talk to themselves or to
other old men. The burials in the cemetery are old and the gravestones
are much worn, some of them like tables, low thick slabs set on squat
legs, others erect, a little tilted perhaps from subsidence, and set
around the walls, tablets; and all, all bearing those legends of
bereavement and parenthetic dates. Lives begun and ended long ago,   10
now layered in random rote of their falling, sons lie upon mothers and
fathers on their daughters, and all finally upon each in a last
interlocking knit, their differences at nought and a lasting affection
replacing the frailty of human love. These under earth anthologies
pervade the place with the monotony of their content and rise in a slow
exhalation, without scent or sight, a breathing of bones, a long
suspiration that wears as emblem the tree on a green ground.

The children call it the dead centre of Greenock, but the town no
longer turns on it, having spilled in a plethora of living east and west
and back up on to the hill. But from its seats the roofs of the older   20
buildings make a sweep in half circle around the horizon, roof slant and
chimney stack, tiering up on to the hill and sending on quiet evenings
countless purlings of dove dun smoke slowly up into the air. At such
moments then the old graveyard does seem a hub, the still centre of the
town's slow revolve.

As to burial there is now another, larger cemetery, a sprawling
overgrown tract, a vast dump for the dead. The bodies here are still
earthbound by the rootings of memory, having not yet divested

themselves of the love of created beings, insertions still appear in the
Greenock Telegraph commemorating their decease, people cut their   30
grasses as penance for being alive and every Sunday, in the good
weather, groups may be seen, walking slowly, with flowers and
composed faces, to look down on graves in recall of lineaments now
dissolved.

Held as they are to the land of the living by such unreciprocal
rememberings the dead invest their domain with a prolix tension of
growth. Visitors lose themselves on unfamiliar lanes and with mild
terror come upon other sepulchral visitors round evergreen corners.
And the sheer volume of death that engulfs the eye, the rows upon
lines of plinths and plaques, of glass-domed immortelles, urns in   40
mottled mock marble 'from the neighbours' and the cenotaphs of the
wealthy which all, no matter how portentous or how pathetic, make
the same piteous utterance to the living gaze, finally to hasten exit, like
the pressure of fathoms compels ascent, up to the air and the light, for
in the bone ground there is no glimpse of the dwellings of the quick,
everywhere grow the gloomy greens of rhododendrons, the never-
greens of conifers and the graygreen gravegrass.

But when at last the threads of memory rot and the rememberers
themselves are tombed, then the liberated dead move in silent flit to the
old open field of the truly buried, and there in sight of the living they   50
relax and at last rest.

A GREEN TREE IN GEDDE *Alan Sharp* □

Arnold Bennett has been praised for his minute observation of people and
places. In the Bennett extract, the description of the place is detailed, but he
uses it (as far as the description of the cottages is concerned) to tell the reader
what Hilda thinks of Mr Skellorn.

Alan Sharp, on the other hand, aims for a kind of poetic realism in his extract;
on the face of it, he is describing a graveyard in Greenock, but with his image-
laden, heightened language he aims to fuse the mundane with a poetic vision.

Bennett's description is concrete and literal; Sharp uses the description to hint
at eternal truths about human existence. That is not to say that Sharp's writing
is better or more profound. Sharp's intention might not be successfully realised
in the writing, whereas Bennett may achieve his more limited aims.

1 How does Bennett use the account which he gives of the cottages to reveal to us what
Hilda thinks of Skellorn?

2 Read the first paragraph of the Alan Sharp extract again. The author is describing the
cemetery, but what other elements does he inject into the writing?

3 Compare the rhythm of Sharp's prose with Bennett's. Account for the difference
between them by reference to the intentions of the two authors.

4 Look at the following quotations from the passages:

'Most of the dwellings were owned by their occupiers, who, each an absolute monarch of the soil, niggled in his sooty garden of an evening amid the flutter of drying shirts and towels. Freehold Villas symbolized the final triumph of Victorian economics, the apotheosis of the prudent and industrious artisan. It corresponded with a Building Society Secretary's dream of paradise.' (25–30)

'Held as they are to the land of the living by such unreciprocal rememberings the dead invest their domain with a prolix tension of growth. Visitors lose themselves on unfamiliar lanes and with mild terror come upon other sepulchral visitors round evergreen corners.' (34–37)

How do these quotations from the extracts reflect the difference in intention, tone and style between the two extracts?

● Describe any one of the following in two versions, in the first one taking a realistic descriptive approach, and in the second version adopting a more poetic, non-realistic approach and style:

your school building   a rubbish dump   the street where you live   a town centre

It has already been seen how writers can enter the minds of their characters and reproduce their thought-processes for the reader through the use of interior monologue (pages 27–29) or the stream of consciousness technique (pages 45–47). Most novelists follow the thoughts of their characters at some point in their books, but with analytical writers such as Virginia Woolf, most of the 'action' of the novel takes place inside characters' heads.

In Woolf's novel *To the Lighthouse*, the action of the novel, such as it is, is revealed almost completely through Mrs Ramsay's consciousness. The people and surroundings are seen through her thoughts and this affects the writing style; it results, for example, in the use of very long sentences.

Mrs Ramsay is holidaying with her husband, children and friends on a Scottish island. James, her youngest son, wants to visit the local lighthouse the next day, but Mr Ramsay, his father, has said that the visit will not be possible because bad weather is coming. At the beginning of this extract, Charles Tansley, one of Ramsay's friends and protégés, echoes his words.

■ 'No going to the Lighthouse, James,' he said, as he stood by the window, speaking awkwardly, but trying in deference to Mrs Ramsay to soften his voice into some semblance of geniality at least.
    Odious little man, thought Mrs Ramsay, why go on saying that?

    'Perhaps you will wake up and find the sun shining and the birds singing,' she said compassionately, smoothing the little boy's hair, for her husband, with his caustic saying that it would not be fine, had dashed his spirits she could see. This going to the Lighthouse was a passion of his, she saw, and then, as if her husband had not said enough, with his caustic saying that it would not be fine to-morrow, this odious little man went and rubbed it in all over again. 10

'Perhaps it will be fine to-morrow,' she said, smoothing his hair.

All she could do now was to admire the refrigerator, and turn the pages of the Stores list in the hope that she might come upon something like a rake, or a mowing-machine, which, with its prongs and handles, would need the greatest skill and care in cutting out. All these young men parodied her husband, she reflected; he said it would rain; they said it would be a positive tornado.

But here, as she turned the page, suddenly her search for the picture of a rake or a mowing-machine was interrupted. The gruff murmur, 20 irregularly broken by the taking out of pipes and the putting in of pipes which had kept on assuring her, though she could not hear what was said (as she sat in the window), that the men were happily talking; this sound, which had lasted now half an hour and had taken its place soothingly in the scale of sounds pressing on top of her, such as the tap of balls upon bats, the sharp, sudden bark now and then, 'How's that? How's that?' of the children playing cricket, had ceased; so that the monotonous fall of the waves on the beach, which for the most part beat a measured and soothing tattoo to her thoughts and seemed consolingly to repeat over and over again as she sat with the children 30 the words of some old cradle song, murmured by nature, 'I am guarding you – I am your support', but at other times suddenly and unexpectedly, especially when her mind raised itself slightly from the task actually in hand, had no such kindly meaning, but like a ghostly roll of drums remorselessly beat the measure of life, made one think of the destruction of the island and its engulfment in the sea, and warned her whose day had slipped past in one quick doing after another that it was all ephemeral as a rainbow – this sound which had been obscured and concealed under the other sounds suddenly thundered hollow in her ears and made her look up with an impulse of terror. 40

They had ceased to talk; that was the explanation. Falling in one second from the tension which had gripped her to the other extreme which, as if to recoup her for her unnecessary expense of emotion, was cool, amused, and even faintly malicious, she concluded that poor Charles Tansley had been shed. That was of little account to her. If her husband required sacrifices (and indeed he did) she cheerfully offered up to him Charles Tansley, who had snubbed her little boy.

One moment more, with her head raised, she listened, as if she waited for some habitual sound, some regular mechanical sound; and then, hearing something rhythmical, half said, half chanted, beginning 50 in the garden, as her husband beat up and down the terrace, something between a croak and a song, she was soothed once more, assured again

that all was well, and looking down at the book on her knee found the picture of a pocket knife with six blades which could only be cut out if James was very careful.
TO THE LIGHTHOUSE *Virginia Woolf* □

Virginia Woolf uses long sentences, for the most part, in the extract. The choice of sentence construction and length is not accidental but emerges from the content. The character, Mrs Ramsay, is contemplating the interaction of the people around her. Her analysing naturally leads to longer, involved sentences; they are the stylistic counterpart to her rational analysis of the events around her.

Sometimes Woolf uses shorter sentences:

. . . he said it would rain; they said it would be a positive tornado. (17–18)

The dogmatism of her husband's statements, and their slavish adoption by the younger men, finds expression in the rather curt style with which Woolf mentions them, which contrasts dramatically with the long sentences that she uses elsewhere in the extract.

1 From 'The gruff murmur' (20) to 'an impulse of terror' (40) is all one sentence. Discuss the reasons for the length of the sentence, taking into consideration the subject-matter and the interior monologue technique.

2 'They had ceased to talk; that was the explanation.' (41)

This is a very short sentence which comes at the beginning of the next paragraph after the sentence you analysed in Question 1. What is the effect of a sentence made up of two short statements after such a long and rambling sentence?

3 In the last paragraph, Woolf again uses a rambling, diffuse sentence construction because of the approach she is taking to her story. Does the style of the writing reflect the content? Is the sentence construction appropriate to the subject-matter?

The private eye story is the American equivalent of the classic English detective story. Private eye novels in the hands of Raymond Chandler, Dashiell Hammett and other American masters of the genre, are worthy of serious consideration as literature. These writers use a 'hard-boiled', witty style, mirroring an urban world that is alienating and corrupt.

Content and style come together perfectly in the novels of a writer like Chandler. His plots are perhaps less important than the picture he creates of a nightmarish city jungle. His writing is also admired because of its wit and intelligence.

In the extract below from Chandler's *The Big Sleep*, Philip Marlowe, a private eye, returns to his apartment one night to find a hoodlum waiting for him. The hood has been sent by his gangster boss, Eddie Mars.

■ It was close to eleven when I put my car away and walked around to
the front of the Hobart Arms. The plate-glass door was put on the lock
at ten, so I had to get my keys out. Inside, in the square barren lobby, a
man put a green evening paper down beside a potted palm and flicked
a cigarette butt into the tub the palm grew in. He stood up and waved
his hat at me and said: 'The boss wants to talk to you. You sure keep
your friends waiting, pal.'

I stood still and looked at his flattened nose and club steak ear.
'What about?'

'What do you care? Just keep your nose clean and everything will be   10
jake.' His hand hovered near the upper buttonhole of his open coat.

'I smell of policemen,' I said. 'I'm too tired to talk, too tired to eat, too
tired to think. But if you think I'm not too tired to take orders from
Eddie Mars – try getting your gat before I shoot your good ear off.'

'Nuts. You ain't got no gun.' He stared at me levelly. His dark wiry
brows closed together and his mouth made a downward curve.

'That was then,' I told him. 'I'm not always naked.'

He waved his left hand. 'Okay. You win. I wasn't told to blast
anybody. You'll hear from him.'

'Too late will be too soon,' I said, and turned slowly as he passed me   20
on his way to the door. He opened it and went out without looking
back. I grinned at my own foolishness, went along to the elevator and
upstairs to the apartment. I took Carmen's little gun out of my pocket
and laughed at it. Then I cleaned it thoroughly, oiled it, wrapped it in a
piece of canton flannel and locked it up. I made myself a drink and was
drinking it when the phone rang. I sat down beside the table on which
it stood.

'So you're tough to-night,' Eddie Mars' voice said.

'Big, fast, tough and full of prickles. What can I do for you?'

'Cops over there – you know where. You keep me out of it?'   30.

'Why should I?'

'I'm nice to be nice to, soldier. I'm not nice not to be nice to.'

'Listen hard and you'll hear my teeth chattering.'

He laughed dryly. 'Did you – or did you?'

'I did. I'm damned if I know why. I guess it was just complicated
enough without you.'

'Thanks, soldier. Who gunned him?'

'Read it in the paper to-morrow – maybe.'

'I want to know now.'

'Do you get everything you want?'   40

'No. Is that an answer, soldier?'

'Somebody you never heard of gunned him. Let it go at that.'

'If that's on the level, some day I may be able to do you a favour.'

'Hang up and let me go to bed.'

He laughed again. 'You're looking for Rusty Regan, aren't you?'

'A lot of people seem to think I am, but I'm not.'

'If you were, I could give you an idea. Drop in and see me down at the beach. Any time. Glad to see you.'
'Maybe.'
'Be seeing you then.'

THE BIG SLEEP *Raymond Chandler* ☐

Chandler wrote smart, racy dialogue in a very American idiom, making use of repetition to achieve a terse, pointed style:

'... You'll hear from him.'
'Too late will be too soon,' I said. (19–20)

He has had hundreds of imitators. He used the genre of the private eye thriller to create a picture of dark, urban violence and betrayals. His style of writing reflects that city environment of tough attitudes, distrust and wry, ironic humour which often masks desperate loneliness beneath the hard-boiled exterior.

1 How does Marlowe insult the man who is waiting for him?

2 'So you're tough to-night,' Eddie Mars' voice said.
'Big, fast, tough and full of prickles.' (28–29)

Chandler specialises in this kind of tough guy banter. What other examples of this kind of humour are there in the conversation between Marlowe and Eddie Mars?

3 Do you think this kind of writing deserves to be taken seriously as literature, or does its subject-matter and style relegate it to the realm of light reading?

4 Chandler's characteristic style is terse and witty. He does not waste words. Pick out examples from the extract of this aspect of his style and comment on how he achieves his effect.

5 'Much of Chandler's writing consists of dialogue rather than narrative, but the dialogue serves a narrative purpose as well.'

Do we learn anything from the dialogue about the characters and about incidents that have happened in the novel?

● Write dialogue for an episode in a novel for any of the following, using a tough guy witty style:

a teacher and a pupil   a policeman and a motorcyclist
a newspaper reporter and a rock star

The answer to the question 'What is a novel?' has become so elastic and all-embracing that it would now be very difficult to create a satisfactory definition that would include all the variations in form and experimental language that novelists have tried out.

A contemporary writer, Russell Hoban, has his narrator use an English language of the future in his novel called *Riddley Walker*: it is a language which is similar enough to our contemporary language for us to be able to understand it, but unfamiliar enough to convince us that it comes from another society and another era.

■ Walker is my name and I am the same. Riddley Walker. Walking my riddels where ever theyve took me and walking them now on this paper the same.
    I dont think it makes no diffrents where you start the telling of a thing. You never know where it begun realy. No moren you know where you begun your oan self. You myt know the place and day and time of day when you ben beartht. You myt even know the place and day and time when you ben got. That dont mean nothing tho. You stil dont know where you begun.
    Ive all ready wrote down about my naming day. It wernt no moren 3   10

days after that my dad got kilt in the digging at Widders Dump and I wer the loan of my name.

Dad and me we jus come off forage rota and back on jobbing that day. The hoal we ben working we ben on it 24 days. Which Ive never liket 12 its a judgd men number innit and this ben 2 of them. Wed pernear cleart out down to the chalk and hevvy mucking it ben. Nothing lef in the hoal only sortit thru muck and the smel of it and some girt big rottin iron thing some kynd of machine it were you cudnt tel what it wer.

Til then any thing big we all ways bustit up in the hoal. Winch a girt big buster rock up on the crane and drop it down on what ever we wer busting. Finish up with han hammers then theywd drag the peaces to the reddy for the melting. This time tho the 1stman tol us word come down they dint want this thing bustit up we wer to get it out in tack. So we ben sturgling with the girt big thing nor the woal 20 of us cudnt shif it we cudnt even lif it just that littl bit to get the sling unner neath of it. Up to our knees in muck we wer. Even with the drain wed dug the hoal wer mucky from the rains. And col. It were only jus the 2nd mooning of the year and winter long in going.

We got hevvy poals and leavering it up jus a nuff to get a roap roun 1 end of it we had in mynd to shif that girt thing jus a littl with the crane so we cud get it parper slung then winch it out of there. It wer a 16 man treadl crane with 2 weals 4 men inside 4 men outside each weal. Userly I wuntve ben on the crane we all ways put our hevvyes on them weals. All we had tho wer 20 in all and we neadit some mussl on the leaver poals so I wer up there on the lef han weal with our hardes hevvy Fister Crunchman we wer the front 2 on that weal. Durster Potter and Jobber Easting behynt us. Straiter Empy our Big Man he wer down in the hoal with Dad and 2 others. Us on the out side of the weals looking tords the hoal and them on the in side looking a way from it.

20

30

40

RIDDLEY WALKER *Russell Hoban* □

Undoubtedly the form and language of the twentieth-century novel has loosened up in comparison with the three-volume tomes of the eighteenth and nineteenth centuries. James Joyce shook the established notions of what a novel is early on in this century, with his novels *Ulysses* and *Finnegan's Wake*. Since then, writers have experimented with numerous forms and techniques – the anti-novel, for example, which deliberately eschewed the novel's conventional elements of story, character and logical order of events.

In *Riddley Walker*, Russell Hoban re-defines what a novel can be, not only in terms of form and content, but also in the language he chooses to communicate his particular vision.

1 Apart from the obvious spelling variations, what other differences are there between the 'English' of the extract and the Standard English used in our time?

2 The characteristics of a language reflect the society or section of the society that uses it. Judged by the language of the extract, what kind of society is being portrayed here?

3 In writing this novel about the future, Russell Hoban could have had his first-person narrator use conventional, contemporary English. What added qualities does the story-telling gain, however, from the employment of the 'English' used in the extract?

The extracts below are by Franz Kafka and John Updike. They both deal with a form of persecution, but the two writers handle the subject very differently.

■ Someone must have been telling lies about Joseph K., for without having done anything wrong he was arrested one fine morning. His landlady's cook, who always brought him his breakfast at eight o'clock, failed to appear on this occasion. That had never happened before. K. waited for a little while longer, watching from his pillow the old lady opposite, who seemed to be peering at him with a curiosity unusual even for her, but then, feeling both put out and hungry, he rang the bell. At once there was a knock at the door and a man entered whom he had never seen before in the house. He was slim and yet well knit, he wore a closely fitting black suit, which was furnished with all sorts of   10
pleats, pockets, buckles, and buttons, as well as a belt, like a tourist's outfit, and in consequence looked eminently practical, though one could not quite tell what actual purpose it served. 'Who are you?' asked K., half raising himself in bed. But the man ignored the question, as though his appearance needed no explanation, and merely said: 'Did you ring?' 'Anna is to bring me my breakfast,' said K., and then with silent intensity studied the fellow, trying to make out who he could be. The man did not submit to this scrutiny for very long, but turned to the door and opened it slightly so as to report to someone who was evidently standing just behind it: 'He says Anna is to bring him his   20
breakfast.' A short guffaw from the next room came in answer; one could not tell from the sound whether it was produced by several individuals or merely by one. Although the strange man could not have learned anything from it that he did not know already, he now said to K., as if passing on a statement: 'It can't be done.' 'This is news indeed,' cried K., springing out of bed and quickly pulling on his trousers. 'I must see what people these are next door, and how Frau Grubach can account to me for such behaviour.' Yet it occurred to him at once that he should not have said this aloud and that by doing so he had in a way admitted the stranger's right to an interest in his actions; still, that did   30
not seem important to him at the moment. The stranger, however, took his words in some such sense, for he asked: 'Hadn't you better stay here?' 'I shall neither stay here nor let you address me until you have

introduced yourself.' 'I meant well enough,' said the stranger, and then of his own accord threw the door open. In the next room, which K. entered more slowly than he had intended, everything looked at first glance almost as it had done the evening before. It was Frau Grubach's living-room; perhaps among all the furniture, rugs, china, and photographs with which it was crammed there was a little more free space than usual, yet one did not perceive that at first, especially as the main 40 change consisted in the presence of a man who was sitting at the open window reading a book, from which he now glanced up. 'You should have stayed in your room! Didn't Franz tell you that?' 'Yes, yes, but what are you doing here?' asked K., looking from his new acquaintance to the man called Franz, who was still standing by the door, and then back again. Through the open window he had another glimpse of the old woman, who with truly senile inquisitiveness had moved along to the window exactly opposite, in order to see all that could be seen. 'I'd better get Frau Grubach –' said K., as if wrenching himself away from the two men (though they were standing at quite a distance from him) 50 and making as if to go out. 'No,' said the man at the window, flinging the book down on the table and getting up. 'You can't go out, you are arrested.'

THE TRIAL *Franz Kafka* ☐

■ Caldwell turned and as he turned his ankle received an arrow. The class burst into laughter. The pain scaled the slender core of his shin, whirled in the complexities of his knee, and, swollen broader, more thunderous, mounted into his bowels. His eyes were forced upward to the blackboard, where he had chalked the number 5,000,000,000, the probable age in years of the universe. The laughter of the class, graduating from the first shrill bark of surprise into a deliberately aimed hooting, seemed to crowd against him, to crush the privacy that he so much desired, a privacy in which he could be alone with his pain, gauging its strength, estimating its duration, inspecting its anatomy. 10 The pain extended a feeler into his head and unfolded its wet wings along the walls of his thorax, so that he felt, in his sudden scarlet blindness, to be himself a large bird waking from sleep. The blackboard, milky slate smeared with the traces of last night's washing, clung to his consciousness like a membrane. The pain seemed to be displacing with its own hairy segments his heart and lungs; as its grip swelled in his throat he felt he was holding his brain like a morsel on a platter high out of a hungry reach. Several of the boys in their bright shirts all colours of the rainbow had risen upright at their desks, leering and baying at their teacher, cocking their muddy shoes on the folding 20 seats. The confusion became unbearable. Caldwell limped to the door and shut it behind him on the furious festal noise.

Out in the hall, the feather end of the arrow scraped on the floor with
every step. The metallic scratch and stiff rustle mixed disagreeably. His
stomach began to sway with nausea. The dim, long walls of the ochre
hall wavered; the classroom doors, inset with square numbered panes
of frosted glass, seemed experimental panels immersed in an activated
liquid charged with children's voices chanting French, singing an-
thems, discussing problems of Social Science.

THE CENTAUR *John Updike* □

1 The events of each of the extracts are seen through the consciousness of one character
– K. and Caldwell. Analyse how the authors achieve this.

2 Neither of the two extracts takes a realistic approach to its theme. Analyse the authors'
treatment of the material with which the extracts deal, quoting briefly from both to
illustrate your analysis.

Both the following extracts present a character in a comic light. Read them
carefully, comparing the authors' comic technique.

■ Kommandant van Heerden had few illusions about himself and a great
many about everything else. And it was thanks to his illusions that he
found himself in charge of the Police station in Piemburg. It was not a
very onerous position. Piemburg's mediocrity was not conducive to
more than petty crime and it had been felt at Police Headquarters in
Pretoria that, while Kommandant van Heerden's appointment might
push the city's crime rate up, it would at least serve to lower the waves
of violence and theft that had followed his posting to other more
enterprising towns.

Besides, Piemburg deserved the Kommandant. As the one town in   10
the Republic still to fly the Union Jack from the Town Hall, Piemburg
needed to be taught that the Government could not be challenged
without taking some revenge.

Kommandant van Heerden knew that his appointment was not due
to his success in the field of criminal investigation. He fondly imagined
it had come to him because he understood the English. It was in fact
due to the reputation of his grandfather, Klaasie van Heerden, who had
served under General Cronje at the Battle of Paardeberg and had been
shot by the British for refusing to obey the order of his commanding
officer to surrender. He had instead stayed put in a hole in the bank of   20
the Modder River and shot down twelve soldiers of the Essex Regiment
who were relieving themselves there some forty-eight hours after the
last shot had been fired. The fact that Klaasie had been fast asleep
throughout the entire battle and had never heard the order to cease fire

was discounted by the British during his trial and by later generations of Afrikaans historians. Instead he was accounted a hero who had been martyred for his devotion to the Boer Republics and as a hero he was revered by Afrikaans Nationalists all over South Africa.

It was this legend that had helped Kommandant van Heerden to his present rank. It had taken a long time for his incompetence to live 30 down the reputation for cunning that had been bequeathed him by his grandfather, and by that time it was too late for Police Headquarters to do anything about his inefficiency except put him in command of Piemburg.

Kommandant van Heerden imagined that he had got the post because it was in an English town and certainly it was just the post he wanted. The Kommandant believed that he was one of the few Afrikaaners who really understood the English mind. In spite of the treatment the British had meted out to his grandfather, in spite of the brutality the British had shown to the Boer women and children in the 40 concentration camps, in spite of the sentimentality the British wasted on their black servants, in spite of everything, Kommandant van Heerden admired the British.

There was something about their blundering stupidity that appealed to him. It called out to something deep within his being. He couldn't say exactly what it was, but deep called to deep and, if the Kommandant could have chosen his place of birth, its time and nationality, he would have plumped for Piemburg in 1890 and the heart of an English gentleman.

RIOTOUS ASSEMBLY *Tom Sharpe* □

■ Shagpoke Whipple lived on the main street of Ottsville in a two-storey frame house with a narrow lawn in front and a garage that once had been a chicken house in the rear. Both buildings had a solid, sober look, and, indeed, no one was ever allowed to create disorder within their precincts.

The house served as a place of business as well as a residence; the first floor being devoted to the offices of the bank and the second functioning as the home of the ex-President. On the porch, next to the front door, was a large bronze plate that read:

RAT RIVER NATIONAL BANK	10
Nathan 'Shagpoke' Whipple	
PRES.	

Some people might object to turning a part of their dwelling into a bank, especially if, like Mr Whipple, they had hobnobbed with crowned heads. But Shagpoke was not proud, and he was of the saving

kind. He had always saved: from the first time he received a penny at
the age of five, when he had triumphed over the delusive pleasures of
an investment in candy, right down to the time he was elected
President of the United States. One of his favourite adages was 'Don't
teach your grandmother to suck eggs'. By this he meant that the   20
pleasures of the body are like grandmothers, once they begin to suck
eggs they never stop until all the eggs (purse) are dry.

As Lem turned up the path to Mr Whipple's house, the sun rapidly
sank under the horizon. Every evening at this time, the ex-President
lowered the flag that flew over his garage and made a speech to as
many of the town's citizenry as had stopped to watch the ceremony.
During the first year after the great man's return from Washington,
there used to collect quite a crowd, but this had dwindled until now, as
our hero approached the house, there was but a lone Boy Scout
watching the ceremony. This lad was not present of his own free will,   30
alas, but had been sent by his father, who was desirous of obtaining a
loan from the bank.

Lem removed his hat and waited in reverence for Mr Whipple to
finish his speech.

'All hail Old Glory! May you be the joy and pride of the American
heart, alike when your gorgeous folds shall wanton in the summer air
and your tattered fragments be dimly seen through clouds of war! May
you ever wave in honour, hope, and profit, in unsullied glory and
patriotic fervour, on the dome of the Capitol, on the tented plain, on
the wave-rocked topmast, and on the roof of the garage!'   40

With these words, Shagpoke lowered the flag for which so many of
our finest have bled and died, and tenderly gathered it up in his arms.
The Boy Scout ran off hurriedly.

A COOL MILLION Nathanael West □

1 What do you think the attitude of the respective authors is to their characters?

2 Analyse the satirical elements in both extracts.

3 'Tom Sharpe and Nathanael West achieve a comic effect by defeating readers'
expectations and by injecting a strong dose of the bizarre into their writing.'

Do you agree? Support your answer by quoting from both extracts.

4 Do you think the author intrudes more directly in one extract than the other? Give
reasons for your answer, quoting briefly where relevant.

Both the following extracts are opening passages to novels written in the first
person. In style, however, they are very different.

■ Under certain circumstances there are few hours in life more agreeable than the hour dedicated to the ceremony known as afternoon tea. There are circumstances in which, whether you partake of the tea or not – some people of course never do, – the situation is in itself delightful. Those that I have in mind in beginning to unfold this simple history offered an admirable setting to an innocent pastime. The implements of the little feast had been disposed upon the lawn of an old English country-house, in what I should call the perfect middle of a splendid summer afternoon. Part of the afternoon had waned, but much of it was left, and what was left was of the finest and rarest quality. Real   10 dusk would not arrive for many hours; but the flood of summer light had begun to ebb, the air had grown mellow, the shadows were long upon the smooth, dense turf. They lengthened slowly, however, and the scene expressed that sense of leisure still to come which is perhaps the chief source of one's enjoyment of such a scene at such an hour. From five o'clock to eight is on certain occasions a little eternity; but on such an occasion as this the interval could be only an eternity of pleasure. The persons concerned in it were taking their pleasure quietly, and they were not of the sex which is supposed to furnish the regular votaries of the ceremony I have mentioned. The shadows on   20 the perfect lawn were straight and angular; they were the shadows of an old man sitting in a deep wicker-chair near the low table on which the tea had been served, and of two younger men strolling to and fro, in desultory talk, in front of him. The old man had his cup in his hand; it was an unusually large cup, of a different pattern from the rest of the set and painted in brilliant colours. He disposed of its contents with much circumspection, holding it for a long time close to his chin, with his face turned to the house. His companions had either finished their tea or were indifferent to their privilege; they smoked cigarettes as they continued to stroll. One of them, from time to time, as he passed,   30 looked with a certain attention at the elder man, who, unconscious of observation, rested his eyes upon the rich red front of his dwelling. The house that rose beyond the lawn was a structure to repay such consideration and was the most characteristic object in the peculiarly English picture I have attempted to sketch.

THE PORTRAIT OF A LADY *Henry James* □

■ I wish either my father or my mother, or indeed both of them, as they were in duty both equally bound to it, had minded what they were about when they begot me; had they duly considered how much depended upon what they were then doing; – that not only the production of a rational Being was concerned in it, but that possibly the happy formation and temperature of his body, perhaps his genius and the very cast of his mind; – and, for aught they knew to the contrary,

even the fortunes of his whole house might take their turn from the
humours and dispositions which were then uppermost: – Had they
duly weighed and considered all this, and proceeded accordingly, – I   10
am verily persuaded I should have made a quite different figure in the
world, from that, in which the reader is likely to see me. – Believe me,
good folks, this is not so inconsiderable a thing as many of you may
think it; – you have all, I dare say, heard of the animal spirits, as how
they are transfused from father to son &c. &c. – and a great deal to that
purpose: – Well, you may take my word, that nine parts in ten of a
man's sense or his nonsense, his successes and miscarriages in this
world depend upon their motions and activity, and the different tracts
and trains you put them into, so that when they are once set a-going,
whether right or wrong, 'tis not a halfpenny matter, – away they go   20
cluttering like hey-go-mad; and by treading the same steps over and
over again, they presently make a road of it, as plain and as smooth as a
garden-walk, which, when they are once used to, the Devil himself
sometimes shall not be able to drive them off it.

TRISTRAM SHANDY Laurence Sterne □

1 'Under certain circumstances there are few hours in life more agreeable . . .' (1)

How does this opening sentence set the tone for the rest of the first extract?

2 Both extracts are written in the first person. Contrast the manner in which the authors
use first person narrative.

3 Analyse the sentence construction used in both extracts. Compare the kind and length
of sentences used and relate that to the content and theme of the extracts.

The passages below both deal with the reactions of a character to the city scene
in which he finds himself.

■ I walked up Half Moon Street. After the gay tumult of Piccadilly it had a
pleasant silence. It was sedate and respectable. Most of the houses let
apartments, but this was not advertised by the vulgarity of a card; some
had a brightly polished brass plate, like a doctor's, to announce the fact
and others the word *Apartments* neatly painted on the fanlight. One or
two with an added discretion merely gave the name of the proprietor,
so that if you were ignorant you might have thought it a tailor's or a
money lender's. There was none of the congested traffic of Jermyn
Street, where also they let rooms, but here and there a smart car,
unattended, stood outside a door and occasionally at another a taxi   10
deposited a middle-aged lady. You had the feeling that the people who
lodged here were not gay and a trifle disreputable as in Jermyn Street,

racing men who rose in the morning with headaches and asked for a hair of the dog that bit them, but respectable women from the country who came up for six weeks for the London season and elderly gentlemen who belonged to exclusive clubs. You felt that they came year after year to the same house and perhaps had known the proprietor when he was still in private service. My own Miss Fellows had been cook in some very good places, but you would never have guessed it had you seen her walking along to do her shopping in   20 Shepherd's Market. She was not stout, red-faced and blousy as one expects a cook to be; she was spare and very upright, neatly but fashionably dressed, a woman of middle age with determined features; her lips were rouged and she wore an eyeglass. She was businesslike, quiet, coolly cynical and very expensive.

The rooms I occupied were on the ground floor. The parlour was papered with an old marbled paper and on the walls were water colours of romantic scenes, cavaliers bidding good-bye to their ladies and knights of old banqueting in stately halls; there were large ferns in pots, and the armchairs were covered with faded leather. There was   30 about the room an amusing air of the eighteen eighties, and when I looked out of the window I expected to see a private hansom rather than a Chrysler. The curtains were of a heavy red rep.

CAKES AND ALE *Somerset Maugham* □

■ It was the hour of twilight on a soft spring day towards the end of April in the year of Our Lord 1929, and George Webber leaned his elbows on the sill of his back window and looked out at what he could see of New York. His eye took in the towering mass of the new hospital at the end of the block, its upper floors set back in terraces, the soaring walls salmon coloured in the evening light. This side of the hospital, and directly opposite, was the lower structure of the annexe, where the nurses and the waitresses lived. In the rest of the block half a dozen old brick houses, squeezed together in a solid row, leaned wearily against each other and showed their backsides to him.   10

The air was strangely quiet. All the noises of the city were muted here into a distant hum, so unceasing that it seemed to belong to silence. Suddenly, through the open windows at the front of the house came the raucous splutter of a truck starting up at the loading platform of the warehouse across the street. The heavy motor warmed up with a full-throated roar, then there was a grinding clash of gears, and George felt the old house tremble under him as the truck swung out into the street and thundered off. The noise receded, grew fainter, then faded into the general hum, and all was quiet as before.

As George leaned looking out of his back window a nameless   20 happiness welled within him and he shouted over to the waitresses in the hospital annexe, who were ironing out as usual their two pairs of drawers and their flimsy little dresses. He heard, as from a great distance, the faint shouts of children playing in the streets, and, near at hand, the low voices of the people in the houses. He watched the cool, steep shadows, and saw how the evening light was moving in the little squares of yards, each of which had in it something intimate, familiar, and revealing – a patch of earth in which a pretty woman had been setting out flowers, working earnestly for hours and wearing a big straw hat and canvas gloves; a little plot of new-sown grass, solemnly 30 watered every evening by a man with a square red face and a bald head; a little shed or playhouse or workshop for some business man's spare-time hobby; or a gay-painted table, some easy lounging chairs, and a huge bright-striped garden parasol to cover it, and a good-looking girl who had been sitting there all afternoon reading, with a coat thrown over her shoulders and a tall drink at her side.

Through some enchantment of the quiet and the westering light and the smell of April in the air, it seemed to George that he knew these people all around him. He loved this old house on Twelfth Street, its red brick walls, its rooms of noble height and spaciousness, its old dark 40 woods and floors that creaked; and in the magic of the moment it seemed to be enriched and given a profound and lonely dignity by all the human beings it had sheltered in its ninety years. The house became like a living presence. Every object seemed to have an animate vitality of its own – walls, rooms, chairs, tables, even a half-wet bath towel hanging from the shower ring above the tub, a coat thrown down upon a chair, and his papers, manuscripts, and books scattered about the room in wild confusion.

The simple joy he felt at being once more a part of such familiar things also contained an element of strangeness and unreality. With a 50 sharp stab of wonder he reminded himself, as he had done a hundred times in the last few weeks, that he had really come home again – home to America, home to Manhattan's swarming rock, and home again to love; and his happiness was faintly edged with guilt when he remembered that less than a year before he had gone abroad in anger and despair, seeking to escape what now he had returned to.

YOU CAN'T GO HOME AGAIN *Thomas Wolfe* ☐

1 Both extracts deal with a description of a city scene.
  a Compare the standpoints of the two descriptions.
  b Which of the two protagonists – the 'I' of the first extract, George in the second – is, in your opinion, more integrated with the scenes described in the extracts? Give reasons for your answer.

2 Compare the language used by the two writers and show how the difference in the kind of language used reflects the different tone of the extracts. In particular, consider how they use descriptive detail.

Chapter 7
The Variety of Poetry

The opening chapter of this section of the book looks at a variety of modern and traditional verse and focuses on some of the poetic techniques employed by writers to express themselves.

Before looking at this section, it is worth looking back at the introduction to the book, where two characters discuss prose and poetry in a passage from a play by Molière and some conclusions are drawn about the nature of prose and poetry.

In the play, one of the characters observes that 'whatever isn't prose is verse and anything that isn't verse is prose.' The distinction between what is prose and what is poetry tended to be fairly clear-cut in past centuries. However, in this century, the scope of the content and subject matter of poetry has broadened to include any theme with which a poet wishes to deal. As a result, many modern poets have also brought prose and poetry much closer together in terms of the language they use and in the form of their poems. Since there are no longer any barriers to the kind of themes with which poetry can deal, poets have naturally sought for language which is suitable for expressing new subject-matter. For this reason, there is no longer a distinct and separate poetic diction. Poetic forms have loosened up as well; poets often create their own forms as an extension of their poems' content.

In the past poets were much more wedded to established forms, such as the sonnet, the lyric and the epic poem. Other traditional shaping influences on poetry are conventional metrical patterns, rhyme and structure of stanzas. All these various aspects of poetic form will be discussed in the coming chapters. An important point to grasp, however, is that the development of English poetry has led poets gradually away from conventional forms, themes and poetic language (diction) to a freedom of form and expression. This poetic freedom does not guarantee better poetry, of course; indeed, the absence of external disciplines of form and diction may have created problems for modern poets, as well as a welcome freedom.

The Ballad

Before poems began to be written down and printed, poetry was mainly an oral art-form; wandering balladeers would tell stories to the community in verse form. To help tell their stories memorably, the balladeers would employ repetition, rhyme and insistent rhythms in the verse. These elements – rhyme, rhythm, repetition – are the most distinctive characteristics of poetry for most people and they developed from the oral tradition of poetry, preserved in ballads like the one below, which we can still read today.

The poem takes the form of a dialogue between a mother and her son, Edward. Edward's replies to his mother's insistent questions eventually lead to a grisly revelation. Read the poem aloud, and as you do, notice the rhythm, rhyme and repetition of the verse.

■ EDWARD, EDWARD

'Why does your brand sae drop wi' blude,
        Edward, Edward?
Why does your brand sae drop wi' blude,
        And why sae sad gang ye, O?' –
'O I hae kill'd my hawk sae gude,
        Mither, mither;
O I hae kill'd my hawk sae gude,
        And I had nae mair but he, O.'   8

'Your hawk's blude was never sae red,
        Edward, Edward;
Your hawk's blude was never sae red,
        My dear son, I tell thee, O.' –
'O I hae kill'd my red-roan steed,
        Mither, mither;
O I hae kill'd my red-roan steed,
        That erst was sae fair and free, O.'   16

Your steed was auld, and ye hae got mair,
        Edward, Edward;
Your steed was auld, and ye hae got mair,
        Some other dule ye dree, O.' –
'O I hae kill'd my father dear,
        Mither, mither;
O I hae kill'd my father dear,
        Alas, and wae is me, O.'   24

'And whatten penance will ye dree for that,
        Edward, Edward?
Whatten penance will ye dree for that?
        My dear son, now tell me, O.' –
'I'll set my feet in yonder boat,
        Mither, mither;
I'll set my feet in yonder boat,
        And I'll fare over the sea, O.'   32

143

'And what will ye do wi' your tow'rs and your ha',
    Edward, Edward?
And what will ye do wi' your tow'rs and your ha',
    That were sae fair to see, O?' –
'I'll let them stand till they doun fa',
    Mither, mither;
I'll let them stand till they doun fa',
    For here never mair maun I be, O.'   40

'And what will ye leave to your bairns and your wife,
    Edward, Edward?
And what will ye leave to your bairns and your wife,
    When ye gang owre the sea, O?' –
'The warld's room: let them beg through life,
    Mither, mither;
The warld's room; let them beg through life;
    For them never mair will I see, O.'   48

'And what will ye leave to your ain mither dear,
    Edward, Edward?
And what will ye leave to your ain mither dear,
    My dear son, now tell me O?' –
'The curse of hell frae me sall ye bear,
    Mither, mither;
The curse of hell frae me sall ye bear:
    Sic counsels ye gave to me, O!'   56

Traditional □

The poem's formal elements (rhythm, rhyme, repetition, the dialogue) are all traditional features of this kind of verse. However, they are there because they each have a part to play in contributing towards the effect the ballad would have on its audience by underlining the mounting tension and horror of the poem. The question-and-answer form is very dramatic and, allied to the story-line, creates the tension of the poem, while the repetition and rhythm emphasise the emotional effect of the ballad. It can easily be imagined how impressively a skilled balladeer could tell this tale to an assembled audience.

Each of the seven verses has the same structure; choose one verse and identify its various formal elements. Consider how the formal elements reinforce the effect of the poem, echoing or underlining the meaning of the words.

Allowing for some minor difficulties of understanding you may have had with the Scots dialect in which the ballad is written, how would you describe the kind of language used in the poem? Does it suit the needs of the story and the kind of occasion and audience for which the ballads were created?

● Read some more ballads and compare their treatment of theme and use of rhythm, repetition, dramatic technique and language with that of *Edward, Edward*.

● Some rock and pop singers such as Bob Dylan are considered by many people to be contemporary ballad singers. Look at the lyrics of some of these modern balladeers and consider whether their verse shares characteristics with the old balladeers.

The Poet's Theme

What poets have to say in their poetry is just as important (most people would say more important) as the way it is said. This may seem an obvious thing to state, but often discussion of a poem becomes an analysis of poetic technique which is divorced from the poem as a whole. It is important to stress early on in this part of the book that although rhythm, language (diction), form and other elements of the poet's technique will be discussed as aspects of poetry, these poetic elements should always be seen as integral parts of the total meaning and impact of the poetry, rather than as features to be considered in their own right.

Two things that people often think about poetry are that it is usually difficult to understand and that it is divorced from real life. However, poetry need not be difficult to understand, as the following poem will show, but this is not to deny that many good poems repay careful, detailed reading and analysis: that is what this book aims to encourage. As for the statement that poetry is usually divorced from real life and is rather airy-fairy, there is such a huge body of poetry that deals with burning issues and people's real concerns that this argument can easily be disposed of.

The following poem deals very directly with an emotional situation faced by many people. The poet is a black American woman and the idiom of the poem reflects Afro-American culture and language.

■ IF HE LET US GO NOW

       let me strap.
the baby in the seat, just don't say
nothing all that while . . .
           I move round to
the driver side of the car. The air
warm and dry here. Lawd know what it be
in L.A. He open the door for me
and I slide behind the wheel. Baby
facin me lookin without even
blinkin his eye. I wonder if he   10
know I'm his mamma that I love him

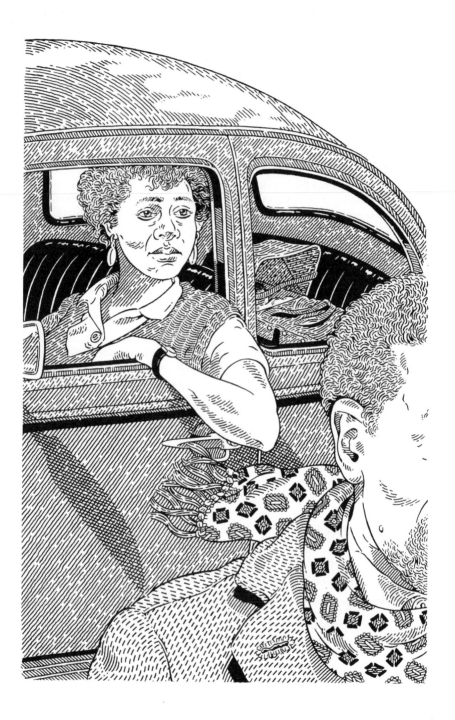

that that his daddy by the door (and
he won't let us go; he still got time
to say wait). Baby blink once but
he only five week old and whatever
he know don't show.
                              His daddy call
my name and I turn to him and wait.
It be cold in the Grapevine at night
this time of year. Wind come whistlin down   20
through them mountains almost blow this old
VW off the road. I'll be in
touch he say. Say, take care; say, write if
you need somethin.
                              I *will* him to touch
us now, to take care us, to know what
we need is him and his name. He slap
the car door, say, drive careful and turn
to go. If he let us go now . . . how
we gon ever take him back? I ease   30
out on the clutch, mash in on the gas.
The only answer I get is his back.

Shirley Williams ☐

The theme of *If he let us go now* is the woman's fear of losing the father of her
child. That is what the poem essentially is about. The poet treats the theme in
terms of an incident when the mother and child are about to leave on a car
journey: this is the content of the poem.

The leave-taking incident is dramatised in the poem; we follow the thoughts of
the woman and we hear the words the man says to the woman. The poem is a
story as well, however slight; there is a narrative element. The story begins
with the mother strapping the baby into the car and ends with her driving the
car away:

                              . . . I ease
out on the clutch, mash in on the gas. (30–31)

All these elements make up the treatment of the poet's theme. It is useful at
times to make a distinction between theme and treatment. The theme is the
core or essence of the poem; the treatment is how the poet realises that theme
in terms of the content of the poem.

How would you describe the kind of language used in the poem? Bearing in
mind what is said in the introduction to the poem about poetry dealing with
people's real concerns, how effective do you think the idiom of the poem is in
communicating the poet's theme?

● In the poem by Shirley Williams, we follow events through the consciousness of the woman in the poem. The poem is written in the first person and the other person involved is seen through the eyes of the woman.

Using a similar technique (first person narrative and the consciousness of one person), write a poem based on one of the following situations:

the parting of two lovers, friends or close relatives

someone leaving home or a place he or she loves

Lyric Poetry

A lyric is a form of poetry that was originally written to be sung to musical accompaniment, but we now ascribe the adjective lyrical to poetry that is a brief expression of love, joy or the beauties of nature.

Below is a poem about youth and its response to nature, written by Robert Buchanan (1841–1901). When reading verse it is important to sub-vocalise (to sub-vocalise is to read aloud in one's head) so that the aural qualities of the poem can be appreciated.

■ THE YOUNG WERE MERRIER

Ah, through the moonlight of autumnal years
How sweet the back-look of our first youth-world!
Freshlier and earlier the Spring burst then:
The wild brook warbled to a sweeter tune,
Through Summer shaws that screened from brighter suns;
The berry glittered and the brown nut fell   6
Ruddier and riper in the Autumn woods;
And Winter drifting on more glorious car
Shed purer snows or shot intenser frost!
The young were merrier when our life was young;
Dropped mellower wisdom from the tongue of age,
And love and friendship were immortal things . . .   12

Robert Buchanan □

Robert Buchanan looks back at the feelings of youth from the slightly melancholy perspective of old age:

Ah, through the moonlight of autumnal years
How sweet the back-look of our first youth-world! (1–2)

An extra value and intensity is added to the strength of youthful feelings when they are put beside the paler emotion of old age.

One of the most important factors in this portrayal is the poem's aural impact. This is frequently achieved by the use of alliteration (see page 95). Alliteration is the repetition of initial consonants in words next to, or in close proximity to, one another; it is a way of emphasising and adding to meaning. It can give rise to sweet-sounding verse or harsh, grating sounds.

> Ruddier and riper in the Autumn woods; (7)

Here the repetition of the 'r' sound emphasises the roundness and fecundity of autumn.

> The wild brook warbled to a sweeter tune,
> Through summer shaws that screened from brighter suns; (4–5)

The alliteration of 'wild/warbled' and 'sweeter/summer shaws/screened/suns' gives a happy, lyrical note to these lines. The sound of this poem is an integral part of its meaning; alliteration is not only a linking device but also helps to underline the tone and theme of the poem.

Are there any other instances of alliteration? What do they add to the poem?

Alliteration is not Buchanan's only way of using language creatively. Look at the second and third lines of the poem. What is unusual about the language here? Why do you think Buchanan does this?

Form and Content

The next poem is by an American poet, Robert Creeley. As you read the poem, notice its form and bear in mind what Creeley himself has written about poetic form:

> Form is never more than an extension of content.

By this he means that the form of a poem is not independent of its content but serves and emerges from the subject-matter.

■ IF YOU

> If you were going to get a pet
> what kind of animal would you get.
>
> A soft-bodied dog, a hen –
> feathers and fur to begin it again.
>
> When the sun goes down and it gets dark
> I saw an animal in a park.
>
> Bring it home, to give it to you.
> I have seen animals break in two.   8
>
> You were hoping for something soft
> and loyal and clean and wondrously careful –

> a form of otherwise vicious habit
> can have long ears and be called a rabbit.
>
> Dead. Died. Will die. Want.
> Morning, midnight. I asked you,
>
> if you were going to get a pet
> what kind of animal would you get.   16
>
> *Robert Creeley* □

The content has something child-like about it. This is reflected in the form of the poem by the rhyming couplets the poet uses and the rondo effect, whereby the poem begins and ends with the same lines. But there is a contrast also between form and theme; beneath the surface theme and the air of simplicity given to the poem by its similarity in form to a nursery rhyme, there are hints of something darker, of innocence cloaking evil. In his choice of form and language, the poet reveals that duality of vision.

Do you find the way the poem develops surprising after the first few lines? Where does the turning point come? What do you think the theme of the poem is? How do the language and form contribute to the poem?

The Use of Imagery

A poet has a theme, which is realised or conveyèd in the content of the poetry. In order to achieve this, the poet searches for diction that expresses concisely what he or she has to say.

Both prose writers and poets seek to express ideas and emotions in their writing, but the language of poetry is more concentrated and weighty than the language of prose, generally speaking. This need to concentrate language leads the poet to find images that will communicate the feelings or ideas that form the theme of the poem to the reader. Imagery is the collective word for images, which are pictures, sounds, tastes or sensations created in the reader's mind by the poet's words. A writer often aims by the use of imagery to develop the theme by making connections for the reader between things that may not have had connections before.

Imagery is generally considered to involve comparison, for example in metaphors and similes. Some people argue, however, that imagery can also be literal and realistic; diction that describes or merely names objects also usually brings forth images in the reader's mind. These literal images may have as much emotional impact on the reader as imagery that is figurative and non-literal, as it is in metaphors.

To illustrate the use of imagery, we are going to look at the lyric of a song written by a twentieth-century master of the popular song, Cole Porter. He uses metaphor after metaphor, image after image, to express the singer's admiration for his love.

■ YOU'RE THE TOP

At words poetic I'm so pathetic
that I always found it best,
Instead of getting them off my chest,
to let them rest unexpressed.
I hate parading my serenading
As I'll probably miss a bar,
But if this ditty
Is not so pretty
At least it'll show how great you are.
You're the top! You're the Colosseum,   10
You're the top! You're the Louvre Museum,
You're a melody
From a symphony by Strauss,
You're a Bendel bonnet, a Shakespeare sonnet,
You're Mickey Mouse.
You're the Nile, you're the Tower of Pisa,
You're the smile on the Mona Lisa;
I'm a worthless cheque, a total wreck, a flop,
But if Baby I'm the bottom,
You're the top!   20
You're the top! You're Mahatma Ghandi,
You're the top, you're Napoleon brandy,
You're the purple light
Of a summer night in Spain,
You're the National Gallery,
You're Garbo's salary,
You're cellophane,
You're sublime, you're a turkey dinner,
You're the time of the Derby winner,
I'm a toy balloon that is fated soon to pop;   30
But if Baby I'm the bottom,
You're the top!

Cole Porter □

Metaphors are the transference of the qualities of one thing to another thing:

> ... You're the Colosseum,
> ... You're the Louvre Museum, (10–11)

In these examples, the qualities of splendour and beauty associated with the Colosseum and the Louvre are transferred to the person being serenaded. The meaning of the metaphors in Cole Porter's lyrics is quite clear; the person is seen as very special and so the serenader gathers together images of excellence from various fields: architecture, art, music, fashion etc.

Look at the portrayal of the subject of the serenade in comparison with that of the serenader. What do the metaphors express about the latter?

As well as admiration and self-denigration, what else does the tone of the metaphors convey?

● Write the lyric for a song with a title beginning *You're the*... (finish the title yourself). The lyric should be addressed to a well-known public figure, for example, a politician or show business star. You must find metaphors that express feelings about this person, as Porter's song does.

Imagery in many poems is not as direct as that in the lyric by Cole Porter; the reader may not at first realise the full meaning or impact of a poem's imagery. It can have an accumulative impact reflecting the emotional tone of the verse. Imagery sometimes conveys meaning in a subtle, elusive manner. Indeed, this elusive quality of poetry is one of its characteristic features: not all poems can be analysed completely in a cut-and-dried fashion, stating that *this* is the meaning. Many, many poems have layers of meaning that escape final definition. Metaphor plays an important part in creating this depth of meaning in poetry. In the poem below by W.R. Rodgers, there is scarcely a line that does not contain a metaphor.

■ WHITE CHRISTMAS

Punctually at Christmas the soft plush
Of sentiment snows down, embosoms all
The sharp and pointed shapes of venom, shawls
The hills and hides the shocking holes of this
Uneven world of want and wealth, cushions
With cosy wish like cotton-wool the cool
Arm's-length interstices of caste and class,
And into obese folds subtracts from sight
All truculent acts, bleeding the world white.   9

Punctually that glib pair, Peace and Goodwill,
Emerge royally to take the air,
Collect the bows, assimilate the smiles,
Of waiting men. It is a genial time.
Angels, like stalactites, descend from heaven;
Bishops distribute their own weight in words,
Congratulate the poor on Christlike lack,
And the member for the constituency
Feeds the five thousand, and has plenty back.   18

Punctually to-night, in cold stone circles
Of set reunion, families stiffly sit
And listen: this is the night, and this the happy time
When the tinned milk of human kindness is
Upheld and holed by radio-appeal.
Hushed are hurrying heels on hard roads,
And every parlour's a pink pond of light
To the cold and travelling man going by
In the dark, without a bark or a bite.   27

But punctually to-morrow you will see
All this silent and dissembling world
Of stilted sentiment suddenly melt
Into mush and watery welter of words
Beneath the warm and moving traffic of
Feet and actual fact. Over the stark plain
The silted mill-chimneys once again spread
Their sackcloth and ashes, a flowing mane
Of repentance for the false day that's fled.   36

W.R. Rodgers □

W.R. Rodgers' poem is realised almost entirely through its imagery. The metaphors, together with the occasional simile, are an integral part of the poem's meaning.

The poet's satirical theme is revealed in the metaphors he uses, from the first:

> ... the soft plush
> Of sentiment snows down ...   (1–2)

to the last:

> ... a flowing mane
> Of repentance for the false day that's fled. (35–6)

For the poem to convey its full import, the reader must be able to interpret the meaning of its metaphors: study the poem's metaphors and discuss how they help the poet to communicate his feelings.

Rhythm and Tension in Poetry

This chapter began with a look at an old ballad and its use of the dialogue form as well as of rhythm, repetition and directness of language was noted. The ballad style has been imitated by some twentieth-century poets; among them is W.H. Auden, who, in the poem below, uses to advantage the repetitive, insistent rhythm of the ballad, with its direct expression and simple form. The poem takes the form of a dramatic duologue; try reading it with someone else, taking one part each.

■ O WHAT IS THAT SOUND?

O what is that sound which so thrills the ear
    Down in the valley drumming, drumming?
Only the scarlet soldiers, dear,
    The soldiers coming.

O what is that light I see flashing so clear
    Over the distance brightly, brightly?
Only the sun on their weapons, dear,
    As they step lightly.   8

O what are they doing with all that gear,
    What are they doing this morning, this morning?
Only their usual manoeuvres, dear,
    Or perhaps a warning.

O why have they left the road down there?
    Why are they suddenly wheeling, wheeling?
Perhaps a change in their orders, dear.
    Why are you kneeling?   16

O haven't they stopped for the doctor's care,
    Haven't they reined their horses, their horses?
Why, they are none of them wounded, dear,
    None of these forces.

O is it the parson they want, with white hair,
    Is it the parson, is it, is it?
No, they are passing his gateway, dear,
    Without a visit.   24

O it must be the farmer who lives so near.
    It must be the farmer so cunning, so cunning?
They have passed the farmyard already, dear,
    And now they are running.

O where are you going? Stay with me here!
    Were the vows you swore deceiving, deceiving?
No, I promised to love you, dear,
    But I must be leaving.   32

O it's broken the lock and splintered the door,
    O it's the gate where they're turning, turning;
Their boots are heavy on the floor
    And their eyes are burning.

W.H. Auden □

Like the traditional ballad, *Edward, Edward* at the beginning of the chapter, *O What is that Sound?* takes the form of a dialogue with a question-and-answer structure, which underlines the growing tension of the poem. The repetition and directness of expression are also very similar.

The reasons why the soldiers are coming are left unexplained, which adds to the menace of their approach. This lack of direct explanation has an echo too in *Edward, Edward*, in the way that the murder in that ballad is revealed gradually, but the motives for the deed are left wreathed in mystery. Feelings of horror and persecution are stirred up by both poems; the best poems have a resonance of meaning that stays with the reader, reverberating in the mind and stirring up emotions.

The rhythm of the verse in *O What is that Sound?* is so emphatic and important to its meaning that it is almost impossible to discuss it as a separate topic from the total meaning of the poem. The mounting tension, the insistent drumming rhythms, the sense of the approaching soldiers, the growing fear – all these elements are integrated in the total aural impact of the poem. Sound, rhythm and meaning are totally one – if the rhythms of the verse were altered in any way, then the meaning of the poem would be changed. This poem is a very apt reminder that the elements usually associated with poetry – rhythm, the aural impact of words, rhyme and repetition – are all interlinked and form part of the whole meaning of the poetry.

Look at the poem again and study Auden's use of rhythm. Is the rhythm the same thoughout the poem or does it speed up and slow down according to the meaning of the words? Does the poet use the rhythm to place stress on the most important words?

Do you think the last two lines of the poem make an effective ending to it?

Ideas in Poetry

Sometimes the reader has to work at a poem to extract its full meaning. Poetry is not only about emotions; ideas can be handled in verse just as they can in prose. Robert Buchanan in *The Young were Merrier* dealt with nature and its immediacy in young people's lives in a direct, lyrical and uncomplicated manner. Denise Levertov in the poem below takes nature as her starting-point but engages the theme not only emotionally but on a philosophical level as well.

■ BEYOND THE END

In 'nature' there's no choice –
               flowers
swing their heads in the wind, sun & moon
    are as they are. But we seem
almost to have it (not just
    available death)   6

It's energy: a spider's thread: not to
'go on living' but to quicken, to activate: extend:
   Some have it, they force it –
with work or laughter or even
   the act of buying, if that's
all they can lay their hands on –
      the girls crowding the stores, where light,
       colour, solid dreams are – what gay
     desire! It's their festival,
       ring game, wassail, mystery.   16

It has no grace like that of
the grass, the humble rhythms, the
falling & rising of leaf and star;
it's barely
a constant. Like salt:
take it or leave it.   22

The 'hewers of wood' & so on; every damn
craftsman has it while he's working
   but it's not
a question of work: some
shine with it, in repose. Maybe it is
response, the will to respond – ('reason
can give nothing at all/like
the response to desire') maybe
a gritting of the teeth, to go
just that much further, beyond the end
beyond whatever ends: to begin, to be, to defy.   33

Denise Levertov □

In the introduction to this chapter it was said that poets often create their own forms as an extension of the content of their poems. Denise Levertov uses the form of her verse to express her subject-matter in her philosophical poem. In order to see this it is necessary to examine how she relates the structure of her verse to her theme.

Some lines in the poem have no pause at the end of the line: the sense of the poetry means that one line flows without pause into the next one. These are examples of run-on lines or enjambment. But where the sense of a line allows for a definite pause at the end of the line, then that is called an end-stopped line.

The flow of a poem is not only affected by whether the lines are run-on or end-stopped. In addition, there is usually a natural resting-place somewhere in a line of poetry:

> In 'nature' there's no choice – (1)

Read the first line of the poem aloud and you will notice that there is a natural break in the sense after 'nature'. Sometimes there is more than one caesura in a line (caesura is the name given to these rests in a line of poetry):

> It's energy: a spider's thread: not to
> 'go on living' but to quicken, to activate: extend: (7–8)

There are two caesuras in the first line, marked by the colons; there are three caesuras in the second line, after 'living', 'quicken' and 'activate'. The first of these two lines is a run-on line; the second line is an end-stopped line.

What does this tell us about the meaning and intention of the poem? In *Beyond the End*, the poet is wrestling with an idea, trying to analyse what choice is in human life, what energy is. The verse, which alternates between a flowing and a staccato rhythm, reflects this struggle by the poet to refine her thoughts. This is the reason for the large number of caesuras in the lines above and for the fragmented rhythms of these lines:

> . . . to go
> just that much further, beyond the end
> beyond whatever ends: to begin, to be, to defy. (31–33)

The rhythm and form of the verse emerge from the content of the poem. The poet is struggling towards a statement about human choice and energy and that very struggle to illuminate, to get at the idea she is groping for, is reflected not only in the language but also in the rhythm and flow of the verse.

Discuss how generally the content, form and rhythm of the verse reflect this thoughtful, analytical intention on the part of the poet. As part of this, consider also why some lines consist of one, two or three words only. Does the way in which the poem is laid out on the page have any importance?

Both Levertov in this poem and Robert Buchanan in *The Young were Merrier* (page 148), express a response to nature. How does the use they make of nature in their poems differ?

Love Poetry

To close the introductory chapter to this part of the book, we turn to two poems about a perennial theme of poets – love between men and women. The first poem, by the nineteenth-century poet Robert Browning (1812–1889), is about two lovers meeting; the second, by the American poet Amy Lowell (1874–1925), is about lovers parting.

■ MEETING AT NIGHT

The grey sea and the long black land;
And the yellow half-moon large and low;
And the startled little waves that leap
In fiery ringlets from their sleep,
As I gain the cove with pushing prow,
And quench its speed i' the slushy sand.

Then a mile of warm sea-scented beach;
Three fields to cross till a farm appears;
A tap at the pane, the quick sharp scratch
And blue spurt of a lighted match,
And a voice less loud, thro' its joys and fears,
Then the two hearts beating each to each!

Robert Browning □

■ THE TAXI

When I go away from you
The world beats dead
Like a slackened drum.
I call out for you against the jutted stars
And shout into the ridges of the wind.
Streets coming fast,
One after the other,
Wedge you away from me,
And the lamps of the city prick my eyes
So that I can no longer see your face.
Why should I leave you,
To wound myself upon the sharp edges of the night?

Amy Lowell □

Contrasting cadences reflect the very different moods and themes of the two poems: cadences are the rises and falls of language. As *Meeting at Night* is full of expectancy and excitement, the cadences are mainly rising:

And the startled little waves that leap
In fiery ringlets from their sleep (3–4)

The mood of *The Taxi* is of resignation and loss; the cadence of the verse is falling:

The world beats dead
Like a slackened drum. (2–3)

When those lines are read aloud, the voice naturally falls.

Other stylistic features also reflect the difference in theme. The diction Browning uses is full of energy: 'startled', 'fiery', 'pushing', 'speed', 'warm', 'quick', 'sharp', 'spurt', 'lighted'. The diction of the Lowell poem is desolate and hard: 'dead', 'slackened', 'jutted', 'ridges', 'wedge', 'prick', 'wound', 'sharp edges'. Both poets have expressed their emotions very directly: their intentions are very different and this is reflected in the diction and rhythms.

Browning and Lowell use imagery strikingly in their poems. Pick out some examples of this and consider what its purpose is.

Meeting at Night consists of two sentences only, while *The Taxi* is composed mainly of very short lines. Are either of these two facts significant for the mood and meaning of the poems?

Chapter 8
Theme and Content

In Chapter 7, the distinction between the theme and content of poems was introduced (page 147).

By theme we mean what the poem is really about, the underlying idea or emotion, the description of the poem as a whole: its essence.

By content we mean the actual treatment the poet gives to the theme, the manner in which the poet realises the theme in the poem.

If a poet is writing a poem about loneliness, it is not enough to state the emotion 'I am lonely' over and over again; he or she must find effective ways of communicating that feeling in the poem's subject matter. Nor, when poetry is being evaluated critically, will a poet be admired merely for having attempted to deal with interesting themes in his or her poetry; we give credit to a poet for realising a theme forcefully, beautifully, wittily or sensitively. A critical analysis of a poem and the way a poet has handled a chosen theme will involve looking at the language, tone, form, imagery, rhythm and other features of the verse.

Before moving on to critical evaluation of poems, however, it is necessary to identify their themes and then go on to analyse the particular treatment the poets have given to those. Only after this should the critical evaluation be made. This chapter takes a look at the way particular poets have realised their themes in the content of their poems. Sometimes poems will be studied in pairs so that it is possible to compare the way different poets have dealt with a similar theme or subject.

The theme of the poem below is realised in the form of one extended metaphor: the battle between winter and spring is described in terms of a commentary on a boxing match.

■ THE FIGHT OF THE YEAR

'And there goes the bell for the third month
and Winter comes out of its corner looking groggy
Spring leads with a left to the head
followed by a sharp right to the body
        daffodils
        primroses
        crocuses
        snowdrops
        lilacs
        violets   10
        pussywillow
Winter can't take much more punishment
and Spring shows no sign of tiring
        tadpoles
        squirrels
        baaalambs
        badgers
        bunny rabbits
        mad march hares
        horses and hounds   20
Spring is merciless
Winter won't go the full twelve rounds
        bobtail clouds
        scallywaggy winds
        the sun
        a pavement artist
        in every town
A left to the chin
and Winter's down!
    1 tomatoes   30
    2 radish
    3 cucumber
    4 onions
    5 beetroot
    6 celery
    7 and any
    8 amount
    9 of lettuce
   10 for dinner
Winter's out for the count   40
Spring is the winner.'

Roger McGough □

There is one simple concept behind *The Fight of the Year*: the tussle between
Winter and Spring is perceived in terms of a boxing match, an extended
metaphor that is used throughout the poem. The theme of the poem is
expressed entirely within the metaphor.

1a How is the metaphor of the boxing match established in the first four lines of the poem?
  b Explain how it is continued through the rest of the poem.

2 What light does the imagery throw on the theme and tone of the poem?

● In *The Fight of the Year*, the poet presents an account of the battle between the forces
of winter and spring in the form of a commentary on a boxing match. Use the same
metaphorical starting-point for a poem dealing with the struggle between any of the
following pairs:

    husband and wife   traffic warden and car owner   parent and child
    salesperson and customer   bureaucrat and ordinary citizen.

The need for a poet not only to choose an interesting theme, but also to handle
it well in the content of the poem has already been stressed in this chapter. The
previous poem, *The Fight of the Year* shows how important a part imagery can
play in realising a poem's theme. Through imagery, a poet can convey both the
emotional and the intellectual content of a poem. This is often done by making
connections between seemingly unlike things and is achieved by the use of
metaphor (and simile). For example, in *The Fight of the Year*, the slow yielding of
one season to another is described in terms of a boxing match.

The term imagery is normally taken to refer to language used in the way
described above: the words are figurative, with a metaphorical application (see
also pages 150–153). However, undoubtedly some poetic language evokes
concrete rather than figurative images in the reader's mind and these too can
have a similar impact. The poet can deliberately use these literal images to
convey thoughts and feelings to the reader; they too can acquire a symbolic
significance.

The following two extracts from the poetry of T.S. Eliot demonstrate the
realisation of theme through imagery and illustrate the similarity as well as the
difference between figurative and literal imagery.

■ PRELUDES

> The winter evening settles down
> With smell of steak in passageways.
> Six o'clock.
> The burnt-out ends of smoky days.
> And now a gusty shower wraps
> The grimy scraps
> Of withered leaves about your feet
> And newspapers from vacant lots;
> The showers beat
> On broken blinds and chimney-pots,
> And at the corner of the street
> A lonely cab-horse steams and stamps.
> And then the lighting of the lamps.

The extract above contains a mixture of concrete and figurative images. In the first line there is the metaphor of the winter evening as a living creature settling down for the night. It has an air of heaviness and inevitability. On the other hand, the 'smell of steak in passageways' is a literal image appealing to the reader's sense of smell. 'The burnt-out ends of smoky days' is a metaphor connecting the dying of the day with cigar or cigarette ends: it is a depressing image which seems to have connotations of waste and futility. The 'gusty shower', 'grimy scraps', 'withered leaves' and 'newspapers from vacant lots' are literal concrete images as are 'showers', 'broken blinds and chimney-pots', 'lonely cab-horse' and 'the lighting of the lamps'. All these images contribute to creating the melancholic atmosphere of the poem. They are used symbolically by the poet to represent aspects of city life on a winter evening. They are intended to provoke an emotional response in the reader.

Compare that extract with another poem by Eliot:

■ MORNING AT THE WINDOW

> They are rattling breakfast plates in basement kitchens,
> And along the trampled edges of the street
> I am aware of the damp souls of housemaids
> Sprouting despondently at area gates.
>
> The brown waves of fog toss up to me
> Twisted faces from the bottom of the street,
> And tear from a passer-by with muddy skirts
> An aimless smile that hovers in the air
> And vanishes along the level of the roofs.

The content, mood and theme of this poem are communicated almost entirely through Eliot's use of literal and figurative imagery. The poem's imagery serves the double purpose of describing the scene and conveying the poet's thoughts and feelings about it.

The literal images with which the poem begins establish its setting as early morning in town ('They are rattling breakfast plates in basement kitchens'), but notice also how the choice of the words 'rattling' and 'basement kitchens' gives a seedy atmosphere to the scene, an impression which is confirmed and developed in the rest of the poem.

Eliot's use of figurative imagery reinforces this picture. The unusual metaphor of the normally hard pavement being trampled under foot creates a bleak picture of the city streets. But the figurative imagery also adds depth to the poem. An insight into the quality of life of the people who inhabit this depressing environment is presented in the following lines:

> I am aware of the damp souls of housemaids
> Sprouting despondently at area gates. (3–4)

Eliot compares the housemaids to the plants which grow in the damp crevices of the basement area. The image combines the idea of growth with despair and decay: 'damp souls' suggests a fundamental rottenness, while 'Sprouting' carries the implication of unwanted and unhealthy growth.

In the second stanza, the imagery contributes on a literal level to the overall impression of hopelessness: the 'brown waves of fog' are used by Eliot to paint an ugly melancholy picture. But the stanza also contains two metaphors. The first of these compares the city to aspects of the sea hostile to man and the second compares the disembodied smile of a passer-by to a bird flying high and free above the earthbound people.

1 Examine Eliot's use of the metaphor comparing city life to the action of the sea in the second stanza of the poem. How do the phrases 'toss up'(5) and 'the bottom of the street' (6) help to develop the poet's theme? Why are the faces of passers-by described as 'Twisted' (6)?

2 In the final two lines of the poem Eliot uses the metaphor of a flying bird as the means of communicating his thoughts. What does this contribute to the mood and theme?

The totality of a poem is made up of various elements. Theme and content are expressed by diction, form and rhythm, and these elements are all intertwined with one another. Form is an extension of content; diction and imagery reflect theme and tone. The next poem is an excellent example of this creative process of content and theme extending into diction, imagery and form.

■ THE ABORTION

Somebody who should have been born
is gone.

Just as the earth puckered its mouth,
each bud puffing out from its knot,
I changed my shoes, and then drove south.

Up past the Blue Mountains, where
Pennsylvania humps on endlessly,
wearing like a crayoned cat, its green hair,

its roads sunken in like a grey washboard;
where, in truth, the ground cracks evilly,
a dark socket from which the coal has poured,   11

Somebody who should have been born
is gone.

the grass as bristly and stout as chives,
and me wondering when the ground would
    break,
and me wondering how anything fragile
    survives;

up in Pennsylvania, I met a little man,
not Rumpelstiltskin, at all, at all . . .
he took the fullness that love began.

Returning north, even the sky grew thin
like a high window looking nowhere.
The road was as flat as a sheet of tin,   24

Somebody who should have been born
is gone.

Yes, woman, such logic will lead
to loss without death. Or say what you
    meant,
you coward. . . this baby that I bleed.

Anne Sexton □

The fertile imagery of the first two stanzas of the poem:

> . . . the earth puckered its mouth,
> each bud puffing out from its knot, (3–4)

gives way to the sombre images of loss:

> a dark socket from which the coal has poured, (11)

> The road was as flat as a sheet of tin, (24)

To emphasise the poem's theme, there is an image of childhood; 'wearing like a crayoned cat, its green hair' as well as a reference to a fairy-tale character, Rumpelstiltskin. Theme, content, diction and imagery are wholly integrated in this poem.

1 'Returning north, even the sky grew thin
like a high window looking nowhere.' (22–23)

How does the imagery of the poem reveal the emotional state of the narrator? What contribution do the images of childhood make?

2 Show how the poet combines narrative and imagery to realise her theme. How successful do you think she is?

3 *'Somebody who should have been born
is gone.'* (1–2, 12–13, 25–26)

Comment on how the form of the poem contributes to its theme, paying particular attention to these lines.

● Anne Sexton's poem deals with the effect of the abortion on the woman. The imagery of the poem reflects her emotional response to the operation.

Imagine that you are in one of the following situations and write a poem about it, using imagery to express your emotional reaction:

attending a funeral of a close relative or friend

recovering from a serious operation

having just heard some news that has changed your life

The next two poems both take as their subject the relationship of marriage, seen from the wife's point of view. The first one, written by a poet of the seventeenth century, is straightforward in tone and is an expression of love and happiness.

■ TO MY DEAR AND LOVING HUSBAND

If ever two were one, then surely we.
If ever man were loved by wife, then thee;
If ever wife was happy in a man,
Compare with me, ye women, if you can.
I prize thy love more than whole mines of gold
Or all the riches that the East doth hold.
My love is such that rivers cannot quench,
Nor ought but love from thee, give recompense.
Thy love is such I can no way repay,
The heavens reward thee manifold, I pray.
Then while we live, in love let's so persevere
That when we live no more, we may live ever.

Anne Bradstreet □

The tone of the poem is loving and tranquil. The diction, form and rhythm of the poem reflect this sense of well-being and balance. Notice how the lines of the poem are balanced harmoniously:

> If ever two were one,/then surely we.
> If ever man were loved by wife,/then thee; (1–2)

In each of these lines the poet is expressing, in different ways, the unity of feeling she and her husband share. Notice how the rhyming couplet helps to link the two lines together; in this way, the form of the poem underlines its theme.

1 'My love is such that rivers cannot quench,
  Nor ought but love from thee, give recompense.
  Thy love is such I can no way repay,
  The heavens reward thee manifold, I pray.' (7–10)

  Show how the rhythm and form of these lines emphasise the poem's theme.

2 How does the content of the poem express its theme? What part does imagery play in this?

The second poem that takes marriage as its subject, by a contemporary Irish writer, is more complex in its attitude and is perhaps deliberately ambiguous.

■ THE WIFE'S TALE

When I had spread it all on linen cloth
Under the hedge, I called them over.
The hum and gulp of the thresher ran down
And the big belt slewed to a standstill, straw
Hanging undelivered in the jaws.
There was such quiet that I heard their boots
Crunching the stubble twenty yards away.   7

He lay down and said 'Give these fellows theirs,
I'm in no hurry,' plucking grass in handfuls
And tossing it in the air. 'That looks well.'
(He nodded at my white cloth on the grass.)
'I declare a woman could lay out a field
Though boys like us have little call for cloths.'
He winked, then watched me as I poured a cup
And buttered the thick slices that he likes.
'It's threshing better than I thought, and mind
It's good clean seed. Away over there and look.'
Always this inspection has to be made
Even when I don't know what to look for.   19

But I ran my hand in the half-filled bags
Hooked to the slots. It was hard as shot,
Innumerable and cool. The bags gaped
Where the chutes ran back to the stilled drum
And forks were stuck at angles in the ground
As javelins might mark lost battlefields.
I moved between them back across the stubble.   26

They lay in the ring of their own crusts and dregs
Smoking and saying nothing. 'There's good yield,
Isn't there?' – as proud as if he were the land itself –
'Enough for crushing and for sowing both.'
And that was it. I'd come and he had shown me
So I belonged no further to the work.
I gathered cups and folded up the cloth
And went. But they still kept their ease
Spread out, unbuttoned, grateful, under the trees.   35

Seamus Heaney □

The poet chooses the incident of the wife bringing lunch to her husband and
his fellow workers in the threshing field to realise his theme – which is perhaps
open to more than one interpretation.

Certainly, Heaney paints a satisfying picture of a country scene with a pleasing
mixture of work and relaxation in which all have their part to play. But there
are indications that the wife, from whose viewpoint events are seen, has
discordant feelings. Various strands of the story indicate this: there is the
deliberate contrast of the wife's activities with those of the men, the remarks of
her husband and the comments from her own point of view. All these should
be taken into account in weighing up the poet's intentions in the poem.

1 In your view, what is the theme of *The Wife's Tale*? Take into account the various
   elements of the poem in your answer, including the viewpoint of the wife, the words of
   the men and the descriptive detail and imagery.

2 Compare the attitudes to marriage revealed in Bradstreet's and Heaney's poems.

3 Compare the tone of the two poems.

● In *The Wife's Tale* by Seamus Heaney, the poet adopts a particular voice for the
   purpose of the poem: that of a slightly detached although obedient wife. It is quite
   common for poets to assume particular voices.

Write a poem based on one of the following suggestions, taking on the voice of a particular person:

a husband or wife complaining about his or her marriage partner

a rebellious teenager expressing anger or resentment against adult authority

someone protesting against the raw deal he or she has had at the hands of the law

Whatever the subject of the poem, the poet must assume a voice to deal with its subject-matter. There are various alternatives open for this. For example, the poet can be an observer of the events of the poem, with no direct presence in it, as in *The Fight of the Year*. A second possibility is for the poet to adopt a persona and talk directly in the first person to the reader as in *To My Dear and Loving Husband* and *The Wife's Tale*. Thirdly, the poet can speak directly as the poet to the reader without adopting any intermediary voice.

The following two poems are about death, a perennial subject for poets. The first is presented in the persona of a child: it attempts to give the reader a child's view of the impact of death.

■ DO THE DYING CRY?

The balcony shakes, the wrought-iron bars
melt as she cries, holding them,
I holding my father's hand
down in the street, looking up, seeing her
mouth swallow her face, and behind her
a silent room. Behind the balcony
with wrought-iron bars.
She's dying. Probably she's dead, my father
says, tries to walk away. I cannot ask
who is dying, who is probably dead.   10

The carob tree begins to move where the leaves
are freest. One leaf touches the balcony;
and from the hill a dog's barking
imitates her dying-cry – the wind carries
both to the sea, drops them there,
returns to the balcony, to me under it,
holding my father's hand with a question:

Do the dying cry on balconies, do they resent
this sudden misplacement? – Come, now,
you are old enough to know: her *mother* must be
dead, behind that balcony, in that silent room.   21

Taner Baybars □

The voice of the poem is that of a child. This is made clear early on in the poem:

> I holding my father's hand (3)

But certain recollections and some of the images seem too adult, too sophisticated, to be a child's viewpoint, for example:

> Do the dying cry on balconies, do they resent
> this sudden misplacement? (18–19)

Clearly this is the adult voice intervening in the child's memory of the incident.

1 The images of the balcony, the wrought-iron bars and the silent room are repeated in the poem. What is the emotional impact of this imagery?

2 What other imagery, literal or figurative, does the poet use and how does it further underline the emotional tone of the poetry?

3 Summarise in your own words how the poet handles the theme in the content of the poem.

4 In your opinion, does the poet successfully convey the viewpoint of a child? In other words, is his adoption of the understanding and outlook of a child convincing or is he perhaps successful in some ways, but not in others?

In the second poem, about the death of an old lady, there is no personal narrator. A large part of the poem is concerned with describing the actions and reactions of a rather detached nurse, but the events are not seen from her point of view.

■ DEATH IN LEAMINGTON

She died in the upstairs bedroom
  By the light of the ev'ning star
That shone through the plate glass window
  From over Leamington Spa.

Beside her the lonely crochet
  Lay patiently and unstirred,
But the fingers that would have work'd it
  Were dead as the spoken word.   8

And Nurse came in with the tea-things
  Breast high 'mid the stands and chairs –
But Nurse was alone with her own little soul
  And the things were alone with theirs.

She bolted the big round window,
  She let the blinds unroll,
She set a match to the mantle,
  She covered the fire with coal.   16

And 'Tea!' she said in a tiny voice
  'Wake up! It's nearly *five*.'
Oh! Chintzy, chintzy cheeriness,
  Half dead and half alive!

Do you know that the stucco is peeling?
  Do you know that the heart will stop?
From those Italianate arches
  Do you hear the plaster drop?   24

Nurse looked at the silent bedstead,
  At the grey, decaying face,
As the calm of a Leamington ev'ning
  Drifted into the place.

She moved the table of bottles
  Away from the bed to the wall,
And tiptoeing gently over the stairs
  Turned down the gas in the hall.   32

John Betjeman □

Although Betjeman is not present in the poem as a first person narrator like the 'I' of Taner Baybars' poem, the way in which he describes the old lady's death, the type of detail which he selects and the intervention of his own voice at one point, make his attitude clear. He uses the nurse and her manner to emphasise the sadness and loneliness of the old lady's death. The imagery, which is mainly literal, symbolises decay and death.

1 How is the mood of the poem brought out by Betjeman's use of imagery?

2 'And tiptoeing gently over the stairs
   Turned down the gas in the hall.' (31–32)

   How effective do you find the detail of the nurse turning down the gas as an ending to the poem?

3 The poem is written in rhyming stanzas. What is the effect of the poem being written in rhyming stanzas of four lines each?

4 What is the theme of the poem and how has Betjeman treated it? What contribution does the intrusion of his own voice make?

5 Compare the attitude to death taken in this poem with that taken in the previous one.

The subject of nature is one of the subjects that people most associate poetry with: poets rhapsodising about its beauty, waxing lyrical with purple verse. But nature poetry comprises many different attitudes and responses. The work of the next four poets will show that nature is not always seen just as a thing of beauty or benevolence, but inspires a more varied and challenging reaction from poets. The first poem of the four is by John Keats (1795–1821).

■ TO AUTUMN

Season of mists and mellow fruitfulness!
   Close bosom-friend of the maturing sun;
Conspiring with him how to load and bless
   With fruit the vines that round the thatch-eves run;
To bend with apples the moss'd cottage-trees,
   And fill all fruit with ripeness to the core;
      To swell the gourd, and pump the hazel shells
   With a sweet kernel; to set budding more,
And still more, later flowers for the bees,
Until they think warm days will never cease,
      For Summer has o'er-brimm'd their clammy cells.   11

Who hath not seen thee oft amid thy store?
  Sometimes whoever seeks abroad may find
Thee sitting careless on a granary floor,
  Thy hair soft-lifted by the winnowing wind,
Or on a half-reap'd furrow sound asleep,
  Drowsed with the fume of poppies, while thy hook
    Spares the next swath and all its twinèd flowers;
And sometimes like a gleaner thou dost keep
Steady thy laden head across a brook;
  Or by a cider-press, with patient look,
    Thou watchest the last oozings hours by hours.   22

Where are the songs of Spring? Ay, where are they?
  Think not of them, thou hast thy music too, –
While barrèd clouds bloom the soft-dying day,
  And touch the stubble-plains with rosy hue;
Then in a wailful choir the small gnats mourn
  Among the river sallows, borne aloft
    Or sinking as the light wind lives or dies;
And full-grown lambs lend bleat from hilly bourn;
Hedge-crickets sing; and now with treble soft
  The red-breast whistles from a garden-croft;
    And gathering swallows twitter in the skies.   33

John Keats ☐

In this poem, Keats masterfully evokes an impression of ripe autumn by combining luxuriant imagery with diction chosen for its expressiveness and aural qualities. Keats' ode repays reading aloud or sub-vocalisation, because the sound of the verse is an integral part of the meaning of the poem:

And fill all fruit with ripeness to the core;
To swell the gourd, and pump the hazel shells (6–7)

Notice especially the long vowel sounds he employs. The sensuousness of the diction emerges fully when its auditory qualities are appreciated.

1 a 'Who hath not seen thee oft amid thy store?' (12)

   Whom is Keats addressing here?

  b The poem is written in three stanzas. Analyse the content of each one to show how the poem is structured.

2 Illustrate Keats' attitude to autumn by showing how he uses imagery (including sound imagery) and sensuous language.

3 What does Keats' use of rhyme and enjambement add to the poem?

4 How does the introduction of spring in the third stanza and the use of sound imagery there introduce a new idea, which changes the mood of the poem and develops its theme?

In the next poem, *Watermelon Breakfast*, the natural environment is quite different to the rural English scene Keats was describing. The South African landscape draws a contrasting response from Robert Greig.

■ WATERMELON BREAKFAST

Green rind,
dark pink flesh glistening
grainy trail
on your face as if
you gave up washing lipstick
halfway.
And the pips
the pips should be mentioned,
the way they speckle the fruit
are left stranded
boats without masts
when their red ocean
slides down the throat.
New they shine on the plate:
if we left them long enough,
they'd harden.   16

Take thread
exchange them for balding chickens
on a hot day
ochre ground
hard as bare feet
the dust lifting
the flies falling
a sharp smell of sweat,
and there, far away, the hills
faint as green rinds
deliquescent
the sea, the Indian ocean.
If you look hard,
how the sharks rip that blue,
apart. If they were large
or not stunned by the day,
you would see the water
fall apart in chunks
and the sharks
neat in their shells, black
watermelon pips.   37

And what about the chickens?
The kraal, the sharks, the ocean?
Surely this leads somewhere?

The chickens? Stringy.
The kraal. Bulldozed.
The houses pus on the hills.
But the ocean is learning ways
to stick together.
That's another country.
They eat the rinds there, down to the quick.   47

The watermelon, back to the watermelon.
Now all that sweet pulp's gone
except for the trail on your chin.
All that's left are two green cuticles
thirty black pips.
We'll string them together in amulets
to ward off the ghosts
and start again, sharing
the vast arced smile
of wet watermelons.   57

Robert Greig □

Notice how the poet mainly uses very short lines, which give a staccato, jerky rhythm to the verse. This reflects the treatment the poet gives to the theme – a meandering flow of thoughts and images started by the eating of a watermelon.

1 How do the sound and rhythm of the poem differ from Keats' ode?

2 What contribution to the poem do the striking images of the natural environment make?

3 How does the poet develop his thoughts in the rest of the poem from the eating of a watermelon described in the first verse?

4 What do you think the theme of the poem is?

5 How does Robert Greig's attitude to nature in this poem differ from that of Keats in *To Autumn*.

William Wordsworth (1770–1850), perhaps more than any other English poet, is associated with the presentation of nature as a benevolent spiritual influence on mankind. Ted Hughes, a contemporary poet, takes a very different view of nature; these contrasting viewpoints come out very strongly in the following two poems.

■ DAFFODILS

I wander'd lonely as a cloud
   That floats on high o'er vales and hills,
When all at once I saw a crowd,
   A host, of golden daffodils;
Beside the lake, beneath the trees,
Fluttering and dancing in the breeze.   6

Continuous as the stars that shine
   And twinkle on the Milky Way,
They stretch'd in never-ending line
   Along the margin of a bay:
Ten thousand saw I at a glance,
Tossing their heads in sprightly dance.   12

The waves beside them danced, but they
   Out-did the sparkling waves in glee:
A poet could not but be gay,
   In such a jocund company:
I gazed – and gazed – but little thought
What wealth the show to me had brought.   18

For oft, when on my couch I lie
   In vacant or in pensive mood,
They flash upon that inward eye
   Which is the bliss of solitude;
And then my heart with pleasure fills,
And dances with the daffodils.   24

William Wordsworth ☐

The poem is partly about the feelings of exhilaration experienced by the poet on seeing 'a host of golden daffodils;' (4). This feeling of exhilaration permeates the diction and rhythm of the poem. Notice how the poet's choice of diction underlines his feelings: 'fluttering and dancing', 'in sprightly dance', 'sparkling waves' and 'jocund company' all express the poet's mood.

1 How does Wordsworth's use of imagery bring out his attitude to the daffodils?

2 Analyse the structure of each stanza; discuss the use that is made of rhyme, run-on and end-stopped lines and caesuras. What do these features add to the picture the poet is creating?

3 How is the content of the first three stanzas drawn together by the emergence of the poem's theme in the fourth?

■ THISTLES

Against the rubber tongues of cows and the hoeing hands of men
Thistles spike the summer air
Or crackle open under a blue-black pressure.

Every one a revengeful burst
Of resurrection, a grasped fistful
Of splintered weapons and Icelandic frost thrust up   6

From the underground stain of a decayed Viking.
They are like pale hair and the gutturals of dialects.
Every one manages a plume of blood.

Then they grow grey, like men.
Mown down, it is a feud. Their sons appear,
Stiff with weapons, fighting back over the same ground.   12

Ted Hughes □

Hughes' attitude to the thistles makes a stark contrast to Wordsworth's
feelings about the golden daffodils. This different attitude is, of course,
reflected in the treatment the theme receives from Hughes. Both poets,
however, use the respective flowers to hint at deeper issues of life –
Wordsworth, the benevolent force that nature can be and Hughes, the struggle
for survival that is life itself.

1 Compare the way in which Hughes views the thistles with the attitude Wordsworth takes
to the daffodils.

2 a Hughes' use of imagery in this poem is often figurative. Discuss his purpose in this
use of imagery.
  b Compare the mood created by the imagery of *Thistles* with that of *Daffodils*.

3 Consider how the form of the poem contributes to its content and theme and compare it
with the form of *Daffodils*.

4 Pick out any examples of Hughes' use of language that you consider to be particularly
expressive and explain why they are effective.

5 'Mown down, it is a feud. Their sons appear'. (11)

What is the theme of the poem?

● Write a poem that takes as its theme aspects of nature that seem to you cruel and
harsh. Then write a contrasting poem that concentrates on more pleasant features of
nature.

Poets write about the society they live in, so it is not surprising that verse has often been used to satirise hypocrisy in society's customs, beliefs and politics. Satirical poetry written in the English language perhaps reached its peak of achievement in the eighteenth century.

The following two poems (both are extracts from longer poems) comment satirically on eighteenth-century society; the first, by Alexander Pope, employs a sophisticated and elegant poetic diction to mock the court and political circles surrounding the monarch of that time, Queen Anne.

■ *From* THE RAPE OF THE LOCK

Close by those meads for ever crowned with flow'rs,
Where Thames with pride surveys his rising tow'rs,
There stands a structure of majestic frame,
Which from the neighbouring Hampton takes its name.
Here Britain's statesmen oft the fall foredoom
Of foreign tyrants, and of nymphs at home;
Here thou, great Anna! whom three realms obey,
Dost sometimes counsel take – and sometimes tea.
   Hither the heroes and the nymphs resort,
To taste awhile the pleasures of a court;   10
In various talk th'instructive hours they passed,
Who gave the ball, or paid the visit last:
One speaks the glory of the British Queen,
And one describes a charming Indian screen;
A third interprets motions, looks, and eyes;
At ev'ry word a reputation dies.
Snuff, or the fan, supply each pause of chat,
With singing, laughing, ogling, and all that.
   Meanwhile declining from the noon of the day,
The Sun obliquely shoots his burning ray;   20
The hungry judges soon the sentence sign,
And wretches hang that jurymen may dine;
The merchant from the Exchange returns in peace,
And the long labours of the toilette cease.

Alexander Pope □

Pope is describing the artificial, affected world of the royal court. To undermine, and underline, the false sophistication of this world, he employs a witty epigrammatic style: his phrases are pointed and pithy. The verse form he uses – the heroic couplet – facilitates this because the pairs of rhyming lines allow him to make a stinging remark within each unit of two lines.

Pope's verses are full of inflated poetic diction. This is language used in poetry and practically nowhere else. It is often thought of as rather artificial and pretentious:

> Here thou, great Anna! whom three realms obey,
> Dost sometimes counsel take – and sometimes tea. (7–8)

He deliberately uses words which are too high-flown for the subject being dealt with and then punctures this pompous tone by juxtaposing very ordinary language or referring to a very humble or ignoble activity. This technique of suddenly descending from the sublime to the ridiculous is called bathos.

1 'Hither the heroes and nymphs resort,
To taste awhile the pleasures of a court;' (9–10)

   a Explain why this language might be thought inappropriate for describing its subject.
   b Pick out other examples of high-flown poetic diction and explain why it is unsuitable in its context. What does Pope achieve by the use of this language?

2 Illustrate the way Pope achieves his effect of bathos.

3 'The hungry judges soon the sentence sign,
And wretches hang that jurymen may dine;' (21–2)

Explain the satirical point Pope is making in these lines. Is there a more biting tone to the satire here than in the rest of the extract?

4 'Here Britain's statesmen oft the fall foredoom
Of foreign tyrants...' (5–6)

According to Pope, what do the politicians and courtiers really spend their time doing?

5 Why should a rather grand verse form such as the heroic couplet be particularly suited to satirical poetry, do you think?

The second satirical poem from the eighteenth century is by the Scots writer Robert Burns. In this poem he takes the opportunity to home in on the hypocrisy of Calvinist churchmen in Scotland.

■ *from* HOLY WILLIE'S PRAYER

> O Thou, that in the heavens does dwell!
> Wha, as it pleases best thysel,
> Sends ane to heaven an' ten to hell,
>   A' for thy glory!
> And no for ony gude or ill
>   They've done before thee.

I bless and praise thy matchless might,
When thousands thou hast left in night,
That I am here before thy sight,
      For gifts and grace,
A burning and a shining light
      To a' this place.   12

What was I, or my generation,
That I should get such exaltation?
I, wha deserved most just damnation,
      For broken laws
Sax thousand years ere my creation,
      Thr' Adam's cause!

When from my mother's womb I fell,
Thou might hae plunged me deep in hell,
To gnash my gooms and weep, and wail,
      In burning lakes,
Where damned devils roar and yell
      Chained to their stakes.   24

Yet I am here, a chosen sample,
To shew thy grace is great and ample:
I'm here, a pillar o' thy temple
      Strong as a rock,
A guide, a ruler and example
      To a' thy flock.

O Lord thou kens what zeal I bear,
When drinkers drink, and swearers swear,
And singin' there, and dancin' here,
      Wi' great and sma';
For I am keepet by thy fear,
      Free frae them a'.   36

But yet – O Lord – confess I must –
At times I'm fashed wi' fleshly lust;
And sometimes too, in wardly trust
      Vile Self gets in;
But thou remembers we are dust,
      Defiled wi' sin.

O Lord – yestreen – thou kens – wi' Meg –
Thy pardon I sincerely beg!
O may't ne'er be a living plague,
      To thy dishonor!
And I'll ne'er lift a lawless leg
      Again upon her.   48

> Besides, I farther maun avow,
> Wi' Leezie's lass, three times – and I trow
> But Lord, that Friday I was fou
>   When I cam near her;
> Or else, thou kens, thy servant true
>   Wad never steer her.

Robert Burns □

The real theme of Burns' poem is the self-righteous religiosity of the church elder. The prayer reveals the shallowness and hypocrisy of the man himself, but he is also representative of the church and society to which he belongs. The individual satirical target becomes a symbol for a joyless, hypocritical and sanctimonious community.

1 'A burning and a shining light
     To a' this place.' (11–12)

Willie shows himself to be vain and self-righteous in these lines. What other defects of character does Willie reveal in himself elsewhere in the extract? Quote from the passage to support your answer.

2 Explain in your own words what Burns is aiming to satirise in focusing on one individual, Holy Willie.

3 Compare the kind of diction that Burns uses in this poem with that which Pope employs in *The Rape of the Lock*.

4 Compare Burns' satirical technique with that of Pope.

5 a Which of the two pieces – the Burns or the Pope – is the more direct in its satire and which is the more subtle?

b Which of these poems do you prefer as a satirical piece?
   Give reasons for your answer.

● Write a satirical poem about one of the following:

   school life   a current political issue or personality   a local issue

You do not need to use rhyme, but remember that rhyme can be a very useful tool in satirical poetry. You may want to imitate Pope's or Burns' style in your poem by using rhyming couplets.

From the First World War emerged some memorable poetry. It was a conflict that began amidst much popular enthusiasm and illusions of military glory. But as trench warfare dragged on and casualties reached monstrous proportions on both sides, any notions that war was a glorious pastime largely disappeared.

This change of attitude to the war is reflected in the poetry written by men who were involved in the trench war themselves. The first of the two poems to be considered here was written by Rupert Brooke in 1914.

■ THE SOLDIER

If I should die, think only this of me:
    That there's some corner of a foreign field
That is for ever England. There shall be
    In that rich earth a richer dust concealed;
A dust whom England bore, shaped, made aware,
    Gave, once, her flowers to love, her ways to roam,
A body of England's, breathing English air,
    Washed by the rivers, blest by suns of home.   8

And think, this heart, all evil shed away,
    A pulse in the eternal mind, no less
        Gives somewhere back the thoughts by England given;
Her sights and sounds; dreams happy as her day;
    And laughter, learnt of friends; and gentleness,
        In hearts at peace, under an English heaven.   14

Rupert Brooke □

The Soldier is an intensely patriotic poem. The theme receives a sonorous emotional treatment by the poet, which is reflected in the diction and imagery. No doubts about the morality of going to war intrude here; the poet's intention is to write a hymn of praise to his homeland. The poem was written not long after the First World War began; it is difficult to see how even such a patriot as Brooke would have been able to write a poem like this from the trenches during the latter stages of the war.

1 Identify the theme of the poem and show how it is handled in the content of the verse.

2 How would you describe the tone of the poem and the attitude of the soldier to his possible death?

3 The rhythm of the verse underlines the poem's sentiments. Read the poem aloud, listening to the rhythm of the language. How does the rhythm reflect the overall tone of the poem?

4 What means does Brooke use to make his theme convincing and attractive?

The next poem was written later in the war and reflects the horrific realisation of what war was really like.

■ THE DEATH-BED

He drowsed and was aware of silence heaped
Round him, unshaken as the steadfast walls;
Aqueous like floating rays of amber light,
Soaring and quivering in the wings of sleep.
Silence and safety; and his mortal shore
Lipped by the inward, moonless waves of death.   6

Someone was holding water to his mouth.
He swallowed, unresisting; moaned and dropped
Through crimson gloom to darkness; and forgot
The opiate throb and ache that was his wound.
    Water – calm, sliding green above the weir.
    Water – a sky-lit alley for his boat,
    Bird-voiced, and bordered with reflected flowers
    And shaken hues of summer; drifting down,
    He dipped contented oars, and sighed, and slept.   15

Night, with a gust of wind, was in the ward,
Blowing the curtain to a glimmering curve.
Night. He was blind; he could not see the stars
Glinting among the wraiths of wandering cloud;
Queer blots of colour, purple, scarlet, green,
Flickered and faded in his drowning eyes.   21

Rain – he could hear it rustling through the dark;
Fragrance and passionless music woven as one;
Warm rain on drooping roses; pattering showers
That soak the woods; not the harsh rain that sweeps
Behind the thunder, but a trickling peace,
Gently and slowly washing life away.   27

    .   .   .   .

He stirred, shifting his body; then the pain
Leapt like a prowling beast, and gripped and tore
His groping dreams with grinding claws and fangs.
   But someone was beside him; soon he lay
   Shuddering because that evil thing had passed.
   And death, who'd stepped toward him, paused and stared.   33

Light many lamps and gather round his bed.
Lend him your eyes, warm blood, and will to live.
Speak to him; rouse him; you may save him yet.
He's young; he hated war; how should he die
When cruel old campaigners win safe through?   38

But death replied: 'I choose him.' So he went,
And there was silence in the summer night;
Silence and safety; and the veils of sleep.
Then, far away, the thudding of the guns.   42

Siegfried Sassoon □

Just as there are in *The Soldier*, there are some seductive images in *The Death-bed*:

    Aqueous like floating rays of amber light, (3)

but Sassoon uses them as a contrast, a kind of counterpoint, to the reality of the soldier dying in a hospital, a victim of senseless and cruel war. The loveliness of some of the verse merely underlines the harshness of the soldier's fate: the poem leaves the reader with a sense of waste.

1 What is the theme of the poem and how does the poet handle his theme in the content of the poem?

2 How does this view of a soldier's death differ from Brooke's vision of his own death in *The Soldier*?

3 Both poems use memories of home. Compare how these memories are used in the poems.

4   'So he went,
And there was silence in the summer night;
Silence and safety; and the veils of sleep.
Then far away, the thudding of the guns.' (40–43)

How does the poet use the sound of words in these lines to create an atmosphere and then to break it abruptly?

5 Which of the two poems means more to you? Give reasons for your answer.

Chapter 9
Diction – the Language of Poetry

The language of poetry carries much more weight than individual words and phrases usually do in prose. The poet has to concentrate meaning and emotions in a selection of language that often aims to communicate deep feelings and profound ideas within the space of a few words.

Some poems elude any precise analysis of their meaning. When you analyse a poem, you are not looking for a correct answer or solution; analysing poetry is not like solving a mathematical problem. Even in mundane matters, language is never completely exact. In poetry the diction and imagery may be deliberately or subconsciously ambiguous. Good poems often have an emotional resonance that lingers with the reader, exposing layers of secondary meaning that affect different readers in various ways. There are very few poems where it can be categorically stated that there is one and only one meaning.

When you analyse poems, always start your analysis by looking closely at the text, before trying to express what makes the poetry meaningful to you. This means studying the diction of the poem in some depth.

The sound of verse, the aural impression made by a poem on the reader or listener, is clearly a very important component in the impact made by poetry. The tonal qualities of words can convey meaning and emotions to a reader, even if the total meaning of the verse is not fully understood, especially at a first reading.

This section begins with two poems that both aim to be sonorous and imposing and to have a resonance of meaning.

■ A REFUSAL TO MOURN THE DEATH, BY FIRE,
OF A CHILD IN LONDON

Never until the mankind making
Bird beast and flower
Fathering and all humbling darkness
Tells with silence the last light breaking
And the still hour
Is come of the sea tumbling in harness   6

And I must enter again the round
Zion of the water bead
And the synagogue of the ear of corn
Shall I let pray the shadow of a sound
Or sow my salt seed
In the least valley of sackcloth to mourn   12

The majesty and burning of the child's death.
I shall not murder
The mankind of her going with a grave truth
Nor blaspheme down the stations of the breath
With any further
Elegy of innocence and youth.   18

Deep with the first dead lies London's daughter,
Robed in the long friends,
The grains beyond age, the dark veins of her mother,
Secret by the unmourning water
Of the riding Thames.
After the first death, there is no other.   24

Dylan Thomas □

Normal word-order is frequently upturned in poetry; in Thomas's poem, the
rules of syntax are largely ignored, which is not necessarily a criticism. This
unusual syntax does however cause some initial difficulties for the reader. In
addition, Thomas both juxtaposes and uses words in a startling manner:

Never until the mankind making
Bird beast and flower
Fathering and all humbling darkness (1–3)

In these opening lines, 'making' and 'Fathering' are adjectives qualifying
'darkness', but what makes the sentence more difficult to untangle is that
'mankind' seems to be qualifying 'making' and 'Bird beast and flower' to be
qualifying 'Fathering'. Thomas is using poetic licence to create unfamiliar word
patterns to force the reader to respond on an emotional level; the words may
not have an exact meaning at first reading, but the sound, the sonorous quality
the diction possesses, has an emotional impact.

Alliteration plays a large part in creating this weighty aural impact. Look at the
following examples of alliteration taken from the first stanza of the poem:

'mankind making'   'Bird beast'   'flower Fathering'   'last light'.

In addition, Thomas uses a repetition of 'l' sounds:

. . . all humbling darkness
Tells with silence the last light breaking (3–4)

This repetition of the same consonant in adjacent words is called consonance. Notice also the sibilance (succession of 's' sounds) in

> . . . the still hour
> Is come of the sea tumbling in harness. (5–6)

This onslaught of sound gives the poem its grandeur.

1 '. . . of the sea tumbling in harness' (6)

'Or sow my salt seed
In the least valley of sackcloth to mourn' (11–12)

The poem is rich in metaphorical language. Analyse some of the poem's imagery, including the examples above, and comment on Thomas' purpose in using it.

2 'After the first death, there is no other'. (24)

What is the effect of ending the poem with the briefest of its sentences? What light does it throw on the poet's theme?

3 Discuss Thomas' use of aural effects, taking examples from the poem.

John Milton (1608–1674) is also famous for writing sonorous verse. His diction usually consists of heightened dramatic language; to appreciate fully the impact of its aural qualities, the verse should be read aloud.

Milton's major work is *Paradise Lost*, a long epic poem; below is an extract from the beginning of this work.

■ *From* PARADISE LOST

> Say first – for Heaven hides nothing from thy view,
> Nor the deep tract of Hell – say first what cause
> Moved our grand Parents, in that happy state,
> Favoured of Heaven so highly, to fall off
> From their Creator, and transgress his will
> For one restraint, lords of the World besides.
> Who first seduced them to the foul revolt?
> The infernal Serpent; he it was whose guile,
> Stirred up with envy and revenge, deceived
> The mother of mankind, what time his pride   10
> Had cast him out from Heaven, with all his host
> Of rebel Angels, by whose aid, aspiring
> To set himself in glory above his peers,

He trusted to have equalled the Most High,
If he opposed, and, with ambitious aim
Against the throne and monarchy of God,
Raised impious war in Heaven and battle proud,
With vain attempt. Him the Almighty Power
Hurled headlong flaming from the ethereal sky,
With hideous ruin and combustion, down   20
To bottomless perdition, there to dwell
In adamantine chains and penal fire,
Who durst defy the Omnipotent to arms.
   Nine times the space that measures day and night
To mortal men, he, with his horrid crew,
Lay vanquished, rolling in the fiery gulf,
Confounded, though immortal. But his doom
Reserved him to more wrath; for now the thought
Both of lost happiness and lasting pain
Torments him: round he throws his baleful eyes,   30
That witnessed huge affliction and dismay,
Mixed with obdurate pride and steadfast hate.
At once, as far as Angel's ken, he views
The dismal situation waste and wild.
A dungeon horrible, on all sides round,
As one great furnace flamed; yet from those flames
No light; but rather darkness visible
Served only to discover sights of woe,
Regions of sorrow, doleful shades, where peace
And rest can never dwell, hope never comes   40
That comes to all, but torture without end
Still urges, and a fiery deluge, fed
With ever-burning sulphur unconsumed.
Such place Eternal Justice had prepared
For those rebellious; here their prison ordained
In utter darkness, and their portion set,
As far removed from God and light of Heaven
As from the centre thrice to the utmost pole.

John Milton ☐

Paradise Lost was written in the era of Oliver Cromwell's power and Milton himself was strongly committed to the Puritan cause. It is not surprising then that the verse of Milton's epic poem has a decidedly biblical ring to it; *Paradise Lost* has the same sonorous grandiloquent quality that many passages of the Bible have.

Notice how Milton uses many strong adjectives to tell his story of the battle of good and evil between God and the Devil:

> ... and, with ambitious aim
> Against the throne and monarchy of God,
> Raised impious war in Heaven and battle proud
> With vain attempt. (15–18)

The polarisation of the forces of good and the forces of evil is reflected in the language of the poem. Notice also the rhythm of the verse based on long, rolling sentences which give Milton room to expand his thoughts.

1 Obviously the language Milton uses is not the language of everyday life. The diction is heightened; it is grand and sonorous. Select examples of diction from the extract that fit this description and explain why they suit Milton's subject.

2 Discuss the imagery, literal or figurative, which Milton uses to convey Satan's fall from grace.

3 Analyse the use Milton makes of enjambment and the type of rhythm he employs in his verse. What do these features add to the realisation of the poem's theme?

4 Analyse Milton's use of adjectives in this extract by choosing examples from the passage and commenting on their impact in the context.

The next two poems provide a striking contrast to the sonorous verse of Milton and Dylan Thomas; they each use a different form of English as it is actually spoken – the everyday speech of ordinary life for a particular social group. Ordinary speech has its own natural rhythms; a skilful poet with a good ear can identify those rhythms and use them within a poetic form to help convey a theme.

The first poem is written in an Irish dialect by Moira O'Neill (1864–1955).

■ HER SISTER

> 'Brigid is a Caution, sure!' – What's that ye say?
> Is it my sister then, Brigid MacIlray?
> Caution or no Caution, listen what I'm tellin' ye ...
> *Childer, hould yer noise there, faix! there's no quellin' ye!* ...
> Och, well, I've said it now this many a long day,
> 'Tis the quare pity o' Brigid MacIlray.   6

An' she that was the beauty, an' never married yet!
An' fifty years gone over her, but do you think she'll fret?
Sorra one o' Brigid then, that's not the sort of her,
Ne'er a *hate* would *she* care though not a man had thought of her.
Heaps o' men she a' had . . . *Here, get out o' that,*
Mick ye rogue! desthroyin' o' the poor ould cat!   12

Ah, no use o' talkin'! Sure a woman's born to wed,
An' not go wastin' all her life by waitin' till she's dead.
Haven't we the men to mind, that couldn't for the lives o' them
Keep their right end uppermost, only for the wives o' them? –
Stick to yer pipe, Tim, an' give me no talk now!
There's the door fore'nenst ye, man! out ye can walk now.   18

Brigid, poor Brigid, will never have a child,
An' she you'd think a mother born, so gentle an' so mild . . .
Danny, is it puttin' little Biddy's eyes out ye're after,
Swishin' wid yer rod there, an' splittin' wid yer laughter?
Come along the whole o' yez, in out o' the wet,
Or may I never but ye'll soon see what ye'll get!   24

She to have no man at all . . . *Musha, look at Tim!*
Off an' up the road he is, an' wet enough to swim,
An' his tea sittin' waitin' on him, there he'll sthreel about now, –
Amn't I the heart-scalded woman out an' out now?
Here I've lived an' wrought for him all the ways I can,
But the Goodness grant me patience, for I'd need it wid that man!   30

What was I sayin' then? Brigid lives her lone,
Ne'er a one about the house, quiet as a stone . . .
Lave a-go the pig's tail, boys, an' quet the squealin' now,
Mind! I've got a sally switch that only wants the peelin' now . . .
Ah, just to think of her, 'deed an' well-a-day!
'Tis the quare pity o' Brigid MacIlray.   36

Moira O'Neill □

The whole poem is written in direct speech. The poet catches the natural flow of the speaker's language and shapes it into a poetic form. Such are the lilting rhythms of the Irish speech that the words of the poem appear very natural and direct; the rhyming couplets seem entirely appropriate and not at all obtrusive. Some dialects of English have this natural poetic quality; it can be harnessed by a skilled poet and shaped to one of the recognised poetic forms.

1 Show how the poet manages to tell us as much about the speaker as about Brigid.

2 What do you think the real theme of the poem is?

3 Comment on the use of dialect in the poem, saying whether you think this feature adds to the impact it makes on the reader.

4 Analyse the rhyming structure that is used in each stanza and comment on how that helps to organise the content for the poet.

5 Briefly and in simple terms, explain how the diction used in this poem differs from the diction of the poems by Thomas and Milton.

Poets frequently adopt a particular voice in a poem. In the following poem, Gavin Ewart takes on the voice of an English army officer; the diction is mainly standard English, but the language is peppered with colloquialisms and idioms associated with the social class and the profession of the owner of the voice of the poem.

■ OFFICERS' MESS

It's going to be a thick night tonight (and the night before was a thick
    one),
I've just seen the Padre disappearing into 'The Cock' for a quick one.
I don't mind telling you this, old boy, we got the Major drinking –
You probably know the amount of gin he's in the habit of sinking –
And then that new MO came in, the Jewish one, awful fellow,
And his wife, a nice little bit of stuff, dressed in a flaming yellow.
Looked a pretty warmish piece, old boy, – no, have this one with me –
They were both so blind (and so was the Major) that they could hardly
    see.
She had one of those amazing hats and a kind of silver fox fur
(I wouldn't mind betting several fellows have had a go at her).   10
She made a bee-line for the Major, bloody funny, old boy,
Asked him a lot about horses and India, you know, terribly coy –
And this MO fellow was mopping it up and at last he passed right out
(Some silly fool behind his back put a bottle of gin in his stout).
I've never seen a man go down so quick. Somebody drove him home.
His wife was almost as bad, old boy, said she felt all alone
And nestled up to the Major – it's a great pity you weren't there –
And the Padre was arguing about the order of morning and evening
    prayer.
Never laughed so much in all my life. We went on drinking till three.
And this bloody woman was doing her best to sit on the Major's knee!   20
Let's have the blackout boards put up and turn on the other light.
Yes, I think you can count on that, old boy – tonight'll be a thick night.

Gavin Ewart □

The voice in Ewart's poem comes from a totally different social and class background to the voice of Moira O'Neill's poem. The rhythms of the speech are quite different; the dialect used in the previous poem could be said to have a natural poetry. The same cannot be said of the upper-class speech of the officer in the mess, although it does have its own rhythms which Ewart skilfully employs in the poem and underlines by equally skilful use of rhyme.

1 What picture of the person speaking (the voice the poet assumes) emerges from the poem? Does he have any prejudices, judging from the evidence of this poem?

2 Select examples of the colloquialisms and everyday speech that Ewart has used in his portrayal of the voice of the poem. What impression of the speaker do these give us?

3 Compare *Her Sister* with Ewart's poem in terms of social class and the concerns of the people involved. Briefly discuss the differences in the kind of language and the rhythms of the verse arising out of these contrasts.

● Write a poem on any subject which uses either a dialect you know and use, or the language of a particular social background with which you are familiar.

T.S. Eliot (1888–1965) believed that a strict analysis of exact meaning is not the only means of understanding poetry, because a poem's language makes an impression on readers through its rhythm and emotional associations. Often, quite obscure diction and imagery in Eliot's own poetry can be understood on an emotional level.

The poem by Eliot which follows is an example of this: on a first reading it is more easily understood through the emotional associations released by the rhythm and tonal qualities of the language than through an examination of the precise meaning of the words.

Although this is a poem which may at first seem discouragingly difficult, it is possible to gain an understanding of it by looking closely at the part played by its diction and imagery and also by its rhythm, since the form of the verse makes an essential contribution to its content.

■ THE WIND SPRANG UP AT FOUR O'CLOCK

The wind sprang up at four o'clock
The wind sprang up and broke the bells
Swinging between life and death
Here, in death's dream kingdom
The waking echo of confusing strife
Is it a dream or something else
When the surface of the blackened river
Is a face that sweats with tears?
I saw across the blackened river
The camp fire shake with alien spears.
Here, across death's other river
The Tartar horsemen shake their spears.

The poem begins with the conflicting sounds of wind and church bells waking the poet from troubled sleep and launching him upon a series of speculations which are inspired by and in turn reflect this initial, contradictory rhythm. The poem takes the form of a flow of thoughts carried along by a repetition of words, phrases and rhythms that skilfully evoke the areas of 'no-man's land' with which the poem is dealing. The battle between wind and bells, the forces of the elements matched against those of order and harmony, sets the pattern for the conflicting ideas contemplated by the poet: day against night, wakefulness against sleep, reality against illusion and, finally – life against death. What the poet feels, as he lies in the uncertain state between sleep and wakefulness, is that just as the wind 'breaks' the bells, so it is the more threatening of each of these ideas which seems to be gaining the upper hand.

It can be seen from the example which follows how Eliot's use of diction, imagery and rhythm continually supports and extends this idea of conflict and the pessimism about its outcome. Mimicking the struggle of the first two lines between wind and bells, the last four lines of the poem fall into pairs of lines that form units of rhythm and sense, each of which presents its own conflict or contrast:

I saw across the blackened river
The camp fire shake with alien spears (9–10)

In the first line, the poet is shown on one side of the river, in the second, a whole army is revealed on the other side – an unequal and threatening foe which has taken concrete shape, a personalization of the vague symbol of chaos represented by the wind. At the same time the images of fire and water, light and dark reinforce the idea of conflict; ominously, the light and fire are on the far bank with the enemy hordes.

The poem is a complex one and will perhaps remain frustrating to those who seek a definitive, precise meaning, because Eliot repeats words, themes and ideas in different combinations adding clusters of associations around them. However, the imagery, rhythms and tone of the language together reveal the central concerns of the poem and point to the poet's position on them.

1 Repetition and alliteration play a very important part in the rhythms and sounds of the verse. Analyse how Eliot uses both of these in the poem.

2 The word 'dream' is used twice in the poem, but perhaps the verse has more the quality of a nightmare than of a dream. Which images have a 'nightmarish' quality to them? What function do these images have in the poem?

3 The use of punctuation is very sparse in this poem. Why is this?

4 Describe briefly what kind of emotional impact the poem has on you.

Church ritual and liturgies are very often based on powerful language with very strong rhythmic qualities, spoken in an emphatic manner. The twentieth-century poet Louis MacNeice takes the liturgical prayer as his model for the poem below.

■ PRAYER BEFORE BIRTH

I am not yet born; O hear me.
Let not the bloodsucking bat or the rat or the stoat or the
    clubfooted ghoul come near me.

I am not yet born; console me.
I fear that the human race may with tall walls wall me,
    with strong drugs dope me, with wise lies lure me,
        on black racks rack me, in blood-baths roll me.

I am not yet born; provide me
With water to dandle me, grass to grow for me, trees to talk
    to me, sky to sing to me, birds and a white light   10
        in the back of my mind to guide me.

I am not yet born; forgive me
For the sins that in me the world shall commit, my words
    when they speak me, my thoughts when they think me,
        my treason engendered by traitors beyond me,
            my life when they murder by means of my
                hands, my death when they live me.

I am not yet born; rehearse me
In the parts I must play and the cues I must take when
   old men lecture me, bureaucrats hector me, mountains   20
     frown at me, lovers laugh at me, the white
       waves call me to folly and the desert calls
         me to doom and the beggar refuses
          my gift and my children curse me.

I am not yet born; O hear me,
Let not the man who is beast or who thinks he is God
   come near me.

I am not yet born; O fill me
With strength against those who would freeze my
   humanity, would dragoon me into a lethal automaton,   30
     would make me a cog in a machine, a thing with
       one face, a thing, and against all those
        who would dissipate my entirety, would
         blow me like thistledown hither and
          thither or hither and thither
           like water held in the
            hands would spill me.

Let them not make me a stone and let them not spill me.
Otherwise kill me.

Louis MacNeice □

The poem, like many prayers, depends on repetition for its hypnotic rhythmic effect; not only are words and phrases repeated, but there are frequent repetitions of constructions. Each stanza starts with the same five words followed by a plea.

Another important factor in creating the sonorous repetitive tone of the poem is the use of internal rhyme, as for example in 'with tall walls wall me' (5). Internal rhyme refers to the effect resulting from words rhyming with one another within the same line of poetry; the multitude of rhymes provide another unifying element in the verse.

1 What features of the poem make it like a prayer or chant?

2   '... my words
when they speak me, my thoughts when they think me,' (13–14)

   What is unusual about this sentence and why does MacNeice choose to use language in this way?

3 Look at the way the stanzas are laid out on the page. Comment on the shape of the stanzas and of the poem as a whole and discuss how both of them affect the emphasis and impact of the poem.

4 The poet uses alliteration frequently. Choose two examples of alliteration from the poem and explain what they add to the point that MacNeice is making.

5 The language MacNeice uses is often powerful and colourful. Select images or diction from the poem that seem to you particularly striking and comment on why these examples are effective in the context.

6 Compare the language and tone of MacNeice's poem with that of Dylan Thomas' poem *A Refusal to Mourn* (page 188).

Cadence is a term used frequently to describe the rise and fall of verse. It can also be used to describe a poem's tone; cadences can be harsh and grating or soft and mellifluous. In the next four poems, cadence plays an important part in the emotional effect of the verse.

Poets sometimes aim to produce a mellifluous quality through a careful choice of diction and this is what Alfred Lord Tennyson (1809–92) seeks to do in the poem below.

■ BLOW, BUGLE, BLOW

    The splendour falls on castle walls
      And snowy summits old in story:
    The long light shakes across the lakes,
      And the wild cataract leaps in glory.
    Blow, bugle, blow, set the wild echoes flying,
    Blow, bugle; answer, echoes, dying, dying, dying.   6

    O hark, O hark! how thin and clear,
      And thinner, clearer, farther going!
    O sweet and far from cliff and scar
      The horns of Elfland faintly blowing!
    Blow, let us hear the purple glens replying:
    Blow, bugle; answer, echoes, dying, dying, dying.   12

    O love, they die in yon rich sky,
      They faint on hill or field or river:
    Our echoes roll from soul to soul,
      And grow for ever and ever.
    Blow, bugle blow, set the wild echoes flying,
    And answer, echoes, answer, dying, dying, dying.   18

         Alfred Lord Tennyson □

The mellifluous quality of the verse is created partly by the soft-sounding diction with its repetitive falling cadences which Tennyson uses:

> And answer, echoes, answer, dying, dying, dying. (18)

But the effect is also achieved by using internal rhyme, half-rhyme, alliteration and assonance:

> The splendour falls on castle walls
> And snowy summits old in story: (1–2)

In these two lines, the rhyme of 'falls' with 'walls' is an example of internal rhyme (when two words in the same line rhyme), while 'snowy' half-rhymes with 'story' (half-rhyme is when two words almost rhyme). The repetition of the vowel sound in 'snowy' and 'old' is an example of assonance.

1 Is there, in your opinion, a theme to the poem or is Tennyson mainly concerned with atmosphere and the creation of mellifluous sounds? Give reasons for your answer.

2 Show how the poet uses repetition, alliteration and rhyme to help create his sound-picture.

3 Which images from the poem seem to you to be particularly effective?

In the next poem, A.E. Housman (1859–1936) takes nature as his subject. The tone and cadence of the verse is similar to that in the previous poem by Tennyson.

■ TELL ME NOT HERE

> Tell me not here, it needs not saying,
>   What tune the enchantress plays
> In aftermaths of soft September
>   Or under blanching mays,
> For she and I were long acquainted
>   And I knew all her ways.   6
>
> On russet floors, by waters idle,
>   The pine lets fall its cone;
> The cuckoo shouts all day at nothing
>   In leafy dells alone;
> And traveller's joy beguiles in autumn
>   Hearts that have lost their own.   12

On acres of the seeded grasses
  The changing burnish heaves;
Or marshalled under moons of harvest
  Stand still all night the sheaves;
Or beeches strip in storms for winter
  And stain the wind with leaves.   18

Possess, as I possessed a season,
  The countries I resign,
Where over elmy plains the highway
  Would mount the hills and shine,
And full of shade the pillared forest
  Would murmur and be mine.   24

For nature, heartless, witless nature,
  Will neither care nor know
What stranger's feet may find the meadow
  And trespass there and go,
Nor ask amid the dews of morning
  If they are mine or no.   30

A.E. Housman ☐

The term poetic diction means language that is considered to be reserved for use in poetry; it is language that is not normally used in everyday life. There are numerous examples of poetic diction in Housman's poem:

'the enchantress' (2)   'blanching mays' (4)   'In leafy dells' (10)

Another feature of the diction Housman uses is the occasional unusual word such as 'elmy' (21), and 'pillared' (23). Housman was writing around the turn of this century when modern poetry with its harsher themes and diction was about to take over from the elegiac sweetness of poets such as Housman and Tennyson.

1 What is the theme of the poem?

2 In your own words, explain what impression the sound of the verse makes on you. What literary techniques does Housman use to achieve this?

3 How would you describe the tone of the poem? How is the tone reflected in the cadence of the verse and the choice of diction?

In the following poem by the nineteenth-century poet, Elizabeth Barrett Browning, there is very little imagery. Although it deals with an emotional subject, the content is intellectual. But the verse still achieves a euphonious quality, like the preceding poems by Tennyson and Housman.

■ SONNET

> If thou must love me, let it be for naught
>   Except for love's sake only. Do not say,
>   'I love her for her smile – her look – her way
> Of speaking gently, – for a trick of thought
> That falls in well with mine, and certes brought
>   A sense of pleasant ease on such a day' –
>   For these things in themselves, beloved, may
> Be changed, or change for thee – and love, so wrought,
> May be unwrought so. Neither love me for
>   Thine own dear pity's wiping my cheeks dry:
> A creature might forget to weep, who bore
>   Thy comfort long, and lose thy love thereby!
> But love me for love's sake, that evermore
>   Thou mayst love on, through love's eternity.

Elizabeth Barrett Browning □

Elizabeth Barrett Browning is writing within an established poetic form, the sonnet, which is a fourteen-line poem. The sonnet will be looked at in detail in Chapter 10, but for now it is worth noticing that this sonnet roughly divides into two sections of 8½ lines (down to 'unwrought so' in line 9) and 5½ lines. Each part is linked together by a rhyming structure.

There is a subtle use of the caesura in the sonnet; the varying resting places in the lines help to give the verse its smooth-flowing, but thoughtful quality.

The poet is dealing with ideas and this is reflected in the poem's economical style of diction; although the words are quite simple, the play of ideas is quite complicated and this gives the poem its taut intellectual quality.

1 Summarise the arguments the poet is putting forward in the sonnet. Is there a couplet which neatly sums up the arguments of the poem?

2 How would you describe the tone and diction of the poem?

3 Would you say that the sound of the poem reflects the attitude of the poet to her theme? If so, how?

The last three poems all had a soft cadence and mellifluous diction. But language in poetry can be harsh-sounding when it is appropriate to the poet's theme and intention. Below is an extract from a poem by Robert Lowell.

■ THE QUAKER GRAVEYARD IN NANTUCKET

A brackish reach of shoal off Madaket, –
The sea was still breaking violently and night
Had steamed into our North Atlantic fleet,
When the drowned sailor clutched the drag-net. Light
Flashed from his matted head and marble feet,
He grappled at the net
With the coiled, hurdling muscles of his thighs:
The corpse was bloodless, a botch of reds and whites,
Its open, staring eyes   10
Were lustreless dead-lights
Or cabin-windows on a stranded hulk
Heavy with sand. We weight the body, close
Its eyes and heave it seaward whence it came,
Where the heel-headed dogfish barks its nose
on Ahab's void and forehead; and the name
Is blocked in yellow chalk.
Sailors, who pitch this portent at the sea
Where dreadnoughts shall confess
Its hell-bent deity,   20
When you are powerless
To sand-bag this Atlantic bulwark, faced
By the earth-shaker, green, unwearied, chaste
In his steel scales: ask for no Orphean lute
To pluck life back. The guns of the steeled fleet
Recoil and then repeat
The hoarse salute.

Robert Lowell □

The subject-matter of this poem is grim: a corpse is caught in a trawler's drag-net. This incident prompts the poet to express some general sentiments about death. The diction Lowell uses reflects the harsh theme – 'brackish' (1), 'breaking' (2), 'matted' (5) 'grappled' (6), 'botch' (8) – these words are all harsh-sounding. The diction of the poem is a reflection of its theme.

9 / Cadence

1 'A brackish reach of shoal off Madaket,'

How well does this opening line set the tone for the poem?

2 'Lowell's choice of diction is both aurally and visually effective.'

Show how the quality of the diction is appropriate to the theme and content of the extract.

3 The 'earth-shaker' (22) is Poseidon, a powerful god who controlled the sea in Greek myth. What is the significance of his appearance here?

4 'The sea was still breaking violently and night
Had steamed into our North Atlantic fleet,
When the drowned sailor clutched the drag-net. Light
Flashed from his matted head and marbled feet,'

The rhyming of 'night' and 'light' partly explains why Lowell has ended these lines with those two words, but what other effect does the placing of these words at the end of the lines have?

In the following poem by Ruth Stone, the harsh rhythms and images express the emotions of the narrator.

■ WINTER

The ten o'clock train to New York;
coaches like loaves of bread powdered with snow.
Steam wheezes between the couplings.
Stripped to plywood, the station's cement standing room
imitates a Russian novel. It is now that I remember you.
Your profile becomes the carved handle of a letter knife.
Your heavy-lidded eyes slip under the seal of my widowhood.
It is another raw winter. Stray cats are suffering.
Starlings crowd the edges of chimneys.
It is a drab misery that urges me to remember you.   10
I think about the subjugation of women and horses,
Brutal exposure. Weather that forces, that strips.
In our time we met in ornate stations
arching up with nineteenth-century optimism.
I remember you running beside the train waving goodbye.
I can produce a facsimile of you standing
behind a column of polished oak to surprise me.
Am I going toward you or away from you on this train?
Discarded junk of other minds is strewn beside the tracks.
Mounds of rusting wire. Grotesque pop-art of dead motors.   20
Senile warehouses. The train passes a station.
Fresh people standing on the platform;
their faces expecting something.
I feel their entire histories ravish me.

Ruth Stone □

Instead of making a direct statement of her feelings, the poet communicates her emotions with a careful selection of images: the imagery of the poem stimulates an emotional reaction in the reader. Thus Ruth Stone's selection of objects and detail from the environment creates the tone and atmosphere of the poem:

'. . . Stray cats are suffering.' (8)

The mood created by the images in this poem is one of unhappiness and sadness.

This process whereby an image is chosen by the poet to create an emotion in the reader is known as the theory of the 'objective correlative'. It was given this name by T.S. Eliot.

1 How does the poet create a picture and an atmosphere in the first five lines of the poem?

2 'Your profile becomes the carved handle of a letter knife.' (6)

What do you think the poet means by this metaphor and explain how she extends the metaphor into the next line.

3 'Mounds of rusting wire. Grotesque pop-art of dead motors.
Senile warehouses. The train passes a station.' (20–21)

a What emotions do these images aim to represent?
b How does the rhythm and type of language used in these lines compare with that of the lines which deal with the speaker's memories of her lover?

4 What do you think the theme of the poem is?

5 Comment on the kind of diction the poet uses in the poem.

● Write a poem with the title *Parting*. Try to use imagery that reflects the emotional content of the poem.

The next three poems show different ways in which poetry can be witty. Talented poets can use poetic techniques to create amusing verse which also engages the intellect of the readers. Two of the poems are from the point of view of men addressing their lovers. Both play with language in a witty manner; both use intellectual arguments and conceits. The first poem is by Andrew Marvell (1621–1678) and the second by Thom Gunn, a contemporary poet.

■ TO HIS COY MISTRESS

Had we but world enough and time
This coyness lady were no crime.
We would sit down, and think which way
To walk, and pass our long love's day.
Thou by the Indian Ganges side
Should'st rubies find: I by the tide
Of Humber would complain. I would
Love you ten years before the flood:
And you should, if you please, refuse
Till the conversion of the Jews.   10
My vegetable love should grow
Vaster then empires, and more slow.
An hundred years should go to praise
Thine eyes, and on thy forehead gaze.
Two hundred to adore each breast:
But thirty thousand to the rest.
An age at least to every part,
And the last age should show your heart.
For lady you deserve this state;
Nor would I love at lower rate.   20
    But at my back I always hear
Time's winged chariot hurrying near:
And yonder all before us lie
Deserts of vast eternity.
Thy beauty shall no more be found;
Nor in thy marble vault, shall sound
My echoing song: then worms shall try
That long preserved virginity:
And your quaint honour turn to dust;
And into ashes all my lust.   30
The grave's a fine and private place,
But none I think do there embrace.
    Now therefore, while the youthful hue
Sits on thy skin like morning dew,
And while they willing soul transpires
At every pore with instant fires
Now let us sport us while we may;
And now, like am'rous birds of prey,
Rather at once our time devour,
Than languish in his slow-chapt power.   40
Let us roll all our strength, and all
Our sweetness, up into one ball:
And tear our pleasures with rough strife,
Through the iron gates of life.
Thus, though we cannot make our sun
Stand still, yet we will make him run.

Andrew Marvell □

The diction in the first section of the poem (down to line 20, 'at lower rate') is gentle. The language is that of praise and love, although its style is deliberately exaggerated:

> My vegetable love should grow
> Vaster than empires, and more slow. (11-12)

In the second section (down to line 32, 'embrace'), an urgency enters the verse as a result of sombre reflections on the brevity of life and the loneliness of the grave. The verse is full of images of death:

> And yonder all before us lie
> Deserts of vast eternity (23-4)

The urgency turns to eager suggestions for vigorously consummating their love in the final section:

> And now, like am'rous birds of prey,
> Rather at once our time devour, (38-9)

1 The poem divides neatly into three sections, in each of which the poet puts one argument. What are these arguments and how does Marvell link the three sections together to form his theme?

2 a Marvell uses diction to create a different mood in each of the three sections of the poem. Show how he creates these varying atmospheres.
  b Is there any general style of writing which runs throughout the poem? Select examples of Marvell's diction which illustrate this.

3 Are there any images in the poem which you find particularly striking? Explain why the ones you choose are especially effective.

■ CARNAL KNOWLEDGE

> Even in bed I pose: desire may grow
> More circumstantial and less circumspect
> Each night, but an acute girl would suspect
> that my self is not like my body, bare.
> I wonder if you know, or, knowing, care?
> You know I know you know I know you know.   6
>
> I am not what I seem, believe me, so
> For the magnanimous pagan I pretend
> Substitute a forked creature as your friend.
> When darkness lies without a roll or stir
> Flaccid, you want a competent poseur.
> I know you know I know you know I know.   12

Cackle you hen, and answer when I crow.
No need to grope: I'm still playing the same
Comical act inside the tragic game.
Yet things perhaps are simpler: could it be
A mere tear-jerker devoid of honesty?
You know I know you know I know you know.   18

Leave me. Within a minute I will stow
Your greedy mouth, but will not yet to grips.
'There is a space between breast and lips.'
Also a space between thighs and head,
So great, we might as well not be in bed.
I know you know I know you know I know.   24

I hardly hoped for happy thoughts, although
In a most happy sleeping time I dreamt
We did not hold each other in contempt.
Then lifting from my lids night's penny weights
I saw that lack of love contaminates.
You know I know you know I know you know.   30

Abandon me to stammering, and go;
If you have tears, prepare to cry elsewhere –
I know of no emotion we can share,
Your intellectual protests are a bore
And even now I pose, so now go, for
I know you know.   36

Thom Gunn □

The tone of the poem is cynical and bitter and this is reflected in the diction in phrases like 'a forked creature' (9) and 'you want a competent poseur' (11). A key line is:

I saw that lack of love contaminates. (29)

A mood of desolate, angry self-disgust permeates the feeling and language of the poem.

1 Summarise the argument that the 'I' of the poem is putting forward to his lover.

2 'Cackle you hen, and answer when I crow' (13)

'... Within a minute I will stow
Your greedy mouth...' (19–20)

What does Gunn's use of this and other imagery and diction in the poem reveal about the 'I' of the poem and his attitude to his lover?

3 Would you say that this poem reflects a sexist attitude in any way?

4 How would you describe the tone of the poem?

5 Compare the attitudes to love and their lovers of the voices of the poems by Marvell and Gunn.

Cynical wit was displayed in both the Marvell and Gunn poems. In the poem below, the humour is dark because the subject is so grave. It is possible that some people might find the use of humour in relation to such themes upsetting and trivialising. Read the poem carefully and make up your own mind whether the humour is appropriate in the context or is offensive in relation to the horrendous events it touches on.

■ APOCALYPSE

'After the New Apocalypse, very few members were still in possession of their instruments. Hardly a musician could call a decent suit his own. Yet by the early summer of 1945, strains of sweet music floated on the air again. While the town still reeked of smoke, charred buildings and the stench of corpses, the Philharmonic Orchestra bestowed the everlasting and imperishable joy which music never fails to give.'

from a German tourist brochure.

It soothes the savage doubts.
One Bach outweighs ten Belsens. If 200,000 people
Were remaindered at Hiroshima, the sales of So-and-So's
New novel reached a higher figure in as short a time.
So, imperishable paintings reappeared;
Texts were reprinted;
Public buildings reconstructed;
Human beings reproduced. 8

After the Newer Apocalypse, very few members
Were still in possession of their instruments
(Very few were still in possession of their members),
And their suits were chiefly indecent.
Yet, while the town still reeked of smoke etc,
The Philharmonic Trio bestowed etc. 14

A civilization vindicated,
A race with three legs still to stand on!
True, the violin was later silenced by leukaemia,
And the pianoforte crumbled softly into dust.
But the flute was left. And one is enough.
All, in a sense, goes on. All is in order. 20

And the ten-tongued mammoth larks,
The forty-foot crickets and the elephantine frogs
Decided that the little chap was harmless,
At least he made no noise, on the banks of whatever river it
    used to be.   25

One day, a reed-warbler stepped on him by accident.
However, all, in a sense, goes on. Still the everlasting and
    imperishable joy
Which music never fails to give is being given.   29

D.J. Enright □

Look at the following two lines from the poem:

One Bach outweighs ten Belsens. . . (2)

A civilization vindicated, (15)

Both these lines are intended to be interpreted ironically. This means that their surface meaning is not their real meaning; in fact, their real meaning is the opposite to what they seem to be saying. Unless the irony in this poem is perceived by the reader, its true meaning will not be understood. The irony is bitter, as befits the grim subject; this bitterly ironic tone is reflected in the terse and mocking diction.

1 'The Philharmonic Trio bestowed etc.' (14)

  This line refers back to the quotation from the tourist brochure that introduces the poem. What is the effect of abbreviating the statement and adding 'etc'?

2 Look at the first four lines of the poem. What point is the poet making here?

3 'True, the violin was later silenced by leukaemia,
  And the pianoforte crumbled softly into dust.
  But the flute was left. And one is enough.
  All, in a sense, goes on. All is in order.' (17–20)

  Is Enright being ironic here, or is he making a factual statement of his beliefs?

4 Some of the diction used is very prosaic and laconic.
  a How does this style undercut the words of the tourist brochure?
  b How does it affect the tone of the poem?

5 The diction of the poem is referred to above as 'terse and mocking'. Pick out examples of words and phrases that seem to you to fit that description.

This chapter ends with two lyrical poems. Contemporary poetry is perhaps seldom lyrical; arguably lyricism is out-of-step with the spirit of the age, the cynicism of modern life.

The poem below was written at about the turn of the century before the First World War ushered in a new, harsher, more prosaic movement in poetry. With the dawning of a less sentimental age, exemplified in the work of poets such as T.S. Eliot, poets have tended to dwell on the more sombre aspects of life rather than subjects like the beauties of nature.

■ NIGHTINGALES

Beautiful must be the mountains whence ye come,
And bright in the fruitful valleys the streams wherefrom
  Ye learn your song:
Where are those starry woods? O might I wander there,
 Among the flowers, which in that heavenly air
  Bloom the year long!   6

Nay, barren are those mountains and spent the streams:
Our song is the voice of desire, that haunts our dreams,
  A throe of the heart,
Whose pining visions dim, forbidden hopes profound,
 No dying cadence nor long sigh can sound
  For all our art.   12

Alone, aloud in the raptured ear of men
We pour our dark nocturnal secret; and then,
  As night is withdrawn
From these sweet-springing meads and bursting boughs of May,
 Dream, while the innumerable choir of day
  Welcome the dawn.   18

Robert Bridges □

The different moods of the stanzas are reflected in the diction used in each. In the first stanza, the poet expresses his admiration for the nightingales; the tone of the diction is uplifting and happy:

 'bright in the fruitful valleys' 'starry woods'

The feeling of emotional desolation in the second stanza is also communicated in the kind of words he uses:

 'spent the streams' 'pining visions dim' 'No dying cadence'

The poem comes to an elegiac close and again the diction underlines this tone:

 'our dark nocturnal secret' 'sweet-springing meads'.

1 Select words or phrases from the poem that belong to a poetic diction; examples of language reserved for poetry and not used in everyday language. What do they add to the poem?

2 What aural impact does the poem make on you?

3 Analyse the structure of each stanza, including the rhyming pattern and line lengths. How does this structure help the poet to convey his meaning?

4 Is the mood of the poem entirely lyrical and optimistic or is there a pessimism present in the poet's treatment of the theme? How do the changing moods of the poem help to develop its theme?

In the following poem the diction is a mixture of the lyrical and the sensuous.

■ A BIRTHDAY

My heart is like a singing bird
   Whose nest is in a water'd shoot;
My heart is like an apple-tree
   Whose boughs are bent with thick-set fruit;
My heart is like a rainbow shell
   That paddles in a halcyon sea;
My heart is gladder than all these,
   Because my love is come to me.   8

Raise me a dais of silk and down;
   Hang it with vair and purple dyes;
Carve it in doves and pomegranates,
   And peacocks with a hundred eyes;
Work it in gold and silver grapes,
   In leaves and silver fleur-de-lys;
Because the birthday of my life
   Is come, my love is come to me.   16

Christina Rossetti □

The structure of the first stanza consists of four pairs of lines, each pair being made up of a simile followed by a describing clause:

My heart is like a singing bird
   Whose nest is in a water'd shoot; (1–2)

The rhythm and sentence structure of the second stanza differ from that of the first. Four of the lines begin with monosyllabic words so the stress is on the first word in the line:

'Raise' 'Hang' 'Carve' 'Work'

This change of rhythm reflects a change in the poem's subject-matter.

1 What is the mood of the poem and how is that mood reflected in the diction and imagery?

2 Show how the poet uses repetition and rhyme to help make an aural impression on the reader.

3 Do you think the imagery of the poem is effective or do you find it clichéd and overdone?

Chapter 10
Form and Meaning

By form we mean the organisation of the verse by the poet. This includes the shape of the poem, length of lines, rhythm, rhyme, stanza structure and metre. All these aspects of form have already been referred to frequently in previous chapters; in this chapter they are considered in greater detail.

However, this salient point should always be borne in mind: form, content and meaning are inextricably linked. The form of a poem is an integral part of the poem as a whole; alter the form of a poem and you alter the content and meaning of the poem. It is useful to analyse the various aspects of poetic form, but that analysis must always be related to the meaning and content of the poetry.

A poem's appearance makes a visual impact on the reader. Several things will be noticed, sometimes subconsciously: the overall shape of the poem, any variation in the length of lines, the division of the poem into stanzas (if any) and the isolation of particular lines. The shape of a poem should be seen in the context of its overall meaning.

Look at the poem called *rain down* by Mary Ellen Solt. The subject-matter and shape of the poem are completely intertwined; the form is the poem and the poem is the form.

Discuss what visual impression the poem makes. The poet also uses the spacing of letters and the typography as a means of expression: what is she seeking to convey by these methods and how successful do you think she is?

● Write a shape poem (a poem that says something about its subject with the shape it forms on the page) on any one of the following;

autumn   gardens   birds   cars   guns

■ rain down

rain down rain down rain down rain down rain dow n rai n b o w
rain down rain down rain down rain down rain dow n rai n b o w
rain down rain down rain down rain down rain dow n rai n b o w
rain down rain down rain down rain down rain dow n rai n b o w
rain down rain down rain down rain down rain dow n rai n b o w
rain down rain down rain down rain down rain dow n rai n b o w
rain down rain down rain down rain down rain dow n rai n b o w
rain down rain down rain down rain down rain dow n rai n b o w
rain down rain down rain down rain down rain dow n rai n b o w
rain down rain down rain down rain down rain dow n rai n b o w
rain down rain down rain down rain down rain dow n rai n b o w
rain down rain down rain down rain down rain dow n rai n b o w
rain down rain down rain down rain down rain dow n rai n b o w
rain down rain down rain down rain down rain dow n rai n b o w
rain down rain down rain down rain down rain dow n rai n b o w
rain down rain down rain down rain down rain dow n rai n b o w
rain down rain down rain down rain down rain dow n rai n b o w
rain down rain down rain down rain down rain dow n rai n b o w
rain down rain down rain down rain down rain dow n rai n b o w
rain down rain down rain down rain down rain dow n rai n b o w
rain down rain down rain down rain down rain dow n rai n b o w
rain down rain down rain down rain down rain dow n rai n b o w
rain down rain down rain down rain down rain dow n rai n b o w
rain down rain down rain down rain down rain dow n rai n b o w
rain down rain down rain down rain down rain dow n rai n b o w
rain down rain down rain down rain down rain dow n rai n b o w

Mary Ellen Solt □

The shape poem by Mary Ellen Solt depends almost entirely on its visual
impact to convey its meaning. The poem overleaf also uses the way it is set out
on the page – its typographical shape and the variations in its line lengths – to
convey its meaning. In addition it makes use of the sound qualities of the
verse, including onomatopoeic words (onomatopoeia is the use of words that
sound like their meaning, such as 'buzz' and 'crash').

■ POEM

For years I've heard
others speak like birds.
                    The words
clicking.
            One day I spoke
articulate
            the words *tic-ed*
in my throat.
            It was
as if love woke   10
                after anger.
The words
                    sure -
                Listen.
(CHURRR)
            Love wakes
at the breakfast table.
                        (CHURRR)
Not that
            the language itself has wings   20
(CHURRR)   Not that
                    (CHURRR)
unfortunate skill.
                Listen.
The words
            sure as a scream.

                    Robin Blaser □

When a poem is printed on the page in a distinctive style as the poem above is,
there is clearly a deliberate intention on the poet's part to communicate
something through its form or shape. One of the most noticeable features of
this poem is the variation in the length of lines and the fact that some lines
begin on the right-hand side of the page:

                    The words
    clicking.   (3–4)

By doing this the poet draws the reader's attention to these words; they are
emphasised by their isolation.

The poem opens quite conventionally in a conversational tone:

    For years I've heard
    others speak like birds. (1–2)

Then there is the isolation of 'The words' and 'clicking' in the next line. The
separation of these words into two lines is a means of emphasis, especially for
the onomatopoeia of 'clicking'.

The manner in which the poem is printed forces the reader to read it slowly and to give due emphasis to words such as 'articulate', 'tic-ed', 'Listen' (repeated) and 'CHURRR' (repeated). By isolating the words 'sure as a scream' as the last line, the poet ensures they carry considerable weight and ends the poem on a dramatic note.

The rhythm of the poem is intertwined with its form. The repetition of 'Listen' as one-word lines stops the poem in its tracks and gives it a stillness, which in turn gives an emphasis to the words that follow:

> 'The words
> sure as a scream.' (24–5)

Discuss what the poem's theme is and how the poet has used the form of the poem to communicate that theme.

Almost everyone responds to rhythm, whether it is in music, in dance or in singing. Some rhythms excite, some soothe; other rhythms provoke sentimental feeling, while some rhythms are restrained and more subtle. Rhythm in poetry can produce a whole range of emotional responses, but it is difficult to analyse or define how this works. The famous poet T.S. Eliot considered the response to rhythm in poetry to be so important that he coined a phrase to describe it. According to Eliot, people respond to a poem's rhythm with the 'auditory imagination.'

The rhythm of a poem's diction is intended to produce an emotional response in the reader. When discussing the rhythm of a poem, the most important factor to be taken into consideration must be how effective it is in underlining or adding to the emotional meaning of the poem as a whole. There is a certain danger in discussing rhythm as a separate component of a poem; diction, rhythm and meaning are intertwined. The discussion of rhythm is a discussion of an aspect of meaning.

It is worth looking first at a poem with a rhythm that is simple and clear; in *Night Mail* by W.H. Auden, the rhythm of the poetry suggests the sound of the steam train so vividly that it is difficult to discuss meaning and rhythm separately. Read the poem aloud.

■ NIGHT MAIL

> This is the Night Mail crossing the Border,
> Bringing the cheque and the postal order,
>
> Letters for the rich, letters for the poor,
> The shop at the corner, the girl next door.
>
> Pulling up Beattock, a steady climb:
> The gradient's against her, but she's on time.
>
> Past cotton-grass and moorland boulder,
> Shovelling white steam over her shoulder,

Snorting noisily as she passes
Silent miles of wind-bent grasses.   10

Birds turn their heads as she approaches,
Stare from bushes at her blank-faced coaches.

Sheep dogs cannot turn her course;
They slumber on with paws across.

In the farm she passes no one wakes,
But a jug in the bedroom gently shakes.

Dawn freshens. Her climb is done.
Down towards Glasgow she descends,
Towards the steam tugs yelping down a glade of cranes,
Towards the fields of apparatus, the furnaces   20
Set on the dark plain like gigantic chessmen.
All Scotland waits for her:
In dark glens, beside pale-green lochs,
Men long for news.

Letters of thanks, letters from banks,
Letters of joy from girl and boy,
Receipted bills and invitations
To inspect new stock or to visit relations,
And applications for situations
And timid lovers' declarations   30
And gossip, gossip from all the nations,
News circumstantial, news financial,
Letters with holiday snaps to enlarge in,
Letters with faces scrawled on the margin,
Letters from uncles, cousins and aunts,
Letters to Scotland from the South of France,
Letters of condolence to Highlands and Lowlands,
Written on paper of every hue,
The pink, the violet, the white and the blue,
The chatty, the catty, the boring, the adoring,   40
The cold and official and the heart's outpouring,
Clever, stupid, short and long,
The typed and the printed and the spelt all wrong.

Thousands are still asleep,
Dreaming of terrifying monsters
Or a friendly tea beside the band in Cranston's or Crawford's:
Asleep in working Glasgow, asleep in well-set Edinburgh,
Asleep in granite Aberdeen,
They continue their dreams,
But shall wake soon and hope for letters,   50
And none will hear the postman's knock
Without a quickening of the heart
For who can bear to feel himself forgotten?

W.H. Auden □

The rhythm of the verse catches the speed, excitement and the insistent noise of the mail train speeding through the night. Just as the train slows down when climbing a gradient, so the rhythm of the poem slows down:

> Dawn freshens. Her climb is done. (17)

Then later, the rhythm picks up again:

> Letters of thanks, letters from banks,
> Letters of joy from girl and boy, (25–26)

Auden thus both avoids repetitive rhythmic monotony and imitates the noise the train makes.

1 Show how the poet uses rhyme, repetition and alliteration to suggest the varying speeds of the train.

2 There are two sections of the poem where rhyme is not used. Compare the rhythm of these sections with the rhyming sections and comment on how this difference in rhythms affects the meaning of the poem.

3 Show how Auden's use of internal rhyme contributes to the impact of the poem.

4 Pick out some examples of imagery from the poem and comment on their effectiveness.

5 This poem was written as a commentary to a Post Office film about the overnight trains taking the mail from London to Scotland. How successful do you think Auden has been in communicating something about that process?

Rhythm in English poetry is based on stressed and unstressed syllables. In speech we naturally stress some syllables and do not stress others. By varying the stress we give to individual words, we can alter meaning:

> Thāt's a good one!
> That's a gōōd one!

A stressed syllable is indicated by the symbol ⁻. Read aloud the two sentences above. If the main stress is put on 'That's' in the first sentence and on 'good' in the second, then the sentences have quite different meanings.

Imagine you are an actor trying to decide how to say this very famous line of Shakespearean dramatic verse:

> To be or not to be: that is the question

You, the actor, have to decide where to put the stresses, i.e. which words and syllables you would stress in saying the line and which you would leave unstressed. You could stress the line in the following way (˘ stands for an unstressed syllable, ⁻ for a stressed syllable):

> Tŏ bē | ŏr nōt | tŏ bē: | thāt ĭs | thĕ q̄ūes | tiŏn.

There are five stresses in the line when it is pronounced in this way. You could, however, choose to put the stresses on different syllables or words:

Tŏ bē | ōr nōt | tŏ bē: | thăt ĭs | thĕ qūes | tiŏn.

Now read the line aloud and listen to how the varying of the stresses alters the meaning of the line. As an actor you might even decide to say the line without stressing any words or syllables. Try that, speaking it aloud. Finally, you could choose to say it in a very eccentric manner:

Tō bĕ | ōr nŏt | tŏ bē: | thăt ĭs | thē qūes | tiŏn.

The point is that different people reading or performing poetry aloud or to themselves might well put stresses on different words, according to their interpretation of the meaning, thus altering the rhythm.

Although there exists this scope for actors and readers to choose where to put the stresses in verse, it is not difficult to recognise patterns of rhythm in poetry. Rhythm is measured in metrical feet. A foot usually consists of one stressed syllable (or monosyllabic word) and one or more unstressed syllables. Some metres in verse fall into recognisable rhythmic units so that we are able to give specific names to them. The basic metrical foot used by Shakespeare for his plays and for the line quoted above is the iambic one; that is an unstressed syllable followed by a stressed one. There are five of these iambic metrical feet in each line. The whole line is called an iambic pentameter.

However, it has already been seen that different actors might well want to pronounce the same line differently, depending on their own interpretation of the needs of the play. Indeed Shakespeare himself makes use of many variations on the basic pattern in order to bring out fully the meaning and emphasis of the words. The rhythm of the iambic pentameter and of all types of metre are there only in order to bring out the meaning, not for their own sake, or to put the verse in a straitjacket.

When the metrical pattern of a poem is analysed, this is called scanning (noun: scansion). There is, however, no point in endlessly scanning lines of poetry in a mechanical manner. The rhythm of poetry is of interest to us because it is an essential tool in the poet's locker; because rhythm and meaning are intertwined.

Here is a list of the most common metrical feet:

iambic foot	˘ ⁻	unstressed syllable followed by a stressed syllable.
trochaic foot	⁻ ˘	stressed syllable followed by an unstressed syllable.
anapaestic foot	˘ ˘ ⁻	two unstressed syllables followed by one stressed syllable.
dactylic foot	⁻ ˘ ˘	stressed syllable followed by two unstressed syllables.
spondaic foot	⁻ ⁻	two stressed syllables.

Note: although a poem may be, for example, mostly written in iambic or trochaic feet, extra syllables or a foot of a different metre can be inserted by the poet as a variation, according to the content and meaning of the verse.

A line of poetry usually consists of several feet. A line of poetry with three feet is a trimeter; with four feet it is a tetrameter; with five feet it is a pentameter; with six feet it is a hexameter or Alexandrine. Poetry written in a basic unit of ˘ ‾ (iambic), with five feet to each line, is employing iambic pentameter, the commonest form of metre used in English poetry.

One of the most famous popular poems to be written in the nineteenth century was Tennyson's *The Charge of the Light Brigade.* He set out to write a memorial to the glorious dead who perished as the result of a monumental military blunder on the part of the British commanders during the Crimean War. The rhythm of the verse plays an essential part in creating the poem's rousing, patriotic mood.

■ THE CHARGE OF THE LIGHT BRIGADE

I

Half a league, half a league,
Half a league onward,
All in the valley of Death
　Rode the six hundred.
'Forward, the Light Brigade!
Charge for the guns!' he said:
Into the valley of Death
　Rode the six hundred.　　8

II

'Forward, the Light Brigade!'
Was there a man dismay'd?
Not tho' the soldier knew
　Some one had blunder'd:
Their's not to make reply,
Their's not to reason why,
Their's but to do and die:
Into the valley of Death
　Rode the six hundred.　　17

III

Cannon to right of them,
Cannon to left of them,
Cannon in front of them
　Volley'd and thunder'd;
Storm'd at with shot and shell,
Boldly they rode and well,
Into the jaws of Death,
Into the mouth of Hell
　Rode the six hundred.　　26

221

IV

Flash'd all their sabres bare,
Flash'd as they turn'd in air
Sabring the gunners there,
Charging an army, while
    All the world wonder'd:
Plunged in the battery-smoke
Right thro' the line they broke;
Cossack and Russian
Reel'd from the sabre-stroke
    Shatter'd and sunder'd.
Then they rode back, but not
    Not the six hundred. 38

V

Cannon to right of them,
Cannon to left of them,
Cannon behind them
    Volley'd and thunder'd;
Storm'd at with shot and shell,
While horse and hero fell,
They that had fought so well
Came thro' the jaws of Death,
Back from the mouth of Hell,
All that was left of them,
    Left of six hundred. 49

VI

When can their glory fade?
O the wild charge they made!
    All the world wonder'd.
Honour the charge they made!
Honour the Light Brigade,
    Noble six hundred! 55

Alfred Lord Tennyson □

The poem's use of repetition is clearly an important aspect of its rhythm, a feature it shares with traditional ballads (compare the poem with the ballads in Chapter 7). Tennyson manages to suggest in his verse the drumming sounds of the horses' hooves as the charge takes place. The poem's rhythm has the obvious emotional effect that a rousing military march or patriotic anthem can have in music.

1 a What is the basic metrical foot that Tennyson employs? Is there any reason why it is particularly suitable for expressing the content of his poem?
  b Show how the rhythm helps to create the battle scene in the reader's mind.

2 What effect does the rhyming scheme of each stanza have?

3 Give your opinion of the poem. Discuss the theme and its treatment, including the poet's use of rhythm and diction.

The ability to use rhyme sensitively is one of the poet's most important skills. Rhyme is used to give a unity to the verse and can also emphasise something a poet wishes to communicate. It can be used almost contradictorily, either to amuse or to heighten emotional response. Rhyme can be blatant doggerel or, on the other hand, it can be subtle in its effect.

The traditional ballad *Edward, Edward* (page 143) showed rhyme used to unify the poem and to help advance the narrative. In Tennyson's hands, it recreates the emotions evoked by the Charge of the Light Brigade (pages 221–222). Rhyme is also a favourite tool of satirical poets such as Pope and Marvell (pages 180 and 206), because it lends itself to epigrammatic use in enabling the poet to make a witty point in a forceful, rounded way. John Betjeman also uses rhyme (pages 170–171) to highlight the sad and lonely death of an old woman.

As well as full rhyme, poets can employ half-rhyme, sight rhyme and internal rhyme. Half-rhyme is when words do not completely rhyme but closely echo one another. Sight rhyme is when words look like one another and as though they ought to rhyme but do not in fact do so. Internal rhyme is when words in the same line of poetry rhyme. In this poem by Wilfred Owen, rhyme is used unobtrusively.

■ FUTILITY

Move him into the sun –
Gently its touch awoke him once,
At home, whispering of fields unsown.
Always it woke him, even in France,
Until this morning and this snow.
If anything might rouse him now
The kind old sun will know.   7

Think how it wakes the seeds, –
Woke, once, the clays of a cold star.
Are limbs, so dear-achieved, are sides,
Full-nerved – still warm – too hard to stir?
Was it for this the clay grew tall?
– O what made fatuous sunbeams toil
To break earth's sleep at all?   14

Wilfred Owen □

Both stanzas follow this rhyming pattern:

... sun *a*
... once *b*
... (un)sown *a*
... France *b*
... snow *c*
... now *c*
... know *c*

This rhyming pattern is worked out as follows; the final syllable of each line is given a letter. A final syllable of a line which rhymes with a preceding final syllable is given the same letter as that syllable. Final syllables which do not rhyme with any preceding syllable are given new letters.

This pattern provides a unit for the poet, a structure in which he can communicate his feelings. For the reader, rhyme can set up pleasing or disturbing echoes; it can also make connections for the reader. The poem is unusual in the number of half-rhymes it has:

sun-sown   once-France   seeds-sides   tall-toil

1 Show how the poet uses full rhymes, half-rhymes and internal rhymes to give unity of sound and meaning to the first stanza.

2 The rhyme contributes greatly to the sound impact of the poem. What other techniques does the poet use to appeal to the auditory imagination of the reader?

3 Has the poet, in your opinion, conveyed the emotion he feels to you or does the poem make little impression on you? Give detailed reasons for your opinion, supporting them with evidence from the poem.

Poets have usually chosen to write within established genres or forms of poetry, although it is true to say that twentieth-century poets have done that less and less. One of the most popular genres or forms is the sonnet, which is a fourteen-line poem. There are two main types of sonnet in English poetry. Firstly there is the Shakespearean sonnet (an example of which appears on page 239) which consists of three quatrains and a closing rhyming couplet. Secondly there is the Petrarchan sonnet, which consists of an octave (eight lines) and a sestet (six lines). Keats found both forms unsatisfactory and experimented with the genre to suit his own poetic needs.

■ TO SLEEP

> O soft embalmer of the still midnight!
>   Shutting with careful fingers and benign
> Our gloom-pleasèd eyes, embower'd from the light,
>   Enshaded in forgetfulness divine;
> O soothest Sleep! If so it please thee, close,
>   In midst of this thine hymn, my willing eyes,
> Or await the amen, ere thy poppy throws
>   Around my bed its lulling charities;   8

> Then save me, or the passèd day will shine
> Upon my pillow, breeding many woes;
> Save me from curious conscience, that still lords
> Its strength for darkness, burrowing like a mole;
> Turn the key deftly in the oilèd wards,
> And seal the hushèd casket of my soul.

John Keats □

In both types of sonnet, the poet often uses the beginning of the sestet to develop a new thought or aspect of the theme; Keats follows this principle.

Also noteworthy is Keats' use of aural effects:

> O soft embalmer of the still midnight! (1)

There is an obvious use of alliteration in this line in the repetition of the initial 's', which is an example of sibilance (see page 190). In this line too, Keats has used repetition of the vowels 'o' and 'i', which is an example of assonance (see page 200).

Notice how Keats varies the flow of the verse in the sonnet: the first and fourth lines are end-stopped, while the ones in between are run-on lines. He maintains this changing flow of verse throughout the sonnet.

1 Read the octave carefully and then the sestet. Is there a definite change in the content or treatment of the theme between the octave and the sestet? If so, what is this change?

2 Follow the sense of the lines and show how the octave and sestet are divided up. Analyse the use that Keats makes of the caesura and of end-stopped and run-on lines. What does the poet intend to convey by this?

3 Pick out examples of alliteration, sibilance, assonance and use of long vowel sounds from the poem and show how the use of these techniques enhances the sound quality of the poetry and contributes to the tone and meaning of the poem.

4 A Shakespearean sonnet is made up of three units of four lines rhyming *a b a b c d c d e f e f*, followed by a closing rhyming couplet. How does Keats vary this rhyming scheme in *To Sleep*?

5 How successful is Keats, in your opinion, in conveying what he feels about sleep?

The modern poem which follows may not seem to have much rhythm to it at first reading, because the rhythm is unobtrusive. However, analysis will show that it has a rhythm that is appropriate to the poet's subject and the tone of the poem.

■ POETRY OF DEPARTURES

Sometimes you hear, fifth-hand,
As epitaph:
He chucked up everything
And just cleared off,
And always the voice will sound
Certain you approve
This audacious, purifying,
Elemental move.   8

And they are right, I think.
We all hate home
And having to be there:
I detest my room,
Its specially-chosen junk,
The good books, the good bed,
And my life, in perfect order:
So to hear it said   16

He walked out on the whole crowd
Leaves me flushed and stirred,
Like *Then she undid her dress*
Or *Take that you bastard*:
Surely I can, if he did?
And that helps me stay
Sober and industrious.
But I'd go today,   24

Yes, swagger the nut-strewn roads,
Crouch in the fo'c'sle
Stubbly with goodness, if
It weren't so artificial,
Such a deliberate step backwards
To create an object:
Books; china; a life
Reprehensibly perfect.   32

Philip Larkin □

Philip Larkin is a thoughtful poet; most of his statements about the human
condition are hedged with doubt and heavily qualified. This tentative tone is
reflected in the rhythm of his verse and is illustrated by the variation in his use
of run-on and end-stopped lines.

At the end of the first line, 'fifth-hand' lends an ironic note to the opening of
the poem. In the second line, 'epitaph' followed by the colon, prepares the way
for the emphasis on the statement that is really the idea behind the poem. The

flow of the verse through the next three lines stopping after 'audacious' and 'purifying' sets up the emphasis for the words 'Elemental move.' The rhythm of the poem is not obtrusive, but it is there and it is wedded to the meaning.

Another subtle aspect of the poem is its rhyming structure; perhaps this should be more accurately referred to as its half-rhyming structure. In the first stanza there are half-rhymes between 'hand–sound,' 'epitaph–off', 'everything–purifying' and a full rhyme between 'approve–move'. In case you think this structure is just accidental, an analysis of the second verse reveals these connections: 'think–junk'; 'home–room'; 'there–order'; 'bed–said'. The same pattern is repeated in each of the final two stanzas. Again it is unobtrusive and is completely integrated into the overall meaning of the poem.

1 Analyse the flow of the verse in the poem, including any use of the caesuras to break the rhythm within a line and any connections between stanzas. What does Larkin achieve by this?

2 'Such a deliberate step backwards
To create an object:
Books; china; a life
Reprehensibly perfect.' (29–32)

By having 'a life' at the end of the line and 'Reprehensibly perfect' as a separate line, does the poet create a special emphasis on the words that would not be there if he had written 'a life reprehensibly perfect' as one line? If so, how does this special stress work? Are there any other instances of this?

3 'The good books, the good bed,' (14)

What tone lies behind the use of 'good' in this line?

4 'Yes, swagger the nut-strewn roads,
Crouch in the fo'c'sle
Stubbly with goodness . . .' (25–27)

What are these details intended to convey to the reader and what part do they play in the development of the poem's theme?

Blank verse is a very common form of metre used in poetry of many periods. The most famous poet to have used blank verse is William Shakespeare who wrote his plays in this metre. Blank verse is unrhymed iambic pentameters – that is, verse with five iambic feet to a line ($\smile$ – five times) which is unrhymed (see also pages 219–221).

Shakespeare, and other dramatists and poets, found blank verse gave them a flexibility within a pattern. The following speech is from Shakespeare's play *Macbeth* in which the 'hero', Macbeth, soliloquises on the rights and wrongs of murdering Duncan, the King of Scotland, in order to gain the throne himself. Guilt, ambition and fear struggle against each other for prominence in Macbeth's mind and this is reflected in the form of the verse.

■ MACBETH *Act I Scene 7*

If it were done, when 'tis done, then 'twere well
It were done quickly; if th'assassination
Could trammel up the consequence, and catch
With his surcease, success; that but this blow
Might be the be-all and the end-all – here,
But here, upon this bank and shoal of time –
We'd jump the life to come. But in these cases
We still have judgement here; that we but teach
Bloody instructions which, being taught, return
To plague th'inventor. This even-handed justice   10
Commends th'ingredients of our poisoned chalice
To our own lips . . . He's here in double trust:
First, as I am his kinsman and his subject,
Strong both against the deed; then as his host

Who should against the murderer shut the door,
Not bear the knife myself. Besides, this Duncan
Hath borne his faculties so meek, hath been
So clear in his great office, that his virtues
Will plead like angels, trumpet-tongued, against
The deep damnation of his taking-off;   20
And pity, like a naked new-born babe,
Striding the blast, or heaven's cherubin, horsed
Upon the sightless couriers of the air,
Shall blow the horrid deed in every eye,
That tears shall drown the wind . . . I have no spur
To prick the sides of my intent, but only
Vaulting ambition, which o'erleaps itself
And falls on t'other –

William Shakespeare □

If the first four lines of the extract are scanned, this metrical pattern is revealed:

Ĭf ĭt | wĕre dōne | whĕn 'tĭs | dŏne, thĕn | 'twĕre wĕll
Ĭt wēre | dŏne quīck | lў; ĭf | th' ăssăss | ĭnāt | ĭŏn
Coŭld trām | mĕl ūp | thĕ cōn | sĕquēnce, | ănd cātch
Wĭth hĭs | sŭrcēāse, | sŭccēss; | thăt būt | thĭs blōw . . .

Although these four lines use an iambic foot, there is some variation in the
number of unstressed syllables. There are resting-places (caesuras) in the first
line after 'were done' and after "tis done', in the second line after 'quickly',
after 'consequence' in the third line, and after 'surcease' and 'success' in the
fourth line. The placing of the caesuras is arranged so that the lines avoid a
plodding monotony and the pauses also help to underline the anxiety in the
tone of Macbeth's speech.

1 Take any section of ten lines of the speech and note where Shakespeare places the
caesura in each line. Is there a variation in the placing which follows the nuances of the
speaker's thoughts?

2 Some lines in this extract are end-stopped and some are examples of enjambment.
Select two examples of each and show how both devices suit the sense and emphasis
that Shakespeare wishes to convey at those points in the speech.

3 Select three examples of striking imagery from the speech and comment on their use.

4 'Striding the blast . . .' (22)
'Vaulting ambition . . .' (27)

Comment on the rhythm of these lines; is it what would be expected in an iambic line?

5 Generally, how does the rhythm of the speech underline the tone and meaning of the
words in the soliloquy?

Sprung rhythm is similar to the free verse of modern poets in that it allows poets the freedom from writing to conventional metres; in sprung rhythm what matters is the way that the stresses in a line are placed. The verse does not conform to a strict metrical pattern. A number of unstressed syllables can be attached to a stressed one and two or more stressed syllables can come one after the other.

Gerard Manley Hopkins (1844–1889) used sprung rhythm in his poetry, together with alliteration and assonance, to create a distinctive sound and rhythm which are integrated with the meaning of the poem. Read aloud the following poem by Hopkins; the sense should lead you to stress certain syllables and words. The poem does not obey a conventional metrical pattern, but it has a definite rhythm which reflects its emotional content.

In the first line, 'my duty' refers to Hopkins' role as a Roman Catholic priest.

■ FELIX RANDAL

Felix Randal the farrier, O is he dead then? my duty all ended,
Who have watched his mould of man, big-boned and hardy-
    handsome
Pining, pining, till time when reason rambled in it and some
Fatal four disorders, fleshed there, all contended?

Sickness broke him. Impatient he cursed at first, but mended
Being anointed and all; though a heavenlier heart began some
Months earlier, since I had our sweet reprieve and ransom
Tendered to him. Ah well, God rest him all road ever he   9
    offended!

This seeing the sick endears them to us, us too it endears.
My tongue had taught thee comfort, touch had quenched thy
    tears,
Thy tears that touched my heart, child, Felix, poor Felix
    Randal;

How far from then forethought of, all thy more boisterous   16
    years,
When thou at the random grim forge, powerful amidst peers,
Didst fettle for the great grey drayhorse his bright and
    battering sandal!
                                        Gerard Manley Hopkins □

Reading the poem aloud should emphasise how unusual the rhythm is compared to more conventional metres. The unfamiliar rhythm and word-order may cause some initial difficulty in understanding the poem. Hopkins also invents phrases – 'hardy-handsome', 'a heavenlier heart' – which give the verse a memorable quality. In the midst of this complexity, the poet also uses some diction which is effective because of its simplicity: 'O is he dead then?'

1 What differences do you notice in the rhythm and stress pattern of *Felix Randal* from more conventional poetry?

2 The verse does not always flow smoothly. How do the changes in rhythm underline the varying mood and subject-matter of the poem?

3 Choose one stanza of the poem to be read aloud. Note where the stresses in each line are and the variation in the number of unstressed syllables.

4 Show how Hopkins emphasises the meaning of his verse with various aural techniques.

Modern poetry, for the most part, has broken away from conventional metres and forms. Just as modern theatre and music (both pop and classical music) have found new forms and broken old rules, so has modern poetry.

Free verse is one of the labels applied to this modern movement in poetry; it is verse that obeys no set metrical pattern and which is usually unrhymed. That does not mean that it is lacks rhythm; the rhythm and the form of the verse emerge from the content and the treatment of the theme. Rarely do modern poets sit down and aim to write a poem in iambic feet within a sonnet or other conventional form. However, that is not to say that they do not use metrical patterns, but most do not feel bound by them. Extra feet can be added where the content demands it, stanzas can be lengthened or shortened, words isolated and stress patterns varied: the general principle is that content and meaning dictate form and versification.

The poem below is an example of free verse.

■ MARY'S SONG

The Sunday lamb cracks in its fat.
The fat
Sacrifices its opacity . . .

A window, holy gold.
The fire makes it precious,
The same fire   6

Melting the tallow heretics,
Ousting the Jews.
Their thick palls float

Over the cicatrix of Poland, burnt-out
Germany.
They do not die.   12

Grey birds obsess my heart,
Mouth-ash, ash of eye.
They settle. On the high

Precipice
That emptied one man into space
The ovens glowed like heavens,
    incandescent.   19

It is a heart,
This holocaust I walk in,
O golden child the world will kill
    and eat.

Sylvia Plath □

Although the meaning of this poem is elusive, the varying rhythm and cryptic style of the verse underline its nightmarish quality with a succession of stark images of fire and destruction. The poet seems to be following a series of ideas set in motion by the lamb cooking in its fat. The short phrases, lines consisting of one word and the spare quality of the diction all add to the intensity of the feeling within this brief poem.

1 The basic metrical unit of the poem is iambic, but extra syllables or different feet are used in numerous lines. Show how the metre varies in the poem and comment on the effect of this.

2 Plath uses lines of varying length. On which words does the poet focus our attention by doing this? What difference does this make to the poem?

3 Each stanza consists of either three or four lines, but their shape and flow vary. Show how the poet varies the rhythm and flow of the verse by the use of end-stopped lines and enjambment, and by the placing of caesuras. Discuss how this affects the meaning of the poem.

4 There are frequent uses of assonance, sibilance and repetition in the poem. Analyse how the poet uses these features to convey the emotion of the poem.

5 a Is there any particular theme the poet is trying to convey?
   b What do you think of *Mary's Song* as a poem?

Chapter 11
Critical Appreciation

This chapter begins by offering practical advice on writing answers to critical appreciation questions. This advice is followed by an example of an answer to a critical appreciation question. Finally, there is the opportunity to practise writing appreciation essays by answering questions which each ask for a comparison of two poems.

General Advice

Throughout your A level course you will be writing critical appreciations in class and at home, but most of the advice here is geared to examination demands in which you have to complete an essay in a restricted time.

Many A level English Literature syllabuses ask you to write a critical appreciation of a poem that you have not seen before or to make a critical comparison of two unseen poems. You may be asked to write a general appreciation, but often the wording of the question directs you to consider specific aspects of the poetry, such as diction, imagery, form and style. Sometimes you are asked to compare poems in terms of how the writers handle similar subject-matter or a similar theme.

In proceeding to answer these questions, it is obvious that you must address yourself to the specified task and not launch into a general critical appreciation, if that is not required of you: make sure you pay attention to the exact wording of the questions in examination papers. This is a cardinal rule for all examination candidates.

Another simple but important rule to remember is to read the passage through several times before starting on your answer and if it is poetry, make sure you listen to the sound of the verse by sub-vocalising. You will not be able to begin your essay impressively and with a coherent plan unless you have a good grasp of your subject-matter.

Whatever the task the question sets, you must find a way of structuring your answer, of organising your material. All English examinations are a test of your ability to write English, including English Literature examinations. An unstructured, rambling essay will largely undo any cogent analysis you may have hidden among the confusion that meets the examiner's eye. Think of all examiners as extremely crotchety individuals, ploughing their way through masses of exam answers: point the way clearly for these important people! Aim for clarity, conciseness and continuity.

Critical appreciation involves giving your opinion about the worth of the writing, but it also involves the analysis of theme, treatment, diction, imagery and form. This analysis should lead naturally to your critical evaluation, sometimes called the value judgement. Do not launch into giving your critical evaluation without first considering the material in some detail, or your opinion will carry little weight.

It is very important to follow this rule in any critical analysis of literature and at every stage of the essay: always back up your analysis and opinions by referring to specific evidence in the text. If a candidate writes; 'The imagery of the poem is rather clichéd and repetitive' and leaves it at that, then the opinion stands on its own, without any evidence from the text to illustrate what is meant. It would be much better to follow the statement above with some appropriate evidence such as; 'For example, the image of the falling leaves as a symbol of decay is over-familiar and the image of the iceberg in the second stanza as a metaphor for emotional coldness is too clichéd to have much impact.' The reports of chief examiners on the performance of candidates in literature exams are full of complaints that candidates make generalisations which they fail to support with relevant references and quotations from the text.

Of course, be careful not to be excessive in the amount you quote in your analysis of unseen literature. You have the text in front of you, so it is not a great feat to be able to lift chunks out of it. Remember also that examiners have the text in front of them as well, so copying out long stretches of text has no point: refer to and quote from the relevant line of the passage briefly.

General Advice Summary

The main points covered can be summarised as follows:

1 Look at the question carefully and make sure you answer only the specific question asked.

2 Read the poem or poems several times before starting your essay so that you have a good grasp of the subject-matter.

3 Aim for clarity, conciseness and continuity in your essay.

4 Do not give your critical evaluation before you have considered the poem fully in your essay.

5 Always back up your analysis and opinions by referring to specific evidence in the text.

6 Refer briefly to the relevant line of a poem or quote briefly when supporting your opinions with evidence from the text. Do not waste time in copying out long passages.

Structuring a Critical Appreciation Essay

There is no one correct formula for writing a structured essay of critical appreciation, but the guidelines which follow will at least give you the basis for a structured approach.

When you start writing your essay, the first rule to remember is: Do not waffle! Don't write an opening paragraph that says nothing at all. If you are writing a general critical appreciation, start by saying what you think the theme of the poem is and commenting on its tone. Then proceed to discuss the treatment the poet gives to the theme in the content of the poem. Analyse the content, not line-by-line, or even stanza-by-stanza, but by tracing the development of the theme through the poem.

Next, discuss the way theme and subject-matter are realised in the poem. Meaning and form, diction, imagery and tone – these can hardly be separated from one another. Yet it is possible to discuss form, imagery and diction separately, as component parts of a poem, as long as they are analysed in terms of their contribution to the meaning and impact of the whole poem. If you are tracing the imagery of a poem, try to show how the images create the emotional tone of the verse and, therefore, crucially affect its meaning. Similarly, an analysis of the form, versification or any other features of the poem is only useful if it is shown how they affect the meaning of the poem.

Only after working your way through a poem in this way, will you be in a position to comment on the writing as a whole. Now it is time to give a value judgement of the whole work. That is not to say that you will not have expressed opinions on some aspects already – the quality of the imagery, the appropriateness of the diction, the rhythm of the verse. By all means, comment on the effectiveness (or the reverse!) of these aspects as you deal with them, but the general critical evaluation should come at the end of the essay.

As you have written your analysis in detail and in a considered manner, you will want to continue this approach in the section where you are expressing your opinions. 'A considered manner' does not mean that you cannot express strong opinions; you should respond to the writing. Whatever the opinions you express, however, avoid sweeping generalisations that totally dismiss or wildly over-praise, especially if you do not back up your opinions with good reasons. Examples of this kind of criticism would be to say that 'This poem is the most boring I have ever read', or 'This poem is the best I have ever read.' Perhaps! But in the way the opinions are expressed, the examiner is bound to sniff hyperbole, the stand-by substitute for real critical analysis.

A much more fruitful approach is to state your response in a clear unvarnished way and then explain your reasons, using the critical terminology with which you have become familiar during your A level course. It is permissible in an A level English Literature exam to state a preference between two unseen poems, but support your opinions with good reasons and back them up with relevant evidence from the text.

Essay Structure Summary

Although, of course, there is no set formula for writing a critical appreciation essay, the following outline may provide a useful skeleton structure:

1 Discuss the theme, including the tone of the poem or poems and the attitude of the poet to the subject-matter.

2 Analyse how the poet handles the theme by tracing its development through the poem.

3 Discuss the component parts of the poem, including imagery, diction, rhythm and form, in relation to the meaning and impact of the poem.

4 Give your own critical evaluation of the writing.

One obvious danger is that section 2 of the structure will take up too much space and become a sterile line-by-line, stanza-by-stanza summary. In this part of your essay, concentrate on covering the most important content: a full-scale summary is not what is wanted.

It should be stressed again that you must find a way of linking these sections together; you are being examined on your ability to write an English essay as well as your critical ability. All good essays have continuity. Paragraphs should be linked together by referring back to a topic discussed in the previous paragraph, using linking phrases such as 'Another aspect of the diction. . .' or 'Not all the imagery, however, is as forceful as. . .'

Of course, you may use your own structure for your essays. The important thing is that you have a discernible plan. As an example of an answer to a critical appreciation question, read the following essay. It is an answer to this question:

Write a critical appreciation of *Winter* by Ruth Stone, discussing the theme of the poem and commenting on any features of its style that contribute to its full effect (the poem can be found on page 204).

The theme of the poem is the sense of loss that the poet, or the 'I' of the poem, feels at the memory of her dead husband. The harsh wintry scene at the station, and on the journey, draw forth sad recollections and her perception of her surroundings is shaped by and at the same time reflects her sadness. The mood is pessimistic and defensive, so that new passengers getting on the train seem to intrude on her – 'ravish me.'

This sombre mood is suggested by the brusque opening of the first line of the poem. The scene is set. There is the picturesque simile of the coaches 'like loaves of bread powdered with snow.' The scene evokes memories of her husband and we learn that she is a widow:

'. . . under the seal of my widowhood.'

The harshness of the winter reflects her mood, her 'drab misery'. Her sense of alienation makes her think of 'the subjugation of women and horses'. The 'brutal exposure' of the cold is both physical and emotional.

There are a few happier images from the past; she describes how she and her husband used to meet in stations 'arching up with nineteenth-century optimism'. But this lifting of the mood ends abruptly in the question:

'Am I going toward you or away from you on this train?'

Her feelings of alienation and her sense of waste are reflected in the images of waste that she sees discarded beside the track. The passengers she sees standing on a station platform, 'their faces expecting something', are somehow menacing in her vulnerable state.

The most compelling aspect of the poem for me is the force of the images the poet uses to convey the speaker's desolation. The diction she uses to describe the station, for instance, not only vividly describes the scene but communicates her solitary grief:

'Stripped to plywood, the station's cement standing room'

There is something cold and unfeeling in those images; this is how the speaker perceives the world in her sadness. The simple but somehow eloquent statement

'It is now that I remember you'

follows on naturally as an extension of the mood established in the first few lines. 'The carved handle of a letter knife' reminds her of her husband's face and she continues the 'letter' metaphor in

'Your heavy-lidded eyes slip under the seal of my widowhood.'

This figurative language is balanced by direct, simple description:

'It is another raw winter. Stray cats are suffering.'

The sibilance of the second half of that line and in the following line:

'Starlings crowd the edges of chimneys'

underlines the sense of sadness. The short sharp phrases

'Brutal exposure. Weather that forces, that strips'

convey the feeling that the poet feels vulnerable, that her emotions are in a raw, exposed state matching the surroundings. She is suffering like the animals she mentions.

As a contrast to this gloom, the diction she uses in her memories of her husband is full of life:

'ornate' 'arching up' 'optimism' 'running'

Even 'the column of polished oak' has a reassuring comfortable feel to it, in contrast to the images of waste that follow:

'Mounds of rusting wire' 'dead motors'

These are the debris of modern industrial civilisation and concrete images of her sense of estrangement from the world and the people in it. The rhythm of the verse underlines the emotional tone of the poem. The stark images of the opening three lines are presented in three end-stopped lines, setting up a mood of alienation. The full stop in the middle of the fifth line leaves an emphasis for

'It is now that I remember you.'

The poet repeats this construction in another key line:

'It is a drab misery that urges me to remember you.'

The fragmented rhythm of 'Brutal exposure. Weather that forces, that strips' reflects the harsh mood of the poem at this point. The rhythm changes when the speaker recalls past occasions she shared with her husband. In the lines describing 'ornate stations' and her husband hiding behind the 'column of polished oak', the flowing verse produced by the use of enjambment emphasises the more confident mood of the speaker. But this rhythm changes in the succession of monosyllabic words that smack almost of desperation:

Am I going toward you or away from you on this train?

The desolate images of the 'Discarded junk' evoke through the rhythm of the verse a feeling of desolation. The final line of the poem and the long vowels of 'entire histories' express the weight of feeling the speaker is suffering.

The poem, in my opinion, very vividly communicates this sense of waste and loneliness. The imagery, both literal and figurative, leaves a lingering impression. How often surroundings seem alienating and dehumanising, especially in a city context and especially if you are feeling sad and lonely. At moments like this, mundane objects are seen more clearly and frequently in a more menacing light. This is the strength of the poem for me. It is evocative and full of atmosphere. A slight criticism might be that some of the images are somewhat too self-conscious and literary. For example, the reference to the station's standing room imitating 'a Russian novel' seems an unnecessary literary reference; it is as though the poet were viewing the experience from a writer's point of view rather than in a directly emotional way from the point of view of the individual in that situation.

The poem also hints at other issues, giving it layers of meaning beyond the expression of grief. The reference to the 'subjugation of women and horses' and the images of industrial waste hint at a dehumanised and uncaring society. Somehow the nineteenth-century optimism has given way to twentieth-century barbarism and alienation. This sense of alienation pervades the poem because the poet's sense of loss has found a convincing counterpart in her immediate surroundings and the waste of the society she finds so menacing. The density of meaning and imagery makes the poem a profound expression of deeply-felt emotions that transcends all expression of personal grief.

In the rest of this chapter, you are given the opportunity to write essays making comparisons between poems. Read the instructions before each one very carefully; make sure you get into the habit of doing what you have actually been asked.

Compare the two sonnets below; how do the attitudes of the two poets differ to the 'lovers' in the poems? Comment on the difference in tone between the two poems and show how this is reflected in the diction, imagery, rhythm and form of the sonnets.

SONNET

When in disgrace with fortune and men's eyes,
I all alone beweep my outcast state,
And trouble deaf heaven with my bootless cries,
And look upon myself, and curse my fate,
Wishing me like to one more rich in hope,
Featured like him, like him with friends possess'd
Desiring this man's art and that man's scope,
With what I most enjoy contented least;
Yet in these thoughts myself almost despising,
Haply I think on thee, and then my state,
Like to the lark at break of day arising
From sullen earth, sings hymns at heaven's gate;
    For thy sweet love remember'd such wealth brings
    That then I scorn to change my state with kings.

William Shakespeare

SONNET

I, being born a woman and distressed
By all the needs and notions of my kind,
Am urged by your propinquity to find
Your person fair, and feel a certain zest
To bear your body's weight upon my breast:
So subtly is the fume of life designed,
To clarify the pulse and cloud the mind,
And leave me once again undone, possessed.
Think not for this, however, the poor treason
Of my stout blood against my staggering brain,
I shall remember you with love, or season
My scorn with pity, – let me make it plain:
I find this frenzy insufficient reason
For conversation when we meet again.

Edna St. Vincent Millay

239

Compare the following two poems from the point of view of theme, treatment of theme, diction and rhythm.

THE ROLLING ENGLISH ROAD

Before the Roman came to Rye or out to Severn strode,
The rolling English drunkard made the rolling English road.
A reeling road, a rolling road, that rambles round the shire,
And after him the parson ran, the sexton and the squire;
A merry road, a mazy road, and such as we did tread
The night we went to Birmingham by way of Beachy Head.   6

I knew no harm of Bonaparte and plenty of the Squire,
And for to fight the Frenchman I did not much desire;
But I did bash their baggonets because they came arrayed
To straighten out the crooked road an English drunkard made,
Where you and I went down the lane with ale-mugs in our hands,
The night we went to Glastonbury by way of Goodwin sands.   12

His sins they were forgiven him; or why do flowers run
Behind him; and the hedges all strengthening in the sun?
The wild thing went from left to right and knew not which was which,
But the wild rose was above him when they found him in the ditch.
God pardon us, nor harden us; we did not see so clear
The night we went to Bannockburn by way of Brighton Pier.   18

My friends, we will not go again or ape an ancient rage,
Or stretch the folly of our youth to be the shame of age,
But walk with clearer eyes and ears this path that wandereth,
And see undrugg'd in evening light the decent inn of death;
For there is good news yet to hear and fine things to be seen,
Before we go to Paradise by way of Kensal Green.   24

Gilbert Chesterton

HOW BEASTLY THE BOURGEOIS IS

How beastly the bourgeois is
especially the male of the species –

Presentable eminently presentable –
shall I make you a present of him?

Isn't he handsome? Isn't he healthy? Isn't he a fine specimen?
Doesn't he look the fresh clean Englishman outside?

Isn't it God's own image? tramping his thirty miles a day
after partridges, or a little rubber ball?
wouldn't you like to be like that, well off, and quite the thing?

Oh, but wait!   10
Let him meet a new emotion, let him be faced with another man's need,
let him come home to a bit of a moral difficulty, let life face him with
    a new demand on his understanding
and then watch him go soggy, like a wet meringue.
Watch him turn into a mess, either a fool or a bully.
Just watch the display of him, confronted with a new demand on his
    intelligence,
a new life-demand.

How beastly the bourgeois is
especially the male of the species –   20

Nicely groomed; like a mushroom
standing there so sleek and erect and eyeable –
and like a fungus, living on the remains of bygone life
sucking his life out of the dead leaves of greater life than his own.

And even so, he's stale, he's been there too long.
Touch him, and you'll find he's all gone inside
just like an old mushroom, all wormy inside, and hollow
under a smooth skin and an upright appearance.

Full of seething, wormy, hollow feelings
rather nasty –   30
How beastly the bourgeois is!

Standing in their thousands, these appearances, in damp England
what a pity they can't all be kicked over
like sickening toadstools, and left to melt back, swiftly
into the soil of England.

D.H. Lawrence

Examine the attitudes to war revealed in the two poems below. Compare also the diction and imagery of the poems and include a critical evaluation of them.

TRENCH IDYLL

We sat together in the trench,
He on a lump of frozen earth
Blown in the night before,
I on an unexploded shell;
And smoked and talked, like exiles,
Of how pleasant London was,
Its women, restaurants, night clubs, theatres,
How at that very hour
The taxi-cabs were taking folk to dine. . .
Then we sat silent for a while
As a machine-gun swept the parapet.   11

He said:
'I've been here on and off two years
And seen only one man killed.'

'That's odd.'

'The bullet hit him in the throat;
he fell in a heap on the fire-step,
And called out "My God! dead!"'

'Good Lord, how terrible!'   19

'Well, as to that, the nastiest job I've had
Was last year on this very front
Taking the discs at night from men
Who'd hung for six months on the wire
Just over there.
The worst of all was
They fell to pieces at a touch.
Thank God we couldn't see their faces;
They had gas helmets on. . .'

I shivered;
'It's rather cold here, sir, suppose we move.'   30

Richard Aldington

PREPARATIONS FOR VICTORY

My soul, dread not the pestilence that hags
The valley; flinch not you, my body young,
At these great shouting smokes and snarling jags
Of fiery iron; as yet may not be flung
The dice that claims you. Manly move among
These ruins, and what you must do, do well;
Look, here are gardens, there mossed boughs are hung
With apples whose bright cheeks none might excel,
And there's a house as yet unshattered by a shell.   9

'I'll do my best,' the soul makes sad reply,
'And I will mark the yet unmurdered tree,
The tokens of dear homes that court the eye,
And yet I see them not as I would see.
Hovering between, a ghostly enemy
Sickens the light, and poisoned, withered, wan,
The least defiled turns desperate to me.'
The body, poor unpitied Caliban,
Parches and sweats and grunts to win the name of Man.   18

Days or eternities like swelling waves
Surge on, and still we drudge in this dark maze;
The bombs and coils and cans by strings of slaves
Are born to serve the coming day of days;
Pale sleep in slimy cellars scarce allays
With its brief blank the burden. Look, we lose;
The sky is gone, the lightness, drenching haze
Of rainstorm chills the bone; earth, air are foes,
The black fiend leaps brick-red as life's last picture goes.   27

Edmund Blunden

Write a critical comparison of the two poems, dealing with theme, treatment of theme, diction and form.

THE MARRIAGE OF BLACK AND WHITE

Marry me
And we shall have children
Who will not need sunbathing
Having been blessed with a skin
The hue that is intermediate:
True representatives
Of the race of the future:
Of the conscience that is to be
A consensus of all there is
Of culture and skins: 10
People who speak a language
That is universal
As the stocks from which it is derived:
The product of prides in races:
The successors over petty bigotry:
The race that will inherit
The best there is from both;
Children grown strong
Tempered by ill-knowledges
That are appendixes
In the two camps
Of colour curtains.   22

And Nietzsche was wrong
Against racial mixing;
He is right – if
There is no psychological homework.

My skin is so black
And potent as the coal
That the miners bring out
From the bowels of the earth,
With plenty of energy entrapped.   31

C'mon.
We are not freaks,
We are of the same species
Despite the protective colouration,
Nature's own invention
For her sons' accommodations
To the various latitudes
Before the sons could conquer
Distance.   40

We are not freaks
I mean you are not and I am not.
And our children won't be mules –
Dead ends of crossbreedings –
On the contrary, very robust,
Best fitted to live in this their world,
A world relative and comparative,
A world shrunk by Orville and Marconi,
A world that knows no boundary,
A world in flux,
With the colour disc in full swing
Blurring the primaries,
A world betterworsened by
I-it.   54

Taban Lo Liyong

A WELSH TESTAMENT

All right, I was Welsh. Does it matter?
I spoke the tongue that was passed on
To me in the place that I happened to be,
A place huddled between grey walls
Of cloud for at least half the year.
My word for heaven was not yours.
The word for hell had a sharp edge
Put on it by the hand of the wind
Honing, honing with a shrill sound
Day and night. Nothing that Glyn Dŵr
Knew was armour against the rain's
Missiles. What was descent from him?   12

Even God had a Welsh name:
We spoke to him in the old language;
He was to have a peculiar care
For the Welsh people. History showed us
He was too big to be nailed to the wall
Of a stone chapel, yet still we crammed him
Between the boards of a black book.   19

Yet men sought us despite this.
My high cheek-bones, my length of skull
Drew them as to a rare portrait
By a dead master. I saw them stare
From their long cars, as I passed knee-deep
In ewes and wethers. I saw them stand
By the thorn hedges, watching me string
The far flocks on a shrill whistle.   27

245

And always there was their eyes' strong
Pressure on me: You are Welsh, they said;
Speak to us so; keep your fields free
Of the smell of petrol, the loud roar
Of hot tractors; we must have peace
And quietness.   33

                Is a museum
Peace? I asked. Am I the keeper
Of the heart's relics, blowing the dust
In my own eyes? I am a man;
I never wanted the drab role
Life assigned me, an actor playing
To the past's audience upon a stage
Of earth and stone; the absurd label
Of birth, of race hanging askew
About my shoulders. I was in prison
Until you came; your voice was a key
Turning in the enormous lock
Of hopelessness. Did the door open
To let me out or yourselves in?   47

R.S. Thomas

Compare the way the following two poems treat their similar themes; examine critically
their rhythm, diction, imagery and form.

THE LAKE ISLE OF INNISFREE

I will arise and go now, and go to Innisfree,
And a small cabin build there, of clay and wattles made:
Nine bean-rows will I have there, a hive for the honey-bee,
And live alone in the bee-loud glade.

And I shall have some peace there, for peace comes dropping slow
Dropping from the veils of the morning to where a cricket sings;
There midnight's all a glimmer, and noon a purple glow,
And evening full of the linnet's wings.

I will arise and go now, for always night and day
I hear lake water lapping with low sounds by the shore;
While I stand on the roadway, or on the pavements grey,
I hear it in the deep heart's core.

W.B. Yeats

TO THE ANCESTRAL NORTH

I

From that elemental land
Of iron whitenesses and long auroras
My Viking fathers sprang
In armoured nakedness.
The rock rang, and cold fire
Sparked at their striding heels.
Their prows plundered and struck, the up-
Ending northern oceans with the smash
Of sword on stone, axe
Biting the pale flesh of the dark pines.
The wintered masts were holy,
Bore flame and fire from the gods,
And all Valhalla thundered in the mystic storm.

II

I love the archaic North,
The gothic loneliness,
The bare cathedral of the cold
Where, in the stunned ice,
The winter woods display
A stripped elegance, and frame the rare
Rose-window of the midnight sun.

III

There, in the blank fastnesses
Of frozen bays, on sands
Sheeted with stony ice,
By the frost-pleated firth, the glassy
Fjord scattered with ashes of snows;
Under the sea-mountain
In the wild moraine of stars
That haul the glazed oceans into heaps
Of shaggy ice, the ancestral ghosts
Of gods and heroes wander,
Melancholy, silent, and remote.

IV

O in the cold and grave and Carolingian forest,
In epic stillness, let me worship in their memory
The falling flake, the long
Larch grove, the lime-white lake
That burns in the trees' black lancets!

The twilight pauses like a stage at bay.
I hear a lost huntsman calling for a hidden castle.
And in the deserted valley
A sad horn echoes in a last, lingering *Hallali*.   *James Kirkup*

247

Both the following poems deal with a theme concerned with animals; compare the attitude of the poets to the subject-matter and write a critical comparison of the two poems.

THE OWL

Downhill I came, hungry, and yet not starved;
Cold, yet had heat within me that was proof
Against the North wind; tired, yet so that rest
Had seemed the sweetest thing under a roof.

Then at the inn I had food, fire and rest,
Knowing how hungry, cold, and tired was I.
All of the night was quite barred out except
An owl's cry, a most melancholy cry   8

Shaken out long and clear upon the hill,
No merry note, nor cause of merriment,
But one telling me plain what I had escaped
And others could not, that night, as in I went.

And salted was my food, and my repose,
Salted and sobered, too, by the bird's voice
Speaking for all who lay under the stars,
Soldiers and poor, unable to rejoice.   16

Edward Thomas

THE HOWLING OF WOLVES

Is without world.

What are they dragging up and out on their long leashes of sound

That dissolve in the mid-air silence?

Then crying of a baby, in this forest of starving silences,
Brings the wolves running.
Tuning of a viola, in this forest delicate as an owl's ear,
Brings the wolves running – brings the steel traps clashing and
  slavering,
The steel furred to keep it from cracking in the cold,
The eyes that never learn how it has come about
That they must live like this,   10

That they must live

Innocence crept into minerals.

The wind sweeps through and the hunched wolf shivers.
It howls you cannot say whether out of agony or joy.

The earth is under its tongue,
A dead weight of darkness, trying to see through its eyes.
The wolf is living for the earth.
But the wolf is small, it comprehends little.

It goes to and fro, trailing its haunches and whimpering horribly.

It must feed its fur.   20

The night snows stars and the earth creaks.

Ted Hughes

Discuss and compare the way the themes of the two poems below are presented and compare the diction, imagery and rhythm of the two poems. Include a critical evaluation of the two poems in your answer.

A WISH

Mine be a cot beside the hill;
    A bee-hive's hum shall soothe my ear;
A willowy brook, that turns a mill,
    With many a fall shall linger near.

The swallow oft beneath my thatch
    Shall twitter from her clay-built nest;
Oft shall the pilgrim lift the latch
    And share my meal, a welcome guest.   8

Around my ivied porch shall spring
    Each fragrant flower that drinks the dew;
And Lucy at her wheel shall sing
    In russet gown and apron blue.

The village church among the trees,
    Where first our marriage vows were given,
With merry peals shall swell the breeze
    And point with taper spire to Heaven.   16

Samuel Rogers

ON THE LAKE

A candle lit in darkness of black waters,
A candle set in the drifting prow of a boat,
And every tree to itself a separate shape,
Now plumy, now an arch; tossed trees
Still and dishevelled, dishevelled with past growth,
Forgotten storms; left tufted, tortured, sky-rent,
Even now in stillness; stillness on the lake,
Black, reflections pooléd, black mirror
Pooling a litten candle, taper of fire;
Pooling the sky, double transparency   10
Of sky in water, double elements,
Lying like lovers, light above, below;
Taking, from one another, light; a gleaming,
A glow reflected, fathoms deep, leagues high,
Two distances meeting at a film of surface
Thin as a membrane, sheet of surface, fine
Smooth steel, two separates, height and depth,
Able to touch, giving to one another
All their profundity, all their accidents,
– Changeable mood of clouds, permanent stars, –   20
Like thoughts in the mind hanging a long way off,
Revealed between lovers, friends. Peer in the water
Over the boat's edge; seek the sky's night-heart;
Are they near, are they far, those clouds, those stars
Given, reflected, pooled? are they so close
For a hand to clasp, to lift them, feel their shape,
Explore their reality, take a rough possession?
Oh no! too delicate, too shy for handling,
They tilt at a touch, quiver to other shapes,
Dance away, change, are lost, drowned, scared;   30
Hands break the mirror, speech's crudity
Then surmise, the divining;
Such things so deeply held, so lightly held,
Subtile, imponderable, as stars in water
Or thoughts in another's thoughts.
Are they near, are they far, those stars, that knowledge?
Deep? shallow? solid? rare? The boat drifts on,
And the litten candle single in the prow,
The small, immediate candle in the prow
Burns brighter in the water than any star.   40

V. Sackville-West

Write a critical appreciation of these two poems, comparing how the poets handle their themes and commenting on diction, form, rhythm and imagery.

ON DEATH

Tell me though safest end of all our woe,
Why wretched mortals do avoid thee so:
Thou gentle drier o' th'afflicted tears,
Thou noble ender of the coward's fears;
Thou sweet repose to lover's sad dispaire
Thou calm t'ambitions rough tempestuous care.
If in regard of bliss thou wert a curse,
And then the joys of paradise art worse;
Yet after Man from his first station fell,
and God from Eden Adam did expel,   10
Thou wert no more an evil, but relief;
 The balm and cure to ev'ry Humane grief:
Through thee (what Man had forfeited before)
He now enjoys, and ne'er can lose it more.
No subtile serpents, in the grave betray,
Worms on the body there, not soul do prey;
No vice there tempts, no terrors there afright,
No coz'ning sin affords a false delight:
No vain contentions do that peace annoy,
No fierce alarms break the lasting joy.   20

Ah since from thee so many blessings flow,
Such real good as life can never know;
Come when thou wilt, in thy afrighting'st dress,
Thy shape shall never make thy welcome less.
Thou mayst to you, but ne'er to fear give birth,
Thou best, as well as certain'st thing on earth.
Fly thee? May travellers then fly their rest,
And hungry infants fly the profer'd brest.
No, those that faint and tremble at thy name,
Fly from their good on a mistaken fame.   30
Thus childish fear did Israel of old
From plenty and the Promis'd Land withold;
They fancy'd giants, and refus'd to go,
When Canaan did with milk and honey flow.

Anne Killigrew

A COUNTRY DEATH

And when her husband died, of course she went
to live in the country with her married
daughter; there the air and food sustained her
well enough, but she missed the London streets.

Her son-in-law was – not rich exactly,
but – he had to spare, and knew of fallow
places where lamp-posts went when finished with,
knew what they did with them when they were old.   8

So, incongruous amongst the Sussex elms,
the lamp-post came and stood before the house,
a London exile itself; alight at
dusk, it was to make her feel less homesick.

All credit to the giver; but still this
old woman's life was fretful, and her death
had nothing of the peace for which they hoped:
what do you do with them when they are old?   16

B.S. Johnson

Glossary

Note: In order to gain a full understanding of the terms explained here it will often be useful to look them up in the general index. This contains references to other places in the book where the terms are used or explained.

alliteration   the repetition of initial letters or sounds in words next to or near to one another. *See* page 95.

allegory   a narrative in which people, objects and events represent moral or spiritual ideas.

anapaestic foot   a metrical foot consisting of two unstressed syllables followed by a stressed one ($\smile \smile -$).

assonance   the repetition of vowel sounds in words next to or near to one another. *See* page 200.

ballad   a spirited poem with a strong and simple rhythm which tells a popular story. Ballads are often of ancient origin and were originally intended for musical accompaniment.

bathos   the ludicrous effect produced by a sudden descent from an elevated tone or sentiment to a banal one.

blank verse   poetry written in unrhymed iambic pentameters.

cadence   a term used to refer to the rise and fall of language and/or its tone.

caesura   the natural resting-place or pause in a line of poetry (there may be more than one); the sense of the words dictates its (their) position in the line.

comic exaggeration   the deliberate stressing or heightening of character traits or incidents for humorous effect.

conceit   an ingenious or witty thought or image.

concrete   concerned with objects that can be perceived by the senses; opposite to abstract, which is concerned with ideas not perceivable by the senses.

consonance   the repetition of the same consonant in words next to or near to one another. *See* pages 189–90.

contemplative writing   a thoughtful type of writing which involves taking a restrained, rational approach to a subject.

content   the treatment of theme by an author.

critical analysis/appreciation   the careful consideration of the various elements of a work of literature, culminating in a judgement of its quality.

dactylic foot   a metrical foot consisting of a stressed syllable followed by two unstressed ones ($- \smile \smile$).

dialect   a variety or form of language peculiar to a district or social class.

diction   the word used to refer to language in poetry.

end-stopped line   a line of verse with a definite pause at its end, normally marked by punctuation. *See also* enjambment.

enjambment   when the flow of the verse does not pause at the end of a line but continues into the next. *See also* end-stopped line and page 156.

epic   a long narrative poem telling of heroic events in an elevated style.

epigrammatic   like an epigram: concise, pointed and witty.

figurative language   language with a meaning going beyond its literal one, involving comparison or metaphor.

first person narrative a story told using the 'I' or 'we' voice. The story-teller is often one of the chief characters. *See also* third person narrative.

foot, metrical the basic unit for measuring patterns of rhythm in poetry. *See also* pages 219–221.

form part of the content of a piece of writing. Form includes both the genre and the detail (such as metre or length of sentences) of the way the writer communicates what he or she has to say.

free verse verse written without the use of regular patterns of metre and rhyme or the traditional types of form.

genre a form or type of literature such as science fiction or lyric poetry.

half-rhyme the term used to describe an incomplete rhyming effect where the sound of the two words is similar but not identical. *See* page 200.

heightened language a phrase used to describe the intensely dramatic, emotional language sometimes used in poetry or prose.

hexameter a line of verse consisting of six metrical feet.

human interest the appeal a news item makes to readers' emotions and curiosity about other people.

iambic foot a metrical foot consisting of an unstressed syllable followed by a stressed one (˘ ¯).

iambic pentameter the commonest metrical pattern in English poetry, consisting of lines of five iambic feet. *See also* pages 219–221.

imagery the use of language to appeal to one of the senses. Imagery is used by a writer to convey sense, tone or emotion and often takes the form of a metaphor which makes connections between previously unrelated things. *See* metaphor and pages 150–3.

interior monologue the narration of a novel, story or poem through the mind of a character, following that person's thoughts. These thoughts tend, however, to be put into a grammatical and ordered form. *See also* stream of consciousness technique.

internal rhyme rhyme that occurs within a line of poetry. *See* page 200.

irony a form of sarcasm. It entails the use of words that say one thing and mean something quite different. Irony involves two layers of meaning: a surface meaning and the real meaning beneath the surface.

literary reference when a writer refers to other writers or works of literature.

lyric (or lyrical) poem a short poem expressing a personal feeling such as joy in love or in the beauty of nature. Originally a lyric was a song to be accompanied by the lyre.

mellifluous sweet-sounding, soothing.

metaphor a comparison which does not use a comparing word such as 'as' or 'like'. It is a figure of speech in which the qualities of one thing are transferred to something else not normally thought of as similar to it, for example: 'Paul was a lion in the fight.' The qualities of the lion (courage, fierceness) are transferred to Paul.

metre the organisation of lines of verse into regular patterns of stressed and unstressed syllables to achieve a rhythmic effect. *See also* pages 219–221.

metrical foot the basic unit for measuring patterns of rhythm in poetry. *See also* pages 219–221.

narrative a story (noun), telling a story (adjective).

monologue a speech delivered by a single speaker or performer.

objective looking at an issue or events without prejudice or bias.

octave an eight-lined poem or stanza: the first eight lines of a sonnet.

onomatopoeia the use of words which resemble what they mean in the way they are pronounced, for example *hiss* or *buzz*.

parody the imitation of a style of writing for humorous effect.

pentameter a line of verse consisting of five metrical feet.

Glossary

periodical essay   an essay written for a publication issued at regular intervals such as a magazine or a journal.

persona   originally a mask worn by actors which was changed according to the different characters represented. It has come to mean the identity or character assumed by an author in a novel, story or poem.

Petrarchan sonnet   *See* sonnet.

protagonist   a main character in a novel, story or play.

pseudonym   a name assumed for the purpose of writing by an author in place of his or her real name.

realism   the attempt to portray ordinary life and people in literature, involving the use of everyday speech and language.

resonance   the effect produced by the selection of language which is not confined to one interpretation but is open to a variety of interpretations and associations.

rhetorical question   a question to which no answer is needed or sought; it is used to make a forceful point.

rhyming couplet   two consecutive lines written in the same metre and which rhyme.

satire   the ridiculing of the follies of people and society, sometimes with the purpose of reforming the faults that are satirised.

scan   (noun, scansion) to analyse the metrical pattern of a line of verse. *See also* pages 219–221.

sestet   the second section (consisting of six lines) of a sonnet or any poem or stanza of six lines.

Shakespearean sonnet   *See* sonnet.

sibilance   the repetition of 's' sounds in words next to or near to one another. *See* page 190.

sight rhyme   words that look as though they should rhyme but do not do so, for example: 'rough' and 'bough'.

simile   an explicit comparison of one thing with another, using 'as' or 'like'.

soliloquy   (verb, soliloquise) a speech delivered by a character in a play who is alone on stage. It can be used to reveal the character's thoughts or as a means of direct communication between the character and the audience in the theatre.

sonnet   a fourteen-line rhyming poem, often written in iambic pentameters. The sonnet often has a clearly marked development of theme in the ninth line which divides the poem into an octave and a sestet.
   Poets have used various different rhyming schemes. The Shakespearean sonnet consists of three quatrains (groups of four lines) followed by a closing rhyming couplet. The Shakespearian sonnet rhymes *abab cdcd efef gg* (*See* page 223 for explanation of letters). The Petrarchan sonnet (there is one on page 202) consists of an octave rhyming *abba abba* and a sestet which may employ any one of several different rhyming patterns.

spondaic foot   a metrical foot consisting of two stressed syllables (‾ ‾).

sprung rhythm   a form of poetic rhythm. The metrical foot consists of one stressed syllable and any number of unstressed syllables. A line may have any number of feet.

Standard English   the English used by official agencies, government, the BBC and most of the media.

standpoint   the point of view from which a story, poem etc. is written.

stanza   stanzas are the groups of lines into which some poems are divided. In many traditional poems stanzas are arranged according to a scheme which governs the metre, number of lines and sequence of rhymes (if any) in the stanza.

stream of consciousness technique   the attempt by an author to reproduce the thought-processes of a person without adapting them to a more grammatical or ordered form than they might have in real life. *See also* interior monologue.

stressed syllables   the syllables in a line of poetry on which the emphasis falls when the line is read or spoken. *See also* pages 219–221.

style   a term used to refer to all or any of a range of things such as the distinctive traits of a particular writer, the clarity and effectiveness of the writing, its aesthetic qualities etc. It is often understood to mean a writer's manner of expression considered separately from the substance of what is said. Style, however, should not be considered in isolation from the substance and content of the writing as it is this which decides its style.

sub-vocalise   to read 'aloud' silently to oneself: to listen in one's mind to the aural qualities of a piece of writing.

tetrameter   a line of verse consisting of four metrical feet.

theme   the essence or central idea of a poem, novel etc.

third person narrative   the most common story-telling technique. The author adopts the role of an anonymous and sometimes omniscient narrator. Sometimes, however, the author intrudes into the narrative to comment directly on events or to make moral judgements about characters. *See also* first person narrative.

tonal qualities   the emotional effect which language has independently of the precise meaning of the words.

tone   the attitude taken by the writer to the subject-matter, for example: satirical, humorous, angry, compassionate.

trimeter   a line of verse consisting of three metrical feet.

trochaic foot   a metrical foot consisting of a stressed syllable followed by an unstressed syllable (ˉ ˘).

versification   the form or style of a poem and its technical aspects such as metre, rhythm, stanza form, line lengths and caesura.

voice   the standpoint adopted by the author.

General Index

Index of Authors
and Titles of Extracts and Poems

Other material